standards and expectancies

Essays in Social Psychology

General Editors: MAHZARIN BANAJI, Harvard University, and MILES HEW-STONE, University of Oxford

Essays in Social Psychology is designed to meet the need for rapid publication of brief volumes in social psychology. Primary topics will include social cognition, interpersonal relationships, group processes, and intergroup relations, as well as applied issues. Furthermore, the series seeks to define social psychology in its broadest sense, encompassing all topics either informed by, or informing, the study of individual behavior and thought in social situations. Each volume in the series will make a conceptual contribution to the topic by reviewing and synthesizing the existing research literature, by advancing theory in the area, or by some combination of these missions. The principal aim is that authors will provide an overview of their own highly successful research program in an area. It is also expected that volumes will, to some extent, include an assessment of current knowledge and identification of possible future trends in research. Each book will be a self-contained unit supplying the advanced reader with a well-structured review of the work described and evaluated.

Published titles

Van der Vliert: *Complex Interpersonal Conflict Behaviour*
Dweck: *Self-Theories: Their Role in Motivation, Personality, and Development*
Sorrentino & Roney: *The Uncertain Mind: Individual Differences in Facing the Unknown*
Gaertner & Dovidio: *Reducing Intergroup Bias*
Tyler & Blader: *Cooperation in Groups: Procedural Justice, Social Identity, and Behavioral Engagement*
Kruglanski: *The Psychology of Closed Mindedness*
Dunning: *Self-Insight*

Titles in preparation

Crisp & Hewstone: *Crossed Categorization, Stereotyping, and Intergroup Relations*
Jost: *A Theory of System Justification*
Mackie: *Emotional Aspects of Intergroup Perception*
Turner: *Social Identity Theory and Self-Categorization*

For continually updated information about published and forthcoming titles in the Essays in Social Psychology series, please visit **www.psypress.com/essays**.

standards and expectancies

contrast and assimilation in judgments of self and others

MONICA BIERNAT

PSYCHOLOGY PRESS
NEW YORK AND HOVE

Published in 2005 by
Routledge
Taylor & Francis Group
270 Madison Avenue
New York, NY 10016

Published in Great Britain by
Routledge
Taylor & Francis Group
2 Park Square
Milton Park, Abingdon
Oxon OX14 4RN

Printed in the United States of America on acid-free paper
10 9 8 7 6 5 4 3 2 1

International Standard Book Number-10: 1-84169-068-6 (Hardcover)
International Standard Book Number-13: 978-1-84169-068-1 (Hardcover)
Library of Congress Card Number 2005006104

Library of Congress Cataloging-in-Publication Data

Biernat, Monica.
    Standards and expectancies : contrast and assimilation in judgments of self and others / Monica Biernat.
            p. cm. -- (Essays in social psychology)
    Includes bibliographical references (p.) and index.
    ISBN 1-84169-068-6 (hardback : alk. paper)
    1. Social perception. 2. Self-perception. 3. Judgment. 4. Comparison (Psychology) I. Title. II. Series.

BF323.S63B542 2005
153.4'6--dc22   2005006104

Taylor & Francis Group
is the Academic Division of T&F Informa plc.

Visit the Taylor & Francis Web site at
http://www.taylorandfrancis.com

and the Routledge Web site at
http://www.routledge-ny.com

For Charlotte and Chris, beyond compare

CONTENTS

PREFACE

I began working on this book by accident. Sometime around 1998, I was asked by Abe Tesser and Norbert Schwarz to contribute a chapter to their volume *Intraindividual Processes*, which was to be part of the Blackwell *Handbook of Social Psychology* (2001). The assigned topic was "standards, expectancies, and social comparison," and I dutifully produced a chapter with the help of my then graduate student, Laura Billings. However, I went a bit overboard and ended up with a document four times as long as the editors had requested. The problem was that I kept discovering interesting research and theory that was disparate in focus but still connected to the theme of standards, expectancies, and judgment. It was Norbert Schwarz who first made me edit the chapter drastically and then encouraged me to consider revisiting the original manuscript and turning it into a monograph for publication in the Psychology Press Essays in Social Psychology series. I am extremely grateful to Norbert for that encouragement and for his comments on the book prospectus, and to series editors Mahzarin Banaji and Miles Hewstone for their support of the project.

The original document went through a lot of changes before emerging in the book form you see here, but it retained an emphasis on how self- and other-judgment are affected by standards and expectancies. The dominant themes of the book are that these judgments may reflect assimilative or contrastive processes (one can be pulled toward or contrasted from a relevant standard), that we can predict which outcome will occur based on knowledge of particular features of the judgment situation, and that these features operate similarly across judgment domains (self and other) and types of standards (the self, other people, social stereotypes).

My own research expertise is on stereotyping, and more specifically, on the role of stereotypes as standards for judging others. Though I discuss this work here, it represents only a small part of what I think is a terribly interesting, general phenomenon: the use of available constructs (be they stereotypes, representations of self or others, contextual cues, or internalized guides) either as interpretive frames that color our impressions in an assimilative fashion (as when stereotypes lead us to judge individual group members as possessing stereotypical traits) or as distinct comparative standards against which judgment is contrasted (as when we view a target person as low in a stereotypical attribute, relative to standards for his or her group). But the fact that this book covers ground where I do not have expertise leads me to a caveat and apology. I have chosen to neglect certain areas and emphasize others that happened to catch my eye, and I have surely simplified areas in which the experts see much more complexity. I hope nonetheless that I have managed to capture some important, general themes about comparison and judgment that run through diverse, and often unconnected, literatures.

I am extremely grateful to colleagues and students who read and commented on this manuscript, and most particularly to Scott Eidelman, Dick Eiser, and Thomas Mussweiler. Eiser's own monograph, *Social Judgment*, served as a model for this book (Eiser, 1990); I referred to it often as I wrote. Thanks are also due to my graduate school mentor, Mel Manis, who taught me much of what I know about assimilation and contrast. I also wish to acknowledge the Kansas graduate students (both former and current) whose work with me is described at various points in this book: Laura Billings, Elizabeth Collins, Scott Eidelman, Kathy Fuegen, Diane Kobrynowicz, Michelle Nario-Redmond, Elizabeth Thompson, and Terri Vescio. Jennifer Ma, a former postdoc, also deserves my thanks, as do my current graduate students and members of the shifting standards research group. The financial support of the National Institute of Mental Health (Grant #R01 MH48844) also contributed to some of the research described here and to my ability to dedicate time to writing. Alison Mudditt at Psychology Press, and later Paul Dukes, were also instrumental in bringing this project to completion. Finally, I thank my husband, Chris Crandall, and my daughter, Charlotte, for their love and support.

Standards and Expectancies: An Introduction and Overview

It is almost a truism to say that *life is relative*—that our experiences and judgments of people, things, and events occur against the backdrop of some comparative standard or frame of reference. My claims that "I'm hungry" or "my daughter is brilliant" or "that haircut is ghastly" are all made with reference to some standard. Indeed, in communicating these things, I assume that you have at least some notion of the standards I have in mind—the contextual background—and can interpret my claims accordingly. Thus, you can pretty readily assume that my hunger level does not require medical attention, that my 5-year-old's brilliance does not qualify her for early admission to an Ivy League school, and that the haircut is unlikely to frighten away small children and animals. Note that this occurs even though the judgment appears absolute—"she's brilliant!"—for such statements imply *more x* (more brilliance) than others, and they are therefore inherently comparative (Huttenlocher & Higgins, 1971).

This theme of relativity has been emphasized by a great number of researchers who have described the wide variety of sources or types of standards that may be used to define and describe our everyday encounters with the world. Beginning with research on such diverse areas as psychophysics (Helson, 1947, 1964; Parducci, 1956; Postman & Miller, 1945; Stevens, 1957; Volkmann, 1951; Wever & Zener, 1928) and the self

(James, 1890/1948), psychologists have long emphasized the relativity of many forms of intra- and interpersonal experience. That judgment is relative or comparative appears in research on attitudes (Sherif & Hovland, 1961) and decision making (Houston & Sherman, 1995; Kahneman & Miller, 1986), as well as in two domains that are highlighted in this book—person perception (Higgins & Lurie, 1983) and self-evaluation (Festinger, 1954a).

Indeed, this book will focus primarily on the role of judgment standards and expectations in evaluations of others and the self. One central theme pervades the book—namely, that the outcome of a comparative process can be conceptualized in terms of either *assimilation* or *contrast*. Assimilation occurs when the target of evaluation (e.g., another person, the self) is pulled toward or judged consistently with the standard or expectation, and contrast occurs when the target is differentiated from (judged in a direction opposite) the comparative frame. By "judgment," I typically refer to a connotative evaluation (e.g., a rating on some trait dimension) but also to outcomes that are affective (such as mood or self-esteem) or behavioral in nature as well.

In person perception, assimilation is reflected in studies in which a target is judged consistently with primed trait adjectives (e.g., Higgins, Rholes, & Jones, 1977), and contrast is reflected in the finding that a member of a stereotyped group is judged to have *less* of a stereotypical trait than a member of the contrasting group (Biernat & Kobrynowicz, 1997). In the domain of self-evaluation, assimilation can be seen when one reacts to an upward social comparison with positive self-evaluations (the self assimilates to a "superstar"; Lockwood & Kunda, 1997), and contrast when one responds with increased sadness upon considering how the actual self is discrepant from an ideal self-state (Higgins, 1987). *Behavioral* assimilation can be seen when one engages in actions designed to meet self-standards (Carver & Scheier, 1998) or in health behaviors that conform with favorably viewed "risk images" (Gibbons & Gerrard, 1995, 1997), and *behavioral contrast* is evident when one behaves or performs counter to a primed exemplar (Dijksterhuis, Spears, Postmes, Stapel, Koomen, van Knippenberg, & Scheepers, 1998) or group stereotype (Schubert & Häfner, 2003). One of the key questions asked throughout this book will be, when does assimilation occur in social judgment, and when does contrast?

A secondary theme of the book is the constructivist nature of comparisons and judgment. Individuals often have leeway to pick and choose their reference points, drawing from a broad knowledge base as well as the specifics of a situation or context to subjectively define evaluative standards (Kahneman & Miller, 1986; Miller & Prentice, 1996). This is particularly evident in the literature on social comparison, which paints an image of the "active comparer," who may selectively choose a target of comparison (or even construct a target of comparison) to meet particular needs (e.g., see Goethals, Messick, & Allison, 1991). On the other hand, the literature on contextual *priming* would seem to suggest that perceivers are subject to the whims of context; constructs may be activated without awareness and affect our judgments through the basic mechanism of knowledge accessibility (Higgins, 1996). Even social comparisons may be thrust upon us—they may occur unintentionally and without awareness (Gilbert, Giesler, & Morris, 1995; Mussweiler, Rüter, & Epstude, 2004; Stapel & Blanton, 2004; Wood, Michela, & Giordano, 2000). The extent to which perceivers control the environment and the comparative standards they use will be highlighted throughout this volume.

Before going further, some working definitions of the terms *standards* and *expectancies* should be offered. Higgins (1990) provides a useful definition of the first construct: "a standard is a criterion or rule established by experience, desires, or authority for the measure of quantity and extent, or quality and value" (p. 302). A *social standard* in particular may be thought of as "any attribute of a person or of a collection of people that serves as a point of comparison for an individual" (Miller & Prentice, 1996, p. 800). Standards are assumed to take a variety of forms. For example, Higgins (1990; Higgins, Strauman, & Klein, 1986) describes three general types: (1) *factual standards* (beliefs about the attributes of others), (2) *guides* ("criteria of excellence or acceptability"; Higgins et al., 1986, p. 30), and (3) *possibilities* (standards regarding what will, could, or might exist).

In this volume, the "factual standards" considered include the *self* as a standard for judging others and *individual others* as standards for judging the self, as well as *group stereotypes* as a source of both self- and other-judgment. Additionally, I will consider *context*—information made accessible in the immediate judgment setting—as a source of standards in both self- and other-judgment (another type of "factual" standard). "Guides" and "possibilities" will be reflected in the examination of *internalized representations* of goals/values/"oughts" as standards for judging the self. It is worth noting, however, that "factual standards" may also function as "guides." For example, group stereotypes may represent not only our beliefs about what groups *are* like but also our prescriptions regarding what group members *should* be like (e.g., see Hogg & Abrams, 1988; Rabbie & Horwitz, 1988; Wilder & Shapiro, 1991). In this sense, standards for judging self and others can be viewed as norms that include both descriptive and prescriptive components (Miller & Prentice, 1996; see also Cialdini, Kallgren & Reno, 1991).

Expectancies have also been broadly defined as "beliefs about a future state of affairs . . . subjective probabilities linking the future with an outcome at some level of probability ranging from merely possible to virtually certain" (Olson, Roese, & Zanna, 1996, p. 211). This definition incorporates the notion of anticipation more than evaluation or measurement, but expectancies are nonetheless similar to standards in that they are mental constructs, based on both memory and current experience, that provide the backdrop against which outcomes and events are experienced. Thus, a social stereotype can be viewed as an expectation about the likely attributes of a group of people (e.g., Hamilton & Sherman, 1994) or as a judgment standard against which individual group members are evaluated (Biernat, Manis, & Nelson, 1991; Biernat & Manis, 1994). Similarly, one's goals and aspirations can be conceptualized in terms of perceived probability or expectation of future success (e.g., Atkinson, 1957; Festinger, 1942; Lewin, Dembo, Festinger, & Sears, 1944) or as future (possible) self-standards (Higgins, 1990; Markus & Nurius, 1986; Schlenker, 1985).

Furthermore, standards and expectancies can be either met or not met, confirmed or disconfirmed, with predictable consequences. For example, the violation of an expectation is likely to produce a negative affect, deeper (more systematic) subsequent processing, attributional search, reduced certainty, and a more explicit knowledge or awareness of the expectation (Olson et al., 1996). Unmet standards are likely to produce at least some of the same effects (e.g., see Stangor & McMillan, 1992; Betten-court, Dill, Greathouse, Charlton, & Mulholland, 1997; and Biernat, Vescio, & Billings, 1999; Higgins, 1987 on self-evaluation). For these reasons, I will often use the terms "standards" and "expectancies" interchangeably.

As will become apparent throughout the book, however, standards are often viewed as conducive to *contrast* effects (e.g., targets are judged relative to and therefore different from the standard), whereas expectations are typically viewed as conducive to *assimilation* (e.g., targets are perceived in line with expectations, because the expectation serves as an interpretive frame; see, e.g., Manis & Paskewitz, 1984a). But this book will make clear that things are not this straightforward or simple, as standards can lead to assimilation (witness anchoring effects), and expectations can lead to contrast as well (as in judgmental extremity produced by expectancy violation). In any case, standards and expectancies are similar in that targets and events are experienced and evaluated in reference to them.

☐ Organization and Overview

This book is organized into three broad sections. The first section includes two chapters that describe basic principles and models of assimilation and contrast. Specifically, Chapter 2 focuses on the role of contextual cues in affecting judgment outcomes and describes some ten factors that have been found to affect whether assimilation or contrast is the dominant pattern in social judgment. This chapter takes a "piecemeal" or bottom-up approach, focusing on empirical findings rather than theoretical accounts of judgment outcomes. Chapter 3, on the other hand, takes the opposite approach and describes a number of recent theoretical models that incorporate and explain the "pieces" identified in Chapter 2. The review of theoretical models highlights *recent* perspectives, but these perspectives, in turn, owe a great debt to a number of classic models of social judgment that do not receive much coverage here. For a deeper consideration of those models, I suggest Eiser's (1990) wonderful monograph *Social Judgment*.

The second broad section of the book contains three chapters on the judgment standards and expectations that guide evaluations of *other people*. Chapter 4 considers the role of *self* and *other exemplars* as standards for judging others. This chapter reviews literature on the role of the self in similarity judgments, the tendency to use our own attributes to describe specific others, false consensus and false uniqueness effects, and the "transference" of attributes of specific exemplars onto other targets. Chapter 5 turns to the role of stereotypes in social judgment and highlights the manner in which stereotypes serve as expectations that color our interpretation of specific members of stereotyped groups, in an assimilative fashion. This chapter considers several models of the stereotyping process and begins to articulate how stereotypes may also produce contrast effects, particularly when individual targets violate stereotypical expectations. Chapter 6 picks up this theme more fully and describes the "shifting standards" model of stereotyping, which I have developed and tested over the last dozen years or so. This model focuses on the role of stereotypes as comparative standards but highlights the fact that both assimilation to and contrast from stereotypes can occur depending on the nature of the judgment being rendered.

The third broad section of the book includes three chapters that focus on standards used in evaluation of the *self*. Chapter 7 considers the role of *personal standards*—internal guides or "rules"—in affecting emotional reactions, judgment, and behavior. This chapter reviews literature on objective self-awareness and self-discrepancy theories and considers the issue of self-regulation more generally as an assimilative process. Not surprisingly, there is overlap in the standards relevant to self- and other-judgment, and thus the two remaining chapters in the "self-judgment" section of this book have their counterparts in the "other-judgment" section. Specifically, Chapter 8 considers the role of *stereotypes* in judgments of the self, focusing on the process of self-stereotyping as an assimilative process. This chapter also considers the role of stereotypes in contributing to contrast effects as well, as when the individual reacts against or compares and distinguishes the self from group characterizations. And Chapter 9 examines another social standard used to judge the self—specific other people, or *social comparisons*. This chapter reviews classic questions that emerge from the social comparison literature, including motives for comparing, choice of comparison targets, and the consequences of engaging in social comparison. It is with regard to this latter topic that the themes of assimilation and contrast can be seen, as emotion, self-evaluation, and behavior can be either consistent with or contrary to the implications of the comparison standard.

The final chapter in this book, Chapter 10, attempts to review the major themes of the book and to offer some ideas about how the range of topics on self- and other-judgment might be integrated into a broader perspective on comparison processes and judgment outcomes in everyday life. I do not promise an integrative model but rather a collection of themes or lessons relevant to judgment regardless of who the target is (self or other), type of judgment, and type of standard or expectation.

What Is Not Here?

Standards and expectancies are relevant to many domains of experience— maybe to *every* domain of experience—and this book cannot possibly review or even touch on literatures relevant to all of these domains. Here, I will highlight a few areas that do not receive coverage in this book. I will not examine the role of expectation as it is outlined in the literature on self-efficacy (Bandura, 1977, 1997), in theories of achievement motivation (Atkinson & Feather, 1966; McClelland, Atkinson, Clark, & Lowell, 1953; Raynor, 1969), or in other expectancy-value models (Abelson & Levi, 1985; Ajzen & Fishbein, 1980; Feather, 1967, 1990; Fishbein & Ajzen, 1975; Heckhausen, 1967; Reisenzein, 1996; Rotter, 1966). I also will not explore the large literature on "self-fulfilling prophecy" (Jones, 1986; Jussim, 1986; Jussim, Eccles, & Madon, 1996; Rosenthal & Jacobson, 1968), which posits (erroneous) expectations as the starting point for behavioral confirmation effects. Counterfactual thinking—which is about comparing realities to alternatives—receives only brief mention in the book as well (Miller, Turnbull, & McFarland, 1990; Roese & Olson, 1997), as does the literature on relative deprivation (Abeles, 1976; Crosby, 1976; Olson & Hafer, 1996; Pettigrew, 1967). Surely many other domains in which standards play a role are missed here as well. These choices to exclude were based on my own knowledge base and interest, and on perceived fit to the theme of *when* assimilation versus contrast occurs. These other literatures dwell on processes and outcomes that I judged to take us too far afield from the primary concern with the role of expectations and standards in self- and other-judgment.

2

CHAPTER

Judging Others and the Self: Contextual Factors Affecting Assimilation and Contrast

As we negotiate our daily lives, opportunities are rife for the assessment and evaluation of others and the self. We often and seemingly effortlessly decide that "Judy is smart," "Eric is annoying," "Donald is hostile," or "I'm not very athletic." No doubt, a number of factors contribute to these types of judgments, including observed information, social stereotypes or other expectations, and contextually activated frames of reference. In this chapter, I will review evidence suggesting that these judgments may be made and can be interpreted in light of *particular* evaluative and comparative *contexts*—that is, information that is made accessible in the immediate judgment setting. I will examine—piecemeal—the features of contexts that have been shown empirically to produce either assimilation or contrast effects. In the next chapter, I will turn to a consideration of several models of social judgment that offer explanations for why these findings emerge.

☐ The Immediate Context, Expectations, and Judgment: An Overview of Findings and Features That Moderate Context Effects

When we form impressions of and make judgments about others, we can be influenced by expectations or standards introduced in the specific setting or context at hand. A classic example is Kelley's (1950) study in which students were led to believe a guest instructor in their economics class was "warm" versus "cold." Judgments of the instructor after the class indicated assimilation to expectations: Those led to believe the instructor was "warm" judged him to be more considerate, informal, sociable, popular, good-natured, humorous, and humane than those led to believe he was "cold." It is worth noting, too, that these effects were not attributable to a general halo effect, as the judgment differences emerged on traits relevant to interpersonal warmth but not on traits more distant from that construct (e.g., intelligence and knowledgeability). Behavior also showed assimilation to expectations: 56% of students given the "warm" expectation entered the discussion led by the instructor, compared to only 32% of those given the "cold" expectation. (Interestingly, Kelley's footnote 3 suggests the possibility of contrast: Those given the "warm" expectation who then encounter an instructor who is [objectively] not warm may show contrast effects—but more on this later!)

Other classic studies have shown comparable patterns of assimilation to experimentally created expectations. These include Langer and Abelson's (1974) study of therapists' impressions of a "patient" versus "job applicant," and Kelley and Stahelski's (1970) and Snyder and Swann's (1978) research on how anticipation of a partner's hostility leads individuals to behave in a competitive and hostile manner themselves (see also Bruner, 1957; Higgins & Chaires, 1980; Higgins & King, 1981; Wyer & Srull, 1980).

The theme of assimilation to a local context or standard is also markedly seen in the domain of *priming* effects. In this research, the "expectation" is typically less explicit than in the research described previously; instead, an initial and/or incidental task activates a construct that is then used to evaluate a subsequently presented target. In a highly cited study by Higgins, Rholes, and Jones (1977), for example, participants were first exposed to positive or negative trait descriptors (e.g., "adventurous" versus "reckless"). Then, in a supposedly unrelated experiment, participants read a description of "Donald," who "drove in a demolition derby" and "planned to learn skydiving," among other things. Donald was evaluated more favorably among individuals initially primed with the trait "adventurous" than with the trait "reckless," but unrelated positive and negative trait primes had no effect on perceptions of Donald (see also Srull & Wyer, 1979).

This basic finding—that an activated construct will be used in subsequent judgment—has been replicated in many subsequent studies, including those that have used behavioral descriptions (Srull & Wyer, 1979, 1980) and person exemplars (Bodenhausen, Schwarz, Bless, & Wänke, 1995; Herr, 1986; Herr, Sherman, & Fazio, 1983) as primes (see Higgins, 1996, for a review). Different mechanisms have been proposed as being responsible for these priming-based assimilation effects, including excitation-transfer (Wyer & Carlston, 1979), storage-bin placement (Srull & Wyer, 1989), and connectionism (Smith & DeCoster, 1998; for a review, see DeCoster & Claypool, 2004). What these have in common is the idea that a primed concept is easier to access and therefore more likely to be used in judgment. In a meta-analysis of assimilative priming effects, the overall effect size (d) was .35 (DeCoster & Claypool, 2004).[1]

In an interesting extension of priming research, it has been documented that *behavior* may assimilate to primed concepts as well. For example, when rudeness versus politeness was primed, individuals were more likely to subsequently interrupt an experimenter (Bargh, Chen, & Burrows, 1996), and when supermodels versus professors were primed, people performed worse in a Trivial Pursuit game (Dijksterhuis et al., 1998). The explanation typically offered for such behavioral effects is automatic behavior priming or, in Jamesian terms, the phenomenon of "ideomotor action" (James, 1890/1948), whereby exposure to concepts related to a behavior activate the behavioral tendency itself. Like priming effects on social judgments, priming effects on behavior are also linked to the basic concept of accessibility. In this case, the accessible construct makes related behavior more likely.

These findings demonstrate assimilation effects, and indeed a number of researchers have argued that assimilation is the predominant form of context effect in the social judgment literature (e.g., Higgins, 1989; Martin, Seta, & Crelia, 1990). Others, however, have suggested that contrast effects are the more typical outcome (Herr et al., 1983; Brown, Novick, Lord, & Richards, 1992; Gilbert, Giesler, & Morris, 1995), and still others have argued that there is no "typical" pattern (Stapel & Winkielman, 1998; Stapel, Koomen, & van der Pligt, 1996, 1997; Wegener & Petty, 1995). Most important in this regard is research that attempts to identify factors that affect whether assimilation *or* contrast occurs. The following text and Table 2.1 summarize some of the major factors that have been identified, along with descriptions and examples of relevant findings.

Features of the Priming Task or Instructions

1. Awareness of Priming Task

Assimilative effects appear to be strongest when primes are subtle, implicit, or unconscious rather than explicit in nature. In the classic study demonstrating this effect (Lombardi, Higgins, & Bargh, 1987, Study 1), participants were primed with the trait concepts "stubborn" and "persistent" through a scrambled sentence task; some participants were primed with "persistent" immediately prior to the critical judgment task, and some with "stubborn." All participants then read a description of a target person that was ambiguous in the sense that pretesting revealed the target to be described with equal frequency as persistent and stubborn (e.g., "once he makes up his mind to do something it is as good as done ..."). In the main study, the participant's task was to indicate the "one word that best described the person." Based on a recall test, participants were classified as unable to recall any of the sentences from the priming task or as able to recall at least one of the primes. The key finding was that participants who had *some* recall of the primes showed contrast from the recently presented prime—i.e., they were more likely to judge the target as persistent when recently primed with "stubborn"—whereas those who had no recall of the primes showed assimilation to the recent primes.

However, a second study that introduced a delay between the priming and judgment task showed assimilation to recent primes by both groups. Lombardi et al. (1987) argue that consciousness of the priming events enabled participants to "adopt flexible strategies in processing subsequent information relevant to the primed constructs. In sum, without consciousness of the priming events, subsequent stimuli are inevitably assimilated to the primed construct, whereas the presence of consciousness may result in either assimilation or contrast effect" (p. 426).

Later research by Strack and colleagues involved manipulating rather than measuring prime awareness (Strack, Schwarz, Bless, Kübler, & Wänke, 1993). When participants were reminded of a primed concept (in this case, positive or negative trait words), judgments of an ambiguous target were contrasted from the prime; when not reminded, assimilation occurred. Explanations for this pattern include the possibility that those who are aware of or recall a priming event "use the events to form a standard that subsequently functioned as a reference point" (Higgins, 1989, p. 92) or because of deliberate attempts to exclude the information (because it is perceived as inappropriate or likely to produce bias) (Bargh, 1992; Martin, 1986; Martin et al., 1990; Petty & Wegener, 1993; Schwarz & Bless, 1992a; Strack, 1992; Wegener & Petty, 1995; Wilson & Brekke, 1994). Additionally,

Skowronski, Carlston, and Isham (1993) have suggested that awareness of primes reinforces extreme standards that do not match the (typically ambiguous) features of the targets being judged. Explicit processing occurs, and the lack of fit between the target and prime produces contrast.

2. Processing Goals and Mind-Sets

Related to the issue of prime awareness is the type of processing goal participants have in mind as they form impressions of others. For example, instructions to be accurate create a desire to make context-independent judgments, and this may lead to overcorrection and contrast effects (Thompson, Roman, Moskowitz, Chaiken, & Bargh, 1994). In one interesting study, Moskowitz and Roman (1992) exposed participants to a set of positive or negative trait-implying sentences and either led them to *memorize* the sentences or to *form an impression* of the actors in the sentences. They were then asked to judge the ambiguous "Donald" (see Higgins et al., 1977). Those asked to memorize showed assimilation effects, whereas those asked to form impressions showed contrast effects (see also Stapel & Koomen, 2000). Moskowitz and Roman (1992) suggest that awareness of the primes was responsible for this effect: Memory participants made spontaneous inferences and therefore were less aware of the primes (Uleman, 1989), with assimilation the result. On the other hand, because the impression formation participants consciously attended to the traits, contrast resulted, presumably for the same reasons underlying the "awareness of prime" effects described previously. Others have suggested, however, that memory instructions prime a broad, abstract, trait category, whereas impression instructions produce specific actor-trait links (Stapel et al., 1996); more on this issue appears in the "Prime/Category Width" section that follows.

In addition to explicit goals, certain mind-sets can affect the direction of context effects as well. In a social comparison study, Stapel and Koomen (2001a) used scrambled sentence priming tasks (Study 4) or a paragraph-writing task (Study 2) to subtly activate either a *comparison* or an *integration* mind-set. Specifically, participants were asked to unscramble sentences or write a paragraph including words such as *compare*, *distinguish*, and *differ* (to emphasize comparison), or *together*, *integrate*, and *harmonize* (to emphasize integration). All participants were then exposed to an upward or downward comparison target, and then they evaluated themselves on dimensions relevant to the comparison information. The comparison mind-set produced reliable evidence of contrast from the social comparison target, whereas integration produced assimilation (see also Stapel & Koomen, 2001b).

Features of the Prime/Context Itself

3. Extremity of Prime

Primes can vary in their extremity; some may activate moderate levels of a concept or trait, whereas others may activate more extreme levels, at either end of the trait/concept continuum. In general, research suggests that when primes are extreme, *contrast* effects on subsequent judgment are more likely to occur. This effect was documented in classic studies of psychophysics (Brown, 1953; Helson, 1964) and in more recent studies of person judgment as well (Manis, Nelson, & Shedler, 1988; Moskowitz & Roman, 1992; Newman & Uleman, 1990; Stapel & Koomen, 1997; Strack et al., 1993). For example, Herr (1986) found that participants primed with extremely hostile person exemplars (Adolf Hitler, Charles Manson) later judged an ambiguously hostile "Donald" to be *less* hostile than did participants primed with extremely nonhostile primes (Peter Pan) or moderately hostile primes (Bobby Knight). The extreme nonhostile primes also resulted in increased hostility ratings of Donald relative to moderately nonhostile primes. Extreme primes produced contrast effects, whereas moderate primes produced assimilation (see also Manis et al., 1988; Philippot, Schwarz, Carrera, De Vries, & Van Yperen, 1991).

The general consensus regarding why these effects occur is that extreme primes operate as standards against which the target is compared; because the target is not as extreme as the prime, contrast occurs. Skowronski, Carlston, and Isham (1993) suggest that this occurs, in part, because processing following extreme primes is *explicit*. On the other hand, moderate primes are likely to be closer to the target, to invite *implicit processing*, and to serve as an interpretive framework, with assimilation as the result. Supporting the "interpretation" perspective, one study found that moderate primes produced assimilation but only if the primes were presented before the target stimulus was encoded (Koomen, Stapel, Jansen, & In 't Veld, 1998; cf., Stapel & Winkielman, 1998).

4. Prime/Category "Width"

Related to prime extremity is the *width* of the prime; some primes are broad and inclusive (e.g., a general trait term such as "conceited"), whereas others are specific or focused (e.g., "Peter is conceited") (Stapel & Koomen, 1996). Research examining the impact of this feature has typically involved manipulations in which either broad, abstract behavior labels are primed or specific actor-trait links or *exemplars* are primed. For example, Stapel and Koomen (1996) exposed participants to trait-implying sentences, in much the same manner as Moskowitz and Roman (1992). In some cases, the sentences described an "impersonal" target, described by pronoun only (e.g., "He knew he could handle most problems that would come up," implying persistence), or a personalized target (e.g., "Peter [depicted in a photo] knew he could handle most problems that would come up"). Participants were primed with either positive or negative trait-implying sentences and with the personalized or impersonalized versions of these sentences. They then judged the same ambiguous Donald paragraph used in Higgins et al. (1977). Those exposed to the personalized primes contrasted Donald from the valence of those primes; those exposed to impersonalized primes showed assimilation to those primes (at least under "memory" conditions; see earlier description of processing goals).

Comparable effects have also emerged in research examining *behavioral responses* to primes or context. In a study that might be called a modern classic, researchers found that priming of an elderly stereotype (through exposure to broad terms associated with that category) led individuals to walk more slowly as they left an experiment—a behavioral assimilation effect (Bargh et al., 1996). In follow-up research, however, others found that priming of *exemplars* rather than broad categories produced behavioral contrast effects (Dijksterhuis et al., 1998). For example, after imagining a specific "professor" (Albert Einstein) versus a specific "supermodel" (Claudia Schiffer), participants' performance on a subsequent "general knowledge" test suffered—performance was contrasted from the activated exemplar (better performance in the Schiffer versus Einstein conditions). In the same study, however, primes of the broad category of "professor" versus "supermodel" produced *assimilation* effects—better test performance in the professor condition (Dijksterhuis et al., 1998, Study 1; see also Dijksterhuis, Spears, & Lépinasse, 2001; Haddock, Macrae, & Fleck, 2002).

Like prime extremity, the width of a prime seems important because narrow primes are more likely to be used as comparative standards of judgment that exclude the target, whereas wide or abstract primes serve as interpretive frames in which the target can be included (Schwarz & Bless, 1992a; Stapel & Koomen, 1996, 1997; Stapel & Schwarz, 1998).

5. Distinctness of Prime/Context

Though it overlaps considerably with prime/category width, it is also worth highlighting *prime distinctness* as a distinct contributor to contrast effects. A prime is distinct to the extent that it "constitutes a separate entity with this clear object boundaries" (Stapel & Winkielman, 1998,

p. 637). In general, the more distinct a prime or context is, the more likely that it will be used as a standard of comparison and produce contrast of more moderate targets (see also Helson, 1964).

The aforementioned research on exemplars versus traits is certainly consistent with this idea, but distinctness can also be introduced in a number of other ways as well. Just some of them are highlighted in the following sections and in Table 2.1.

5a. Unitizing

Distinctness may be created by "unitizing" the context and the target—that is, presenting them together or having them judged at the same time rather than separately. In an illustrative study on this point, participants rated their attraction toward two briefly described individuals (Martin & Seta, 1983). Half the time, the first target (who provided the instantiation of context) was rated prior to the other, and half the time both targets were reviewed, in turn, before either was rated. The first target was always depicted as moderately similar in attitudes to the participant (sharing 3 of 6 attitudes), and the second was depicted as highly similar and therefore more likeable overall (sharing 6 of 6 attitudes). The key finding was that judgments of the likeability of the target (the second person) were *assimilated* to those of the first person when the targets were "unitized"—rated after reviewing both—whereas judgments were *contrasted* from the first person when judgments were separated.

Other studies have relied on other "order of judgment" variations of this sort (Manis, Paskewitz, & Cotler, 1986; Stapel & Spears, 1996; Stapel & Winkielman, 1998). It seems clear that when presentation of a contextual cue and the target occur simultaneously, *assimilation* results, but that a serial presentation of context and target is more likely to produce *contrast* (e.g., Manis et al., 1986; Manis et al., 1988; Wedell, Parducci, & Geiselman, 1987). Furthermore, contrast is likely when the contextual stimulus is explicitly judged (versus not judged), presumably because judging the context makes it a distinct unit (Parducci, 1992; Parducci & Wedell, 1990; Stapel & Winkielman, 1998; Upshaw & Ostrom, 1984).

5b. Interruption

Distinctness can also be manipulated through procedures designed to keep a construct activated for later use or not. For example, Martin (1986) interrupted participants (or not) as they took part in a mood induction task designed to instantiate a positive or negative context. Participants later judged an ambiguously adventurous/reckless target (the famous Donald). In the case when the priming task was completed, mood state served as a distinct construct to be used as a standard of comparison for judging the target, resulting in contrast effects: Donald was judged more favorably by those in a negative mood than by those in a positive mood. But interruption made the context indistinct; furthermore, the lack of closure kept the primed mood active and available for use in interpreting the target (see Zeigarnik, 1935). That is, assimilation resulted from the indistinct prime, as the effects of the unfinished context extended to the target.

5c. Communication Rules

Conversational norms typically prohibit redundancy and require that participants add new information as conversations unfold (the "given-new" contract) (Clark & Haviland, 1977; see also Clark, 1985; Grice, 1975). What this means for social judgment is that an evaluation of one person or event may normatively preclude its use in the evaluation of another person or event. For example, if people are asked about their marital satisfaction and then about their job satisfaction, it is implicit that these domains of life should be considered as separate, nonoverlapping entities—that judgment of one should not be used to render judgment of the other (Schwarz, Strack, & Mai, 1991). Because these entities are *distinct*, there should be a null effect of context, or perhaps a slight contrast effect, such that the first judgment (the context) is uncorrelated or negatively correlated with the second (the target). Under some circumstances, however, norms of nonredundancy may be relaxed, thereby allowing for a blending or assimilation of the two judgments. Under these circumstances, the events or people are nondistinct, and assimilation is the result.

In a study on question ordering and question implications that addressed these issues, Schwarz et al. (1991) asked participants to rate their happiness with marriage and their happiness with life in general. If the global rating preceded the specific marital rating, the finding was assimilation: Judgments of general life satisfaction correlated .67 with ratings of marital satisfaction. In this case, the question ordering indicated, implicitly, that marital happiness should be considered a part of general life happiness (i.e., the norm of nonredundancy was relaxed). In another condition, however, the question wording made it explicit that marital happiness and general life happiness were distinct entities: "Now we would like to learn about two areas of life that may be important for people's overall well-being: a) happiness with marriage, b) happiness with life in general." With this wording, the correlation reduced to a nonsignificant $r = .18$ (see also Ottati, Riggle, Wyer, Schwarz, & Kuklinski, 1989; Schwarz & Bless, 1992a; Strack, Martin, & Schwarz, 1988; Tourangeau & Rasinski, 1988). Conversational norms have their impact in this case through indicating the distinctness or nondistinctness of context and target.

5d. Temporal Distance

For similar reasons, assimilation might be expected if the context is temporally close rather than distant. For example, in a study on life satisfaction, those reminded of positive or negative past events (presumably from a distinct time period of personal history) showed contrast effects in their judgments of current life satisfaction: They viewed themselves as happier now if they previously remembered a past sad event (Strack, Schwarz, & Gschneidinger, 1985). But those reminded of a "present" life event—presumably nondistinct from their current lives—showed assimilation of their current life satisfaction judgments to the primed event.

6. Consistency or Entitativity of Prime/Context

Entitativity refers to the extent to which an object or group is perceived as a unified entity (see Campbell, 1958). In the context of social judgment research, some contextual cues or categories may be highly entitative in nature (as when they involve a specific person [i.e., an exemplar]), whereas other categories are more diffuse or nonentitative (as when they represent a broad and diverse group of people). One generally expects consistency from highly entitative objects, whereas, by definition, less entitativity means less consistency or coherence in the attributes of the object. Research examining entitativity as it affects social judgment generally suggests that if an expectation or context is highly entitative, assimilation of new information is likely to occur; otherwise, contrast is the outcome.

In one relevant study, context was manipulated by creating high or low expectations about the level of psychopathology of an individual (highly entitative), a family (slightly less entitative), or a random group of people (nonentitative) (Hilton & von Hippel, 1990, Study 2). Participants then were asked to judge the psychopathology evidenced in a set of "vocabulary definitions" that had supposedly been provided by the context category (the individual, the family, or the group). These definitions came from a set previously used by Manis and Paskewitz (1984b) to indicate various levels of thought disturbance. The items used in this study had been rated by pretest participants as *moderate* or *ambiguous* with regard to their level of psychopathology (e.g., "APPLE: Nourishment for the stomach"). The researchers found assimilation of the midrange behaviors to the created expectation in the highly entitative condition; that is, the definitions were judged as indicative of high pathology when the context created the expectation that the individual was pathological and of low pathology when the context created the expectation that the individual was "normal." But the "family" produced a mild contrast effect and the random group a marked contrast effect in judgments of the midrange definitions. According to the researchers, "the pressure to assimilate unexpected behaviors should diminish" if a category or context is nonentitative (Hilton & von Hippel, 1990, p. 445).

The careful reader might note an apparent inconsistency in this set of findings and those reported by Stapel and Koomen (1996; see "Prime/ Category Width" section). Specifically, whereas Hilton and von Hippel found *assimilation* to a specific exemplar (an individual) compared to a group, Stapel and Koomen found *contrast* from exemplar primes relative to general trait primes. The difference in these findings may be traced to the degree of connection that existed between the context and target in each study. In Hilton and von Hippel, the category activated in the context phase was also the target; that is, the judged behaviors were supposedly performed by the same actor(s) about whom expectations were created. This connection produced the variations in expectations regarding consistency, such that, for example, one perceived the highly pathological *individual* as still pathological when he or she offered midrange vocabulary definitions. However, in Stapel and Koomen (1996), the context (exemplar or trait) was supposedly unrelated to the target (the ambiguous Donald). This separation allowed for the narrow construct—the exemplar—to serve as a standard of comparison and produce contrast, whereas the broad construct—the trait—served as a diffuse interpretation frame for the subsequent target judgment. In short, the connection between the context and target may moderate the extent to which specific and entitative versus diffuse and nonentitative constructs produce assimilation.

Features of the Target and Judgment

7. Similarity, Appropriateness, and Applicability/ Relevance: Context/Target Overlap

The contextual features discussed thus far focus on the nature of the prime itself and only hint at the importance of *target* features in producing assimilation and contrast. Research on prime/target overlap addresses this point more explicitly. In general, comparison between context and target is more likely if the two belong to the same category— if comparing seems appropriate (Martin et al., 1990). In Brown's (1953) classic study of weight estimation, judges showed contrast from extreme weight anchors of the same type as the targets but not from an equally heavy *tray* that was also lifted. Brown (1953) stated, "The anchor, to be effective, must be perceived as a member of the same class" as the target (p. 210;

see also Parducci, Knobel, & Thomas, 1976; Suls & Wills, 1991; Upshaw & Ostrom, 1984).

Similar findings have emerged in research on social judgment. For example, friendly or hostile animal exemplars (such as "bunny" or "shark") did not seem to serve as standards of comparison for an ambiguously friendly/hostile *human* target (Stapel et al., 1997), and women's self-judgments of attractiveness were not contrasted from very attractive exemplars if those exemplars were described as professional models—presumably a different category (Cash, Cash, & Butters, 1983). More recently, heightened relevance of a comparison (induced by considerations of similarity to a prime) produced behavioral contrast whether the comparison target was an exemplar or a broad category (LeBoeuf & Estes, 2004). This phenomenon of contrast-inducing target-context similarity echoes themes introduced in Kahneman and Miller's (1986) concept of "local norms," Manis and Paskewitz's (1984a) concept of "norm specificity," and Biernat, Manis, and Nelson's (1991) discussion of "within-group standards."

Whereas target-context similarity may set the stage for comparison and contrast, a primed concept must be both accessible and relevant (applicable) to the target being judged for *assimilation* effects to occur as well (see Banaji, Hardin, & Rothman, 1993; DeCoster & Claypool, 2004; Fazio, Powell, & Herr, 1983; Higgins, 1996; Higgins & King, 1981; Higgins & Chaires, 1980; Sedikides, 1990; c.f., Stapel & Winkielman, 1998). For example, after unscrambling sentences that primed the concept of "aggression," *male* but not female targets were judged more aggressive; after unscrambling sentences that primed "dependence," *female* but not male targets were judged more dependent. Targets were assimilated to primes only if they were linked to the prime, in this case, via group stereotypes (Banaji et al., 1993). Others have suggested that judgments may also shift toward the *valence* of evaluatively congruent primes even when there is no denotative similarity between the prime and the target (DeCoster & Claypool, 2004; Martin, 1986; Skowronski et al., 1993; Srull & Wyer, 1980).

Furthermore, Stapel et al. (1997) found some evidence of assimilation of judgements of humans to animal primes in their study (see also Stapel & Winkielman, 1998). What this suggests is that similarity or applicability in itself may not distinguish *whether* assimilation or contrast occurs, but rather that prime–target similarity, relevance, or applicability is necessary for *any* type of context effect (assimilation *or* contrast) to occur. Instead, other factors in conjunction with similarity may matter. For example, a number of researchers have argued that appropriateness of context *and* context extremity are preconditions for contrast (Eiser, 1990; Helson, 1964; Parducci, 1992; Parducci & Wedell, 1990; Schwarz & Bless,

1992a; Sherif & Hovland, 1961). Contrast is also more likely than assimilation if the prime is distinct (see previous section) and is relevant to the dimension of judgment (see next section). Presumably, these factors increase the use of the prime or context as a comparison standard rather than an interpretive frame (Stapel & Winkielman, 1998).

8. Relevance of the Judgment Dimension

As noted earlier, for primes or contextual stimuli to have any effect on subsequent judgment, they must be relevant or *applicable* to the target being judged. That is, weight judgments are likely to be affected by the heaviness of contextual objects but not by their color or size, and judgments of a person on dimension X are likely to be affected by primes relevant to dimension X but not by primes relevant to dimensions Y or Z. Similarly, when a prime relates to one dimension, judgments of the target along *that* dimension, but not others, should be affected. Thus, for example, primes having to do with hostility should affect judgments of a target's hostility but not his or her other attributes (Bargh & Pietramonaco, 1982; Erdley & D'Agostino, 1988; Herr, 1986; Higgins et al., 1977; Moskowitz & Skurnik, 1999).

However, like similarity, dimensional relevance in itself may not determine whether assimilation or contrast effects emerge. For example, in the study by Higgins et al. (1977) described previously, primes relevant to adventurousness or recklessness produced *assimilation* in judgments of the ambiguously adventurous/reckless Donald, whereas unrelated trait primes had no effect (see also Srull & Wyer, 1979). But in a study by Stapel and Winkielman (1998), relevant (compared to irrelevant) primes produced *contrast* (see also Schwarz, Münkel, & Hippler, 1990; Manis & Paskewitz, 1984a), a finding that is fairly common in research on psychophysical judgment as well (Brown, 1953; Helson, 1947, 1964; Postman & Miller, 1945).

The key to distinguishing which effect—assimilation or contrast—occurs seems to be the *explicit linking* or not of the contextual stimuli to the target of judgment. In psychophysical research, the contextual stimuli are often explicitly pointed to as a standard of comparison (e.g., "how heavy is this new object compared to the anchor?"). And in person judgment studies, an explicit link between a relevant contextual cue and the target can be made by asking participants to explicitly rate the contextual stimulus on the dimensions of interest (Stapel & Winkielman, 1998; Upshaw & Ostrom, 1984). In these cases, the relevant primes/contexts tend to produce contrast because the context provides a standard of comparison. In studies that use subtler primes, or primes that are intentionally disconnected from the target judgment phase, assimilation to a relevant contextual cue is the more likely outcome (Banaji et al., 1993; Higgins et al., 1977; Srull & Wyer, 1979). This echoes themes described under the topic of "prime awareness"—obvious links or comparisons may produce contrast, whereas subtler connections between prime and target may produce assimilation.

9. Ambiguity/Extremity of Targets

The features described in the preceding section primarily have to do with the nature of the context as it affects judgment outcomes, but attributes of the judgment *targets* themselves clearly matter as well. Perhaps the most important feature in this regard is target ambiguity versus target extremity on the dimension of interest. Some target stimuli are more extreme or less ambiguous than others. In general, context effects of any kind may require ambiguous stimuli: "Context information will be a guide to interpretation only when there is something to be interpreted, that is, when the target stimulus is ambiguous rather than unambiguous" (Stapel & Winkielman, 1998, p. 635).

Ambiguity can be operationalized in a number of ways. In the priming study by Lombardi et al. (1987), the description of "Donald" was ambiguous in that it was equally likely to be characterized (by nonprimed, pretest participants) as "persistent" or "stubborn." In other research, ambiguous targets are unknown individuals, or even unreal animals (Herr et al., 1983), or they are targets whose standing is "moderate" or "midrange" on the dimension of interest (Manis et al., 1988).

Many social judgment studies have used only ambiguous targets fact that context in implicit recognition of the fact that context effects require a stimulus open to interpretation (e.g., Higgins et al., 1977; Srull & Wyer, 1979, 1980). Finding more evidence of assimilative priming for "more ambiguous" versus "less ambiguous" behavioral stimuli, Srull and Wyer (1979) suggested that "the effect of category accessibility on the encoding of behavioral information is much more pronounced when the implications of this behavior are relatively ambiguous" (p. 1670).

But some studies have explicitly compared judgments of ambiguous and unambiguous targets. For example, Herr et al. (1983) found assimilation effects when moderate primes (i.e., moderately ferocious or unferocious animals [wolves or cats]) preceded ambiguous targets (unreal animals, such as "jabos"). They also found contrast effects in judgments of the same ambiguous targets when these were preceded by extreme primes such as grizzly bears versus kittens (see "Extremity of Prime" section). In other words, both assimilation and contrast effects occurred with ambiguous stimuli, with the direction depending on the extremity of the prime. When unambiguous stimuli—real animals such as foxes and porcupines—were judged, contrast was the result regardless of the prime type. Herr et al. (1983) suggest that for unambiguous targets, "the primed category may still provide an external standard of comparison to which the stimulus is contrasted" (p. 327; see also Philippot et al., 1991; Stapel et al., 1997).

What this line of research suggests is that ambiguous stimuli are open to interpretation, and the context may provide that interpretation, resulting in assimilation at *encoding* (at least under some conditions, such as moderate or "wide" primes). Unambiguous stimuli do not require interpretation, so assimilation to context does not occur. However, assuming that the context is relevant to judging the target, it may serve as a comparison standard that may be "independent of whether the target requires interpretation" (Stapel et al., 1997, p. 53). The result is contrast at the judgment phase.

It is worth noting, however, that in the Herr et al. studies, the unambiguous stimuli (real animals) were nonetheless *moderate* with regard to the dimension of ferocity—they had been pretested as such. Extreme stimuli, however, may be immune to context effects. Albert Einstein, for example, is likely to be judged intelligent regardless of the context in which he is considered; that is, a ceiling effect, relatively immovable by context, might be expected. Interestingly, in a study that used a well-known stimulus— the participant's "good friend"—as the unambiguous target, no context effects emerged in judgments of hostility. That is, whether primed with hostile or nonhostile cues, the good friend was rated quite favorably (around 7.5 on a 9-point scale). This may indeed reflect a ceiling effect in judgments of an extreme (unambiguously nonhostile target) (Stapel et al., 1997).[2]

10. Judgment Language/Form

In addition to features of the context and target, the nature of response language may also affect whether assimilation or contrast effects emerge in social judgment. Judgments of social stimuli can take many forms, but the most typical is the subjective trait rating—how adventurous is Donald?, how psychopathological is Bill? In general, both early psychophysical research and later social judgment research documents that subjective ratings are more likely to produce contrast effects than are more "objective" or "common rule" ratings. The latter type of responses can be characterized as "judgmental languages that supposedly cannot be redefined, in that they have an external reference independent of subjects' perceptions" (Eiser, 1990, p. 15).

For example, Krantz and Campbell (1961) asked participants to judge the length of lines either in inches or in more subjective units (above or below "average"). Context was manipulated by virtue of having the target stimulus (a 20-inch line) located within a set of shorter lines or longer lines. Both types of judgments showed contrast effects—the line was judged longer in the short-line context—but the key finding was that this effect was strongest in subjective ratings compared to objective units.[3]

My own research on stereotyping, though perhaps more relevant to topics addressed later in this book, supports a similar conclusion (e.g., Biernat & Kobrynowicz, 1997). Social stereotypes may operate as a feature of context, in that, for example, knowledge of a target person's sex establishes expectations for his or her likely behavior or performance. We have found that judgments of men and women for sex-typed jobs reflect *assimilation* effects when made in common-rule units (e.g., estimated scores on standardized tests) but *contrast* effects when made in subjective (e.g., "good" to "bad") units. That is, when evaluating targets for a masculine job, men were judged better than women in common-rule units but less good than women in subjective units; the converse occurred when considering targets for a feminine job (Biernat & Kobrynowicz, 1997). Because subjective judgments are slippery and open to shifts in meaning depending on context (in this case, the group membership of the target), contrast effects are more likely.

☐ Summary and Some Big Issues

To summarize, context—in the form of explicit expectations, subtle and not-so-subtle primes, and situational cues—serves as the backdrop against which subsequent stimuli (e.g., persons) are experienced and judged. Both assimilative and contrastive tendencies are possible in any given context, and the judgment outcome appears to depend on the features of context, target, and response language described in this chapter. Furthermore, *memory* for a target judgment can be influenced by a combination of context effects at the time of initial judgment and context effects at later recall, as suggested by research on the "change of standard" effect (Higgins & Liberman, 1994; Higgins & Lurie, 1983; Higgins & Stangor, 1988). For example, "Judge Jones" may be characterized as "harsh," initially, relative to other judges who give objectively shorter sentences for criminal offenses (Higgins & Lurie, 1983). But if later seen in a different context (e.g., judges who give longer sentences), memory for Judge Jones's original sentencing decisions may be distorted in the direction of the new context. In short, the context-bound nature of judgment may accumulate over time in the evaluation of any one target.

The list of ten factors described in this chapter is surely not an exhaustive catalog of features that contribute to context effects. The factors are also *not* mutually exclusive; distinctness of prime, for example, is highly related to prime/category width. Furthermore, many of these factors may produce their effects in tandem with other features—e.g., contrast effects may require both an extreme and applicable prime; assimilation may require both a wide prime and an ambiguous target; extremity of prime and prime breadth may interact to produce a complex pattern of results (Moskowitz & Skurnik, 1999). Nonetheless, the list provides a fairly broad inventory of features relevant to whether assimilation or contrast effects emerge.

A central theme in both this list and this volume is that context may have one of two broad classes of effect: The context (e.g., a primed trait concept) may serve either as an interpretive frame toward which the target is drawn (assimilation) or as a comparison standard against which the target is contrasted (see Stapel & Winkielman, 1998, for recent presentations of this perspective). Virtually all of the features previously described have their impact through this proximal mechanism. To take just a few examples, prime awareness and prime distinctness set the context apart as a standard of comparison, whereas prime width allows the target to be included in the activated category (Schwarz & Bless, 1992a). To the extent that ten factors can be boiled down to one, this is it!

The next chapter will discuss a variety of judgment models that take this theme of frame versus referent, interpretation versus comparison, to heart. Before moving to this discussion, however, it is worth addressing a few major issues that emerge in any discussion of context effects.

Perceptual versus Semantic?

Are context effects perceptual in nature—is Donald really *perceived* as less hostile following an exposure to Hitler?—or are they semantic, response-based phenomena? This has been a perennial issue in the literature on psychophysics and is certainly relevant to social judgment as well. Helson (1964), in his theory of adaptation level, represents the perceptual view most clearly. The classic example of a contrast effect from this perspective is the experience of tepid water as "hot" following immersion in cold water, or as "cold" following immersion in hot water. This experience is described by Helson as a "sensory change" that reflects a basic adaptive process (Helson, 1964, p. 136).

Best representing the semantic perspective is variable perspective theory, introduced by Upshaw and his colleagues (e.g., Upshaw, 1962, 1969; Upshaw & Ostrom, 1984) and based on principles put forth in Volkmann's

(1951) "rubber band" model. Essentially, the argument is that judges develop a frame of reference or "perspective" based on the context or their own subjective experience and then define response categories to map onto this perspective. The endpoints of a rating scale (whatever its form) are anchored to the endpoints of the judge's perspective, and in this sense, context effects reflect judgment, not perceptual, phenomena. That is, Donald may be judged less hostile only because the contextual priming of "Hitler" created a perspective in which Hitler anchored the high end of the "hostility" scale.

Many researchers have noted the difficulty of definitively teasing apart these possibilities (Manis & Paskewitz, 1984a; Parducci, 1992; Strack, 1992; Upshaw & Ostrom, 1984). One can conduct the kinds of comparisons of judgment language described in point 10 in this chapter, arguing, for example, that context effects on common-rule scales reflect perceptual events whereas context effects on subjective scales *may be* merely semantic in nature. But this is problematic, as it assumes that common-rule estimates provide a *direct index* of perception, an untenable position. As Eiser (1990) notes, "no response mode is more than an *indicator* of any subjective representation" (p. 15).

One can also compare judgments of novel versus well-known targets. The logic here is that well-known targets do not require interpretation or deep encoding, and therefore any context effects must be purely *semantic* or *judgmental* in nature. In one relevant study, exemplar primes produced contrast effects in judgments of both novel, ambiguous targets and well-known individuals (participants' roommates) (Philippot et al., 1991). This is suggestive of a semantic effect. However, another study reported in the same article included broad trait concept primes along with the exemplars. In this case, assimilation effects emerged but only in judgments of the unknown target, suggesting a *perceptual* effect (i.e., due to encoding rather than judgment processes). The empirical evidence ultimately does not resolve the issue, as both phenomena may occur under very similar conditions.

Additionally, one can compare judgment to some "gold standard" such as paired choice estimates. For example, if I judge Alice as taller than David on a subjective "short–tall" scale but later indicate, in a direct comparison, that David is taller than Alice, it suggests that my subjective judgment was *only* judgmental rather than perceptual (Manis, Biernat, & Nelson, 1990). But this too has its problems, as it denies, for example, the "reality" of the experience of Alice as tall (in a particular context, i.e., "for a woman"). Importantly, too, we have argued that even when judgments of the same target differ depending on the response language used, these judgments may both be important in predicting different kinds of outcomes for that target (Biernat, Vescio, & Manis, 1998; Biernat & Vescio,

2002). For example, judging Alice as subjectively tall may lead me to discuss with her the difficulties in finding women's clothing that fits; judging David as (objectively) taller than Alice may lead me to ask him to reach a book on a high shelf. Both judgments are real or genuine, with real implications for the target.

But perhaps Eiser (1990) summarizes the "perceptual versus semantic" discussion best. He writes:

> About all one can safely assume is that changes in judgment *may* reflect changes in subjective representation, and if there are changes in subjective representation, they *may* be due to sensory adaptation. However, it is very easy to observe changes in judgment in situations where we would not wish to introduce any notion of perceptual adaptation. Indeed, the significance for psychology of principles of judgment is their generalizability for many different kinds of situations and their *independence* from any model of perception (pp. 15–16, emphasis in original).

Contrast as Comparison versus Correction?

When contrast effects occur, they may be due to substantively different processes. One is a *correction* process, whereby one desires to remove a contextual influence out of one's evaluation of a target stimulus. For example, the earlier descriptions of prime awareness and conversational norms point to situations in which the judge views a contextual influence as inappropriate and desires to partial it out of any subsequent judgment (see Martin et al., 1990; Moskowitz & Skurnik, 1999; Petty & Wegener, 1993; Wilson & Brekke, 1994). It is important to note that consciousness or awareness is not a necessary requirement for correction contrast to occur; that is, one can engage in correction without being able to verbally report that a context is being partialled out of a judgment (for a discussion, see Moskowitz & Skurnik, 1999). Nonetheless, the correction process requires the availability of cognitive resources.

These active correction processes can be distinguished from what we might call "comparison contrast" (e.g., Stapel & Winkielman, 1998), as when information is used as a standard of comparison—perhaps effortlessly or automatically. Many classic studies of psychophysics have assumed—implicitly or explicitly—that contrast is an effortless process, developing naturally out of the situation at hand, as have some models of social judgment (e.g., Manis & Paskewitz, 1984a). But others have assumed that assimilation is the default process, with contrast always requiring extra effort or energy (e.g., Martin, 1986). Still others have argued that either assimilation or contrast may be the default (relatively automatic) outcome, and either assimilation or contrast may be achieved through effortful correction (Petty & Wegener, 1993; Wegener & Petty, 1997; see also Moskowitz & Skurnik, 1999). This theme of automaticity versus effort will be apparent in many of the models discussed in the next chapter. For now at least, we will assume that both assimilation and contrast effects may be observed through relatively automatic mechanisms as well as through controlled correction processes.

TABLE 2.1. Factors Affecting Whether Assimilation to or Contrast from Primed Concepts/Standards Occurs

Concept/Factor	Illustrative Source	Finding/Account	Operationalization
1. Prime awareness	Strack et al. (1993)	When reminded of prime, contrast occurs; not reminded = assimilation Those who are aware of or recall a priming event (a) "use the events to form a standard that subsequently functioned as a reference point" (Higgins, 1989, p. 92) or (b) deliberately attempt to exclude primed/contextual information (Martin et al., 1990)	Prime is positive or negative trait dimension; DV = impression of ambiguous target
2. Processing goals: memorization vs. impression formation instructions	Moskowitz & Roman (1992)	Instructions to memorize prime lead to assimilation; instructions to form impression of primed targets lead to contrast Memorization leads to spontaneous inference of traits; lack of awareness produces assimilation; impression formation produces consciousness of primes and contrast	Participants read trait-implying positive or negative behaviors under different instructional sets; they then judge ambiguous "Donald"
3. Extremity of context/prime	Herr (1986)	Contrast is more likely when primes are extreme; assimilation when moderate Extreme primes serve as the standard of comparison to which ambiguous target is compared; moderate primes serve as the interpretive frame	Ambiguous target person's hostility is judged in context of extreme standards of hostility (Adolf Hitler vs. Shirley Temple) or moderate standards (Joe Frazier vs. Billie Jean King)

TABLE 2.1. Factors Affecting Whether Assimilation to or Contrast from Primed Concepts/Standards Occurs (*Continued*)

Concept/Factor	Illustrative Source	Finding/Account	Operationalization
4. Prime width (especially traits vs. exemplars)	Stapel, Koomen, & van der Pligt (1996)	Wide contextual categories (e.g., traits) are likely to produce assimilation; narrow categories (e.g., exemplars) act as standards and produce contrast	Participants read positive or negative trait-implying sentences about an impersonal target/ trait concept or a personalized exemplar; then judge ambiguous "Donald"
5. Distinctness of context		Contrast more likely if prime/ context is distinct from target	
5a. Unitizing context and target/ presentation mode	Wedell, Parducci, & Geiselman (1987)	Sequential/successive presentation of context and target tends to produce contrast, whereas paired presentation produces assimilation; in the latter case, inclusion occurs, and there is a "failure to separate the individual stimulus from other stimuli that are simultaneously present" (p. 231)	Faces are presented successively vs. in pairs; DV = judged attractiveness of (average) target face
5b. Completion of task	Martin (1986, Study 3)	Zeigarnik effect produces assimilation as effects of unfinished context/prime extend to target; contrast occurs when priming task is completed	Pos or neg self-relevant statements are written (primed mood) and interrupted vs. not; DV = impression formed of ambiguously adventurous/ reckless target
5c. Conversational norms	Schwarz, Strack, & Mai (1991)	Given-new contract (Clark, 1985; Grice, 1975) and norm of nonredundancy indicate that judgments of one target should exclude judgment of previously described/ evaluated target (contrast or null effect)	DV = correlation between happiness with marriage and happiness with life in general; correlation is strong when marriage question precedes "life in general" question (assimilation), but if both are presented as separate areas of life, correlation is reduced

TABLE 2.1. Factors Affecting Whether Assimilation to or Contrast from Primed Concepts/Standards Occurs (*Continued*)

Concept/Factor	Illustrative Source	Finding/Account	Operationalization
5d. Temporal distance of events	Strack, Schwarz, & Gschneidinger (1985)	Distant events are more likely to be excluded from a representation, resulting in contrast; close events result in assimilation	Prime is pos or neg events in present life or past DV = current life satisfaction
6. Consistency/ entitativity of category/context	Hilton & von Hippel (1990, Study 2)	If an expectation/context is highly entitative (e.g., it involves an individual as opposed to a diverse group), assimilation of new, unexpected information occurs; otherwise, contrast "The pressure to assimilate unexpected behaviors should diminish" if a category or context is nonentitative (p. 445)	Expectations created about psychopathology of individual, family, or random group DV = judgments of psychopathology of moderate/ ambiguous behaviors that differ from induced expectation
7. Similarity/ applicability of context to target	Brown (1953)	Contrast and assimilation may both require that the context/ prime and target overlap or belong to the same category	Weight is anchor; judgments of other weights are contrasted from it, but "tray" weight is not
8. Relevance of judgment dimension	Schwarz, Münkel, & Hippler (1990) vs. Higgins et al. (1977)	Contextual cue must be relevant/linked to target being judged for any context effect: contrast if relevant prime/context is explicitly linked to target (context as standard); assimilation if relevant prime is subtle or not explicitly linked (context as interpretive frame)	Schwarz et al. (1990): Contrast in judgment of the "Germanicness" of beverages when Ps previously estimate how many Germans drink vodka or beer (relative to when Ps previously estimate caloric content of vodka or beer) Higgins et al. (1977): Judgments of ambiguously reckless/ adventurous Donald are assimilated to primes related to these traits but are not affected by unrelated primes

TABLE 2.1. Factors Affecting Whether Assimilation to or Contrast from Primed Concepts/Standards Occurs (*Continued*)

Concept/Factor	Illustrative Source	Finding/Account	Operationalization
9. Ambiguity/ extremity of target	Stapel et al. (1997)	Ambiguous or moderate targets are assimilated to existing context/expectation; unambiguous (or extreme) targets are not assimilated, sometimes contrasted	Participants judge ambiguous "Donald" or unambiguous "good friend" on valenced traits following friendly or hostile trait primes
10. Judgment language (subjective or common rule)	Biernat & Kobrynowicz (1997)	Objective judgments are more likely to reveal assimilation to standard; subjective judgments may reveal reduced assimilation or contrast	Male and female applicants for sex-typed jobs are evaluated using either objective or subjective language; objective judgments show assimilation effects, whereas subjective judgments show contrast

Note: DV = dependent variable; Ps = participants.

☐ Notes

1. In this meta-analysis, the researchers treated assimilation, anchoring contrast, and correction contrast as three separate phenomena considered in separate data sets. Thus, this effect size of .35 does *not* reflect the overall direction of priming effects (across all priming studies) but rather the effect size in studies in which the original researchers were theoretically or empirically oriented toward assimilation (e.g., by setting up experimental situations that favored assimilation).
2. These researchers did find some evidence of contrast effects in judgments of good friends when extreme person exemplars served as primes; however, these effects were generally weak.
3. Interestingly, a later phase of the study involved a switch in context: The target stimulus remained the same, but those first exposed to the "long line" context were transitioned to the "short line" context and vice versa. At this new phase, the effect of context was generally the same for those making judgments in inches versus subjective rating units. Krantz and Campbell (1961) offer a two-process interpretation for this pattern, the specifics of which are beyond the scope of this chapter. Nonetheless, a key feature of their argument is that the findings in the inches condition "represent the operation of a single *perceptual* contrast process" (p. 40, emphasis added), whereas the subjective rating condition also involves a second *semantic* or "definitional contrast" effect.

CHAPTER

Models of Assimilation and Contrast

The previous chapter focused on specific features of contexts and targets that may determine whether assimilation or contrast effects emerge in judgment. But even a list of ten such features leaves one with a dizzying array of possibilities and permutations that one might need to consider to predict the form of a context effect in any given situation. This is where theoretical models are so important and useful.

This chapter will highlight relatively recent models that have been developed in the literature on social judgment. However, it is important to note that these recent models owe a great debt to psychophysicists including Fechner (1860), Helson (1947, 1964), and Stevens (1957), as well as attitude scalers such as Thurstone (1928) and Hovland and Sherif (1952), information integrators such as Anderson (1974), and "perspective" modelers such as Volkmann (1951), Upshaw (1965, 1978), and Parducci (1956; Parducci & Wedell, 1986).

For example, Helson (1947, 1964) argued that the relevant standard in a given judgment setting is the adaptation level (AL)—the "point of perceived neutrality" or, technically, the weighted logarithmic mean of previous stimulation on some dimension. In other words, the context (past experience or exposure) provides the standard. Essentially Helson's model is about *contrast* effects—that is, judgment (and perception) shifts away from the AL, as when a "moderately bright" room appears *very bright* to one who has been adapted to the dark and appears *very dim* to one adapted to the bright sunlight.

Volkmann's (1951) "rubber band model" introduced the notion of a frame of reference: Participants set endpoints of a judgment scale to capture the stimulus range they expect to see. Anchoring and reanchoring is done as the stimulus range extends and restricts (see Parducci, 1956; Postman & Miller, 1945). The context again provides the standard, though not in the *sensory* manner described by Helson. These ideas were also reflected in the "range" principle of Parducci's (1963) "range-frequency" model, but Parducci also suggested that judges make judgments to reflect the frequency—the rank order position—of items in a stimulus range. For both Volkmann and Parducci, judgments of stimuli are generally *contrasted* from extreme anchors—with the extension of a range in one direction, judgments move toward the other. Upshaw's (1962, 1969) variable-perspective model also extended some of Volkmann's ideas to the domain of attitudinal judgment. Response scales are anchored to the expected range of stimuli on a dimension—this is the judge's "perspective." But if the judge's own position on the dimension is outside the range, the perspective gets extended to encompass his/her position, and the result is enhanced contrast effects.

Also with regard to attitudinal judgment, the idea of own attitude as an anchor that might produce contrast *or* assimilation was introduced by Hovland and Sherif (1952). One's own position on an issue serves as an anchor so that all other attitudinal positions are judged relative to it. This ultimately led to the development of the social judgment or "assimilation-contrast" model (Sherif & Hovland, 1961), which posited that stimuli *close to* the anchor (i.e., within the "latitude of acceptance") are assimilated, whereas those further away from the anchor (within the "latitude of rejection") are contrasted.

All of these earlier models receive excellent consideration and treatment in Eiser's (1990) book, *Social Judgment*. Because I cannot improve on that review, I will simply direct the interested reader to this book (as well as the original model descriptions) for more details. Instead, this chapter will focus on more recent judgment models that emphasize *social* judgment (judgments of others and the self). Each of these models again asks the central question, *"when* assimilation and when contrast?" Where possible, I will explicitly indicate how the principles and issues outlined in Chapter 2 are incorporated in these theoretical approaches.

☐ The Set/Reset Model

Martin and his colleagues (Martin, 1986; Martin & Achee, 1992; Martin et al., 1990) have offered a general model of context effects that focuses on the overlap that exists between an ambiguous target and the surrounding context. In a process termed "setting," a judges' representation of an ambiguous target can be pulled toward that overlapping context. In essence, assimilation occurs because reactions to the context can be mistaken for reactions to the target. But if the judge realizes s/he is affected by context, an attempt may be made to avoid using the context—to "partial out" or subtract its effects. However, because of the overlap between the context and target, this correction may involve subtracting out some of the "true" reaction to the target. The result of this "resetting" process is reduced assimilation or *contrast* from the context. A schematic representation of the setting and resetting process appears in Figure 3.1.

An illustrative example of the set/reset process appears in Martin (1986, exp. 3). Participants first experienced an explicit priming task in which they wrote sentences about themselves that were either positive or negative in tone. All participants were stopped after writing four statements, but some were led to believe that they were being interrupted—that they would have to write four more statements later. Following the prime, participants were asked to form an impression of a target person (the ubiquitous Donald) based on a written description; the target was depicted ambiguously with regard to the traits "adventurous" and "reckless." In place, then, was the ambiguous target, the potential for overlap between context (positive or negative self-thoughts or mood) and the target, and, manipulated between-subjects, the subtraction cue—the finished task versus the still-active task.

In the interruption condition, participants' open-ended impressions of Donald were assimilated to the prime: Donald was viewed more favorably following the positive self-primes than the negative self-primes. But in the "finished" condition, impressions were contrasted from the context. Presumably this occurred because interrupted participants were experiencing a Zeigarnik effect, continuing to think about the contents activated during the writing task (see Zeigarnik, 1935). They then found their impressions pulled toward that context. On the other hand, finished participants could better recognize that their own moods should not affect their judgment of Donald and could therefore "partial out" the effects of the prime on their impressions. Their overcorrection produced contrast effects.

In this model, contrast effects are posited to require more cognitive effort than assimilation effects. To test this assumption of their model, Martin et al. (1990) exposed participants to a priming procedure identical to that used in the "interruption" condition described above (Martin, 1986). That is, participants wrote four self-relevant sentences that were positive or negative in tone (and had clearly finished that task) and then formed impressions of the ambiguous target. As in Martin (1986), this

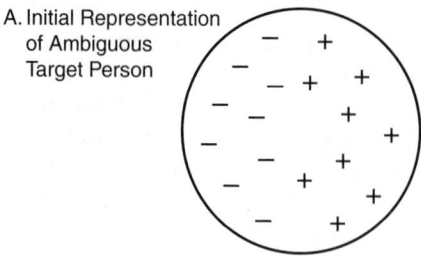

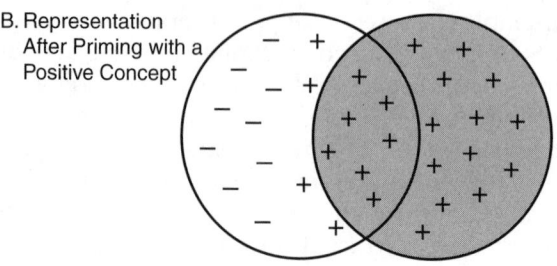

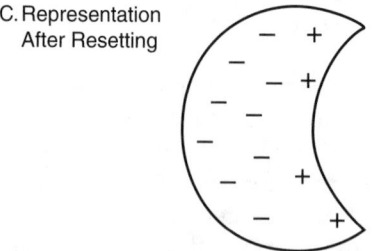

FIGURE 3.1. Schematic representation of set/reset model, with contrast as the result. (From Martin, L. L., Seta, J. J., & Crelia, R. A. [1990]. *Journal of Personality and Social Psychology, 59,* 27–37. With permission.) Plus signs represent positive features/impressions of a target person; minus signs represent negative features/impressions.

condition produced contrast effects (the target judged more favorably following negative than positive self-referent statements), presumably based on an explicit partialling of the context from the judgment. However, in another condition, participants were distracted as they formed an impression of the target. This condition produced a reliable *assimilation* effect. That is, without enough cognitive resources, the resetting process could not occur; only setting—assimilation—was possible. According to

Martin et al. (1990), these results "support the set/reset hypothesis prediction that the processes involved in contrast demand more cognitive effort than do the processes involved in assimilation" (p. 30).

It is worth noting, explicitly, how the set/reset model maps onto the factors described in the previous chapter. First, it should be clear that for "setting" to happen, the target must be *ambiguous* and the context must be relatively *broad and indistinct*, such that *overlap* between context and target can occur. Resetting requires both cognitive effort and some sort of cue that the effects of the context should be partialled out of the evaluation of the target. In addition to the interruption/completion technique described in the studies above, this cue could presumably include prime awareness and conversational norms, among other things. For example, Moskowitz and Skurnik (1999) discuss the role that context extremity may play in cueing a correction or resetting process. They argue that *moderate* trait primes may trigger resetting processes because they are "more likely to be seen as having contaminated one's reaction to a target" (p. 914). Extreme trait primes may be perceived as inappropriate as well, but because they are distinct and do not overlap with the target, they are not likely to be perceived as relevant at all to characterizing a target.[1] The set/reset model provides some initial basis, then, for predicting the role of context in guiding judgment: The context, if applicable, and the target, if ambiguous, set the stage for assimilation; contrast (or reduced assimilation) requires additional mental resources.

☐ The Inclusion/Exclusion Model

The basic prediction of the inclusion/exclusion model is simple: that "assimilation effects are likely to emerge when the target stimulus and the context stimuli are assigned to the same category, whereas contrast effects may emerge when they are assigned to different categories" (Schwarz & Bless, 1992a, p. 218). The former process—jointly categorizing context and target—reflects *inclusion*, and the latter reflects *exclusion*. In this model, inclusion is the default mode, as long as the context includes information that is potentially relevant to the representation of the target (obviously irrelevant information is ignored). But if features of the task or situation at hand suggest that contextual information should not be used, "exclusion" or subtraction occurs, resulting in contrast. The inclusion/exclusion model is highly similar to the setting/resetting model, and indeed both of these models can be thought of as "partialling" models that involve a relatively automatic assimilation mode and a more effortful correction process.

Schwarz and Bless' model is more specific, however, in its emphasis on categorization processes as the key contributor to assimilation and contrast effects. In addition, the inclusion/exclusion model adds the proposition that excluded information can serve as a standard of comparison. And because it is likely to be an *extreme* standard, this use of the context as standard can contribute to a contrast effect. Which form of contrast occurs (exclusion [correction] or comparison) depends on whether the context stimulus is directly *linked* to the dimension of judgment. If it is, it will serve as a standard of comparison. If not, it is merely subtracted from the representation but is unlikely to be used as a standard (Schwarz et al., 1990).

An example illustrating the exclusion process appears in Schwarz and Bless (1990, reported in Schwarz & Bless, 1992a). German participants were first asked (or not asked) to recall the name of the political party that included a respected politician (Richard von Weizsäcker, who was serving as president of the Federal Republic of Germany at the time). Presumably, this created a situation in which participants' representation of politicians of the Christian Democratic Party included von Weizsäcker. When then asked to evaluate Christian Democrats as a group, an assimilation effect occurred—those led to think of von Weizsäcker's party judged the group more favorably than those not asked the initial question (inclusion = assimilation). In another condition of the study, however, participants were asked a different question about von Weizsäcker: Which office does he hold "that sets him aside from party politics?" This question was designed to lead to an exclusion of the respected politician from the representation of the group. Indeed, when next asked to judge Christian Democrats as a group, contrast occurred (the group as a whole judged less favorably in the exclusion condition relative to the no-question condition).

Schwarz and Bless suggest that this pattern of effects was due to a subtraction process rather than to the use of von Weizsäcker as a standard of comparison. What is their evidence? When the same "prior question" conditions were created but participants were asked to judge members of another political party (the Social Democratic Party), there were no context effects. This suggests that von Weizsäcker was *not* serving as a general standard of comparison for evaluating politicians but rather was subtracted out of the particular representation of Christian Democrats by virtue of his exclusion from that category when his presidency was highlighted.

Other research, however, has documented contrast based not on subtraction but on the use of context information as a standard of comparison (Schwarz & Bless, 1992b). German participants were asked to recall the names of politicians involved in a Watergate-like scandal (or not) and then to evaluate either the trustworthiness of German politicians in general or the trustworthiness of three specific politicians who were uninvolved in the scandal. Evaluations of trustworthiness of politicians in general showed assimilation effects: Politicians were judged less trustworthy when the scandal was activated versus not, presumably because of an inclusion process. But evaluations of the three specific politicians revealed contrast effects—they were judged more trustworthy when participants had been reminded of the scandal versus not. In this case, the "scandalous" politicians served as an extreme standard of comparison against which the three other politicians fared well. The evidence against subtraction in this case is based on the fact that "the information that was primed by the scandal questions was presumably never part of the subjects' representations of the specific politicians they had to evaluate" (Schwarz & Bless, 1992a, p. 222). Thus, the excluded information was not subtracted (it was never included), but it did serve to anchor the "scandalous" scale.

Relating the inclusion/exclusion model to the factors outlined in Chapter 2 requires considering what leads to inclusion versus exclusion. As Schwarz and Bless (1992a) themselves write, "One of the key variables that determines the inclusion or exclusion of information is the perceived representativeness of the information for the target category" (p. 229). Representative information is likely to be included, resulting in assimilation, whereas nonrepresentative information is likely to be excluded, resulting in contrast. Clearly, a number of factors outlined in the previous chapter are relevant to this issue of "representativeness." For example, less *extreme*, less *distinct*, and *broader* contexts are conducive to inclusion, as are *context/target overlap* and context *consistency*. The *relevance* of the judgment dimension may also determine whether a context is excluded or not and whether it can serve as a standard of comparison. Furthermore, features that directly indicate that information should be excluded—such as prime *awareness* or *conversational norms*—should prompt exclusion and contrast. In short, many of the features and findings outlined in Chapter 2 can be incorporated in the inclusion/exclusion model. As a general organizing principle, the inclusion = assimilation, exclusion = contrast takes us a long way toward understanding assimilation and contrast effects. However, there are some complexities that the inclusion/exclusion model may fail to address; more on this appears below.

☐ Flexible Correction Model

The previous two models make the assumption that assimilation is the "default," less effortful mode of processing. In contrast, the flexible correction model suggests that *either* assimilation or contrast may be the default;

one is not more effortful or more likely than the other (Petty & Wegener, 1993). This approach suggests that perceivers have naïve theories about how contexts might affect their subsequent judgments and that they then engage in steps to correct these biases (preemptively, online, or after the fact). If a theory suggests that a context may produce assimilation, those who are motivated and able to do so will correct their judgments away from this assimilative bias. But if a theory suggests a context will produce contrast, correction will occur away from this contrastive bias.

Predicting patterns of contextual influence from the perspective of this model requires an assessment of the naïve theories people hold about contexts. In one demonstrative study, Petty and Wegener (1993) first identified, through pretesting, some contexts that people believed were likely to produce contrast (e.g., considering dream vacation spots before judging average locations) and those likely to produce assimilation (e.g., being in a good mood and then judging the pleasantness of everyday activities). In another study, the "vacations" theme was used, and participants were exposed to either a positive or negative context by being asked to consider either five exciting vacation locations (e.g., Hawaii, Paris) or five neutral cities (e.g., Minneapolis, Houston). After rating how much they would like to spend two weeks in each location, they then rated two more neutral locations (Kansas City and Indianapolis) on the same "I'd like to spend two weeks there" scale. Half of the participants immediately rated these two cities after exposure to the context cities (no correction instructions), while half were asked not to let their perceptions of the first set of locations influence their ratings of the final set (correction instructions).

The "no correction" condition revealed evidence of contrast—neutral cities were judged less favorably if exciting rather than neutral locales had been considered first. This finding demonstrates that people's naïve hunches about how this context would affect their judgments were correct. And importantly, the correction instructions produced a significant reduction of the contrast effect and even some (nonsignificant) evidence of assimilation: When explicitly asked to *not let* the earlier ratings affect later judgments, participants corrected (or perhaps even overcorrected) for the negative impact of first considering Paris on impressions of Kansas City. Studies such as these counter the notion that assimilation is a default process and that corrections occur in the direction of contrast.

Other tenets of this model include the assumptions that (1) motivation and ability are necessary prerequisites to correction; (2) correction can be undermined by factors such as the perception that the theory is inapplicable to a particular judgment setting, the (in)accessibility of the theory, and the goals of the perceiver; and (3) although correction generally require more effort than lack of correction, both can vary in the amount of effort involved (see Wegener & Petty, 1997, for a complete listing of model tenets).

How might this model be linked to the features outlined in the previous chapter as conducive to assimilation versus contrast effects? Many of these features are likely to be relevant in that they affect the theories people hold about context effects. For example, *prime extremity* and *distinctness* are likely to activate a theory of contrast—we have the sense, as noted above, that Paris makes Indianapolis seem dull or that Hitler makes Donald seem nonhostile. Other features may affect whether the relevant theory is activated or applied. For example, to the extent that a prime or context seems dissimilar from or *inappropriate* for use in judging the target, the theory may not become accessible, or if accessible, it may not be used to correct the judgment. Prime *awareness* and *distinctness*— e.g., language that separates or unitizes the context and target—may operate similarly to activate a theory and make it seem applicable in a given setting. Finally, as Wegener and Petty (1997) note, "many variables might ... impact both the motivation to identify and to correct for perceived biases" (p. 197). *Processing goals* of the sort identified in the previous chapter, along with accountability concerns and fear of invalidity (Kruglanski & Freund, 1983), may make the correction process—whether it means correction for assimilation or correction for contrast—more likely.

☐ Interpretation–Comparison Model (ICM)

In the previous chapter, considerable attention was paid to research by Stapel and colleagues on factors contributing to assimilation versus contrast effects. In general, Stapel and colleagues' approach can be characterized in terms of an "interpretation–comparison" model. Specifically, the model suggests that accessible and applicable contextual cues are likely to be used as an interpretation frame and produce *assimilation* effects, whereas factors that lead the context to be used as a comparison standard will produce contrast. Thus, interpretation = assimilation, comparison = contrast (see Stapel & Koomen, 1998).

Many features contributing to a context's use as an interpretation frame were outlined in the previous chapter. Perhaps most obviously, mind-sets that reinforce comparison versus integration or interpretation should lead to contrast and assimilation effects, respectively (Stapel & Koomen, 2001a, b). Additionally, for primed/contextual information to be used as a comparison standard, it must be *distinct* and *similar* to (i.e., belonging to the same category as) the target of interest (Brown, 1953;

Helson, 1964; Stapel et al., 1996, 1997). *Extremity* also contributes to the use of a context as standard (e.g., Herr, 1986), as does the *appropriateness* of the contextual information (Strack et al., 1988). In turn, the use of primed/contextual information as an interpretation frame is enhanced by *nondistinct, moderate,* and/or *broad* contextual cues.

For example, in a study focusing on distinctness and category similarity as contributors to contrast effects, Stapel and Koomen (1998) primed the trait "dependence" using a scrambled-sentence task in which dependence-related words were embedded (see Banaji et al., 1993). For one-third of the participants, female exemplars were primed (e.g., "Linda conforms inward others to"); for another third, male exemplars were primed in the same fashion; and for others, the trait alone was primed, with no reference to a particular exemplar. As noted previously, exemplars—because they are more distinct—should be more likely to be used as standards of comparison than broad traits. After the priming procedure, participants judged a moderately/ambiguously dependent target person who was depicted as male (Peter) or female (Petra). This created a situation in which some participants were primed with exemplars of the same category as the target and some with exemplars from a different category than the target. The ICM predicts that prime-category similarity should increase the use of the exemplar as a standard of comparison and produce contrast in judgments of the target's dependence.

However, in this study, the dependent male exemplar prime had reduced "social applicability" and was therefore less likely to be used as a standard of comparison: "A counter-stereotypical exemplar may belong to the same category as the target, but because the trait this exemplar exemplifies lacks social applicability, this exemplar is less likely to be included in the target's reference class when a judgment is constructed … in other words, when *same*-category exemplar information is counter-stereotypical of the target's social category, it will actually be perceived as *different*-category information and thus is unlikely to yield contrastive comparison effects" (Stapel & Koomen, 1998, p. 144). Furthermore, because a dependent male is counterstereotypical, this "makes the possibility of counterstereotypical behavior relatively accessible" and may produce *assimilation* effects (Stapel & Koomen, 1998, p. 145). This led to the complicated prediction that female targets would be contrasted from the female exemplar prime but assimilated to the other two primes, whereas male targets would be assimilated to the male exemplar prime.

Results of two studies suggested that the female target *was* contrasted from the female exemplar prime: She was judged reliably less dependent relative to the male exemplar and broad trait conditions. Judgments of the male target showed a nonsignificant effect of context, though it was the case that *assimilation* was most evident in the male exemplar condition.

Though complex, these findings do indicate that when the prime is *distinct* (exemplar versus trait), AND prime-target *similarity* is high (they belong to the same category) AND *applicability* is high (the primed exemplar fits the social stereotype), *contrast* is the result, presumably because the distinct, similar, applicable context serves as a standard of comparison.

It is worth noting that the concept of an interpretation frame is quite similar to the "inclusion" principle in Schwarz and Bless's (1992a) inclusion/exclusion model. That is, the same principles that lead a context to serve as an interpretation frame also lead the target to be "included" in the context, with assimilation as the likely result. However, the "comparison standard" portion of the ICM is *not* analogous to Schwarz and Bless's "exclusion" principle (which implies more active correction). Instead, comparison in the ICM is very similar to the separate comparison process posited by Schwarz and Bless (1992a; see above). The ICM also does not make any claims about the "default" context effect or the relative ease/effort involved in these outcomes.[2] In my mind, the real value of the ICM is in its broad characterization of two functions context can serve—the interpretation/framing function versus the comparison function. Occasionally the specific features that give rise to each of these modes are not transparent (e.g., the counterstereotypical, similar, distinct prime may actually produce *assimilation*), but the general framework serves well for understanding the basic "why" of assimilation and contrast effects.

□ The Selective Accessibility Model (SAM)

The selective accessibility model, recently formalized by Mussweiler (2003a, b), highlights how knowledge that is made accessible through comparison processes influences judgment of targets. Specifically, the model suggests that there are three phases involved in rendering a comparative judgment. First, a standard must be selected; second, the comparison must occur—one assesses the similarity/dissimilarity of the target object to the standard; and third, knowledge that is made accessible by the earlier phases must be integrated to produce an evaluation of the target.

The standard selection phase may be affected by a number of factors. In some instances, the standard is explicitly or implicitly suggested, as when a specific comparative question is asked (e.g., "Do you use more or less drugs than Frank Zappa?"; see Mussweiler & Strack, 2000). Some standards are likely to be accessible because of recent activation, as often occurs in basic anchoring effects (e.g., Wilson, Houston, Etling, & Brekke, 1996). There may also be normative considerations involved in standard selection; that is, one may be led to choose "appropriate" or diagnostic standards (as in social comparison theory's focus on the advantages of using similar standards; Festinger, 1954b; Wheeler, Martin, & Suls, 1997).

Although the standard selection phase is important, the key contribution of the SAM lies in its articulation of what occurs in subsequent steps. The comparison step first involves an initial, holistic assessment of similarity between the target and the standard, and based on that decision, the judge then engages in either "similarity testing" or "dissimilarity testing." The model, depicted in Figure 3.2, proposes that this testing leads to the selective accessibility of evidence consistent with the hypothesis. That is, if one is testing the hypothesis that the target = the standard, standard-consistent knowledge of the target will become accessible. And conversely, when one tests the hypothesis that the target does not equal the standard, standard-*inconsistent* knowledge about the target becomes accessible.

In the final judgment stage, the model predicts that similarity testing, and the resultant accessibility of standard-consistent knowledge about the target, leads to *assimilation* (the target will be judged consistently with the target), whereas dissimilarity testing, and the resultant accessibility of standard-inconsistent knowledge, leads to *contrast*. In the SAM, then, the direction of context effects depends on whether accessible information makes the target seem like or unlike the standard (see Figure 3.2).

In a study focusing on the selective accessibility hypothesis, participants were first asked to compare their athletic ability to either a moderately high

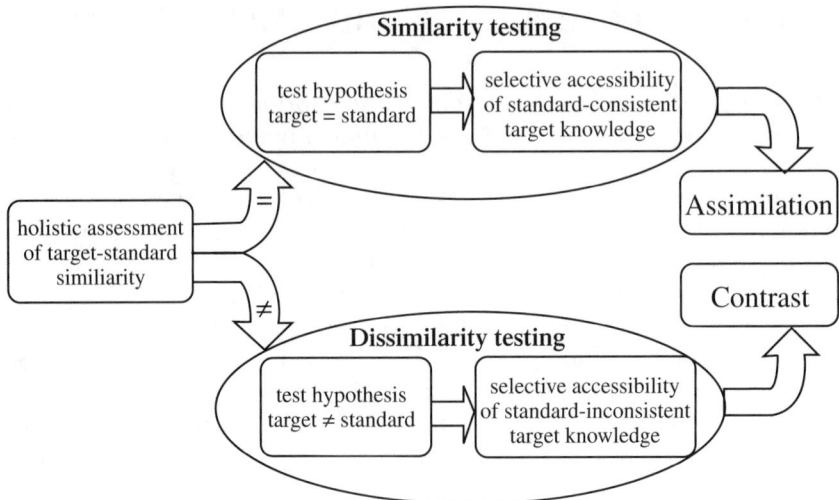

FIGURE 3.2.   The Selective Accessibility Model (SAM). (From Mussweiler, T. [2003a]. *Psychological Review, 110,* 472–489. With permission.)

standard of athleticism (Nicki Lauda, a German race car driver) or a moderately low standard (former U.S. President Bill Clinton; Mussweiler & Strack, 2000, Study 1). Because the standard was provided by the experimenter and a comparison was explicitly requested, the assumption was that similarity testing would occur. In a subsequent lexical decision task, participants viewed words associated with low athleticism (e.g., weak, heavy) or high athleticism (e.g., dynamic, athletic) that were preceded by subliminal self-primes or control primes. Participants in the high-athletic-standard condition were faster to recognize the athletic words than the low-athletic words (when preceded by the self-primes), whereas participants in the low-athletic-standard condition were faster to recognize the low-athletic words than the athletic words (again when preceded by the self-primes). In short, self-linked information that was consistent with the judgment standard was rendered more accessible.

In another study that focused on the last stage of the model—the judgmental outcome—college freshmen were led to engage in either similarity or dissimilarity testing in one task and then were asked to compare their own adjustment to college with either a high or low standard (a college student who was either very competent or incompetent in adjusting to college; Mussweiler, 2001b). Those who had been primed to engage in similarity testing judged their own adjustment to college to be better after comparison with a high standard than with a low standard (assimilation to the standard condition). And consistent with the notion that dissimilarity testing leads to contrast, those primed to engage in this mode of testing judged their own adjustment to college to be *worse* in the high-standard condition than in the low-standard condition (see also Häfner, 2004).

As Mussweiler (2003b) notes, the novel aspect of the SAM relative to the other models reviewed in this chapter lies in the second stage of the model—similarity vs. dissimilarity testing. Here, Mussweiler relies on the literature on hypothesis testing (e.g., Snyder & Swann, 1978; Pyszczynski & Greenberg, 1987; Trope & Liberman, 1996) to suggest that hypothesis-consistent evidence is selectively sought, leading to support of the hypothesis that context and target are similar (resulting in assimilation) or dissimilar (resulting in contrast). Thus, once a hypothesis is formed, many of the factors outlined in the previous chapter are irrelevant to this model. However, these factors can certainly affect standard selection and the holistic assessment of similarity between target and standard. For example, *prime-target overlap*, *distinctness*, and *prime extremity* may all factor into the holistic assessment (e.g., extreme primes are less likely to be viewed as similar to the target, and therefore dissimilarity testing and contrast result). As Mussweiler (2003b) notes, "many of the factors that have been found to determine whether a comparison produces assimilation or contrast may be linked to the same mechanism, namely, similarity versus dissimilarity testing" (p. 486).

Mussweiler's model also acknowledges that the comparison process, in addition to producing selective accessibility effects, provides a reference point—a standard—against which the accessible knowledge can be compared. Thus, considering whether one is adjusting well to college compared to a very well-adjusted student might activate knowledge of one's own good adjustment (and therefore prompt assimilation) at the same time that a high standard is invoked (facilitating contrast). Although contrast effects can sometimes be semantic rather than perceptual in nature, Mussweiler (2003b) acknowledges that "reference point use may well constitute an additional mechanism that influences the evaluative consequences of comparison independently of selective accessibility ... the same comparison may involve both the assimilative tendencies of selective accessibility and the contrastive tendencies of reference point use" (p. 483). This theme will be taken up in the next formal model to be considered in this chapter, the expectation and contrast model of social judgment (Manis & Paskewitz, 1984a, b; Manis, Biernat, & Nelson, 1991).

☐ Expectation and Contrast

In some of the models reviewed above, the suggestion is that assimilation is a relatively effortless process, whereas contrast requires both motivation and capacity to proceed (e.g., Martin et al., 1990; see similar themes in Gilbert, Pelham, & Krull's [1988] three-stage model of attributional judgment). In the flexible correction model, *either* assimilation or contrast is the default, depending on naïve theories about the impact of context. In contrast to these perspectives, Manis and Paskewitz (1984a, b) suggest that contrast and assimilation operate in parallel, with no exclusive processing advantage for either: Judgments are affected by both expectational influences and contextual comparison strategies. For example, a priming experience can create an expectation about what future experiences will be like, promoting assimilation; at the same time, the prime creates an anchor against which subsequent stimuli are judged, promoting contrast (see Manis et al., 1991). The net judgment result depends on which tendency is strongest.

In an illustrative study, participants were first exposed to a series of word definitions that illustrated either high or low pathology and were asked to indicate which had been produced by schizophrenic patients (Manis & Paskewitz, 1984a). This induction series was designed to create *expectations* about the kinds of definitions likely to be seen later in the study, and indeed, measures indicated that those in the high-pathological induction condition expected more psychopathology in a subsequent group of targets. When participants then judged a test series of moderately psychopathological definitions, a marked contrast effect emerged, with the moderate definitions judged more pathological by those originally exposed to the nonpathological induction set. Furthermore, expectations were positively correlated with judgments. Thus, the induction phase produced corresponding expectations that positively predicted judgments, at the same time these judgments were *contrasted* from that initial context.

This model is schematically depicted in Figure 3.3. The "continuity" path reflects the idea that contexts create expectations—e.g., that a definition will be pathological (see also Newman & Benassi, 1989). The "confirmation bias" path reflects the typical assimilative influence of expectations on judgments—we see what we expect to see. And the "contrast" path reflects that use of context as a standard against which new targets are compared. Thus, in this model, the same priming experience or context can produce two opposing effects,[3] and again, the relative strength of these paths may determine the ultimate judgment outcome. For example, to the extent that an expectation is extremely strong (e.g., one knows that all the definitions come from patients in a psychiatric hospital), subsequently encountered moderate definitions may not show the typical pattern of contrast; the confirmation bias is too hearty. Additionally, Manis and Paskewitz (1984a) have proposed that the time course of the expectation and contrast paths operate differently; namely, the contrastive tendency may decline more rapidly than the assimilative one. Indeed, with a time delay introduced between a contextual induction of expectations and target judgments, assimilation rather than contrast is a typical result (Manis & Blake, 1963; Manis & Moore, 1978).

The expectation and contrast model does not speak directly to the specific factors (outlined in the previous chapter) that affect assimilation and contrast effects. However, implicit in the model is that context effects in general require that an unambiguous—perhaps *extreme*—expectation be induced, and contrast effects require that the target be *ambiguous or moderate* on the dimension of interest, or discrepant from the context. The real value in the model is its premise that assimilative and contrastive tendencies work in tandem—that they may "derive from the same eliciting experience" (Manis et al., 1991, p. 210). Less clear is whether one can reliably predict, *a priori*, the relative strength of the two tendencies, whether null effects can be interpreted as due to the combination of assimilative and contrastive tendencies, and whether the *processes* themselves can be reliably captured. Thus far, the "expectation" route has been assessed through explicit measures of expectations and the use of path

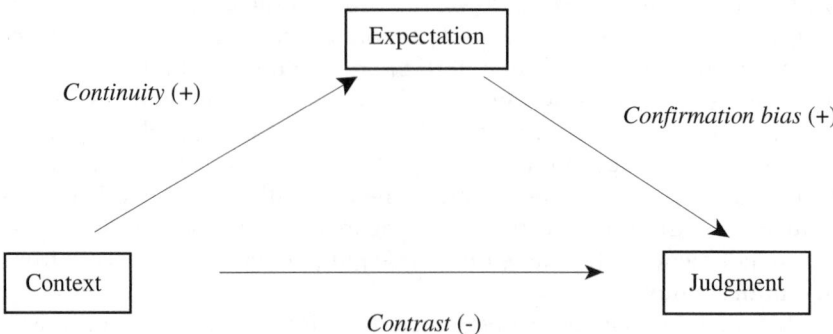

FIGURE 3.3. Paths in the Manis-Paskewitz expectation and contrast model. (Adapted from Manis, M., Biernat, M., & Nelson, T. [1991]. *Journal of Personality and Social Psychology, 61*, 203–211. With permission.)

analysis; more direct evidence for the simultaneity of assimilative and contrastive tendencies would be valuable.

☐ General Model of Informational Biases

Drawing on a number of these earlier models, a dual-process model of memory and information processing (Smith & DeCoster, 2000), and a meta-analytic database, DeCoster and Claypool (2004) offered a model designed to explain patterns of assimilation and contrast in priming studies. Specifically, the model builds on Smith and DeCoster's (2000) distinction between "associative" and "rule-based" processing. Associative processing "operates automatically and makes use of simple memory traces that are formed whenever two stimuli occur together in the environment" (DeCoster & Claypool, 2004, p. 19). In this mode, when a prime or contextual cue is present in the environment, the default mode of associative processing is engaged. The direction of bias—assimilation or contrast—is posited to depend on the *distinctiveness*—e.g., the degree of prime–target overlap and the extent to which the prime is a narrow entity (as in exemplars vs. traits; see Chapter 2). Low distinctive concepts produce inclusion, resulting in assimilation (labeled "incorporation" in the model), whereas highly distinctive concepts result in exclusion, producing contrast (labeled "anchoring"). Thus, this aspect of the model incorporates basic principles of the Interpretation–Comparison Model (Stapel & Koomen, 1998, 2000) and the Inclusion–Exclusion Model (Schwarz & Bless, 1992a).

The second mode of processing—"rule-based" processing—is an effortful mode that "operates with conscious attention and makes use of more complex, linguistic information" (DeCoster & Claypool, 2004, p. 19). This process is engaged in only with awareness, motivation, and capacity, and in social judgment it amounts to a "corrective" mode of processing, similar to correction as outlined in Martin's (1986) set/reset model and Petty and Wegener's (1993) flexible correction model. Indeed, DeCoster and Claypool's (2004) rule-based mode fully incorporates the flexible correction model's emphasis on naïve theories (see also Wegener & Petty, 1995). To the extent that one's theory about the effect of a prime is assimilative, the correction mode will lead to "corrective contrast," and to the extent that the theory is contrastive, the correction model will lead to "corrective assimilation."

DeCoster and Claypool's (2004) model suggests that the two modes of processing occur in parallel, with each mode contributing to the judgment rendered about a target. Indeed, the judgment outcome is based on adding together the influences of (default) associative and rule-based processing. However, this parallelism is different from that posited in Manis and Paskewitz's (1984a) expectation–contrast model. For DeCoster and Claypool (2004), "a single piece of information cannot be both included in and excluded from the target when making an evaluation … therefore, we do not believe that information can be simultaneously incorporated with the target and used as a standard of comparison" (p. 21). But this is precisely what Manis and Paskewitz posit *does* occur.

I am not sure how DeCoster and Claypool (2004) would interpret the path models produced by Manis and Paskewitz (1984a) or Manis et al. (1991), documenting both continuity (assimilative) and contrastive tendencies prompted by the same stimulus set. But perhaps the latter path might be interpreted as *corrective contrast*—a phenomenon not discussed by Manis and Paskewitz (1984a, b) but which could theoretically operate in tandem with default assimilative processing in DeCoster and Claypool's (2004) model. In any case, the "general model of informational biases" (which could use a catchier name!) is important in its positing of multiple processes and its incorporation of both earlier models and factors known to contribute to assimilation and contrast effects.

☐ Reflection and Evaluation Model (REM)

Another general model of "comparative thinking" was recently proposed by Markman and McMullen (2003). I am describing this model last because it shares much in common with the inclusion–exclusion model

(Schwarz & Bless, 1992a) and explicitly borrows from Mussweiler's (2003b) SAM the argument that self-knowledge *accessibility* is the critical determinant of comparison outcomes. It also picks up the theme of simultaneity in comparative processes articulated by Manis and Paskewitz (1984a,b). However, the heart of this model is the notion of *mental simulation*—"the consideration of alternatives to present reality" (p. 244; see Kahneman & Miller, 1986), and the theory is concerned primarily with *self*-judgments (counterfactual comparison research providing the main empirical base). In general, the model proposes two "psychologically distinct modes of mental simulation [that] operate in parallel during comparative thinking" (p. 245). The *reflection* mode involves "as if" thinking, in which one "simulates that information about the comparison standard is true of, or part of, the self" (p. 245). Note that this mode is quite similar to Mussweiler's (2003b) notion of "similarity testing" and that the likely outcome of this process is also *assimilation*. The second mode of simulation is *evaluation*, in which the standard operates as a point of reference against which the self is evaluated, likely leading to *contrast*. Markman and McMullen (2003) note that "reflection occurs when information about the standard is included in one's self-construal, and evaluation occurs when such information is excluded" (p. 245), a statement that highlights the strong connection to Schwarz and Bless's (1992a) inclusion–exclusion model.

One distinction between "reflection" in the REM and "selective accessibility" in the SAM is that the information one comes up with in reflection may be *imaginary* rather than selected from an assortment of facts about oneself. For example, when considering how athletic I am relative to tennis great Serena Williams, Mussweiler suggests that I will selectively call to mind athletic facts about myself (e.g., the one time I made a stunning return of a serve). But Markman and McMullen (2003) suggest that instead I might *imagine* that I was like Serena Williams. Here, nothing in my past is made accessible, but nonetheless standard-consistent cognitions are at the fore of my thinking. Rather than the biased hypothesis-testing mechanism posited by Mussweiler, this imagination effect is akin to findings in the imagination-explanation literature, whereby coming up with explanations for possible future events increases estimates of the probability those events will occur (Koehler, 1991; Ross, Lepper, Strack, & Steinmetz, 1977).

The REM then posits parallel yet independent processes of reflection and evaluation (see Figure 3.4). The ultimate outcome of these processes (i.e., whether assimilation or contrast occurs) depends on the relative strength of these processes, which, in turn, is based on "the extent to which contextual features encourage one to think about the self and the standard together, as a single unit or entity (i.e., inclusion), or the extent to which one thinks about the self and the standard separately, as two distinct entities (i.e., exclusion)" (p. 249). That is, context will determine whether a mode of inclusion or exclusion operates. What are the contextual features that matter here? Many of the features described in Chapter 2: Similarity between standard and target or temporal closeness will prompt the reflection process and assimilation; distinctness of the standard or immutability of the self will prompt evaluation and contrast. Markman and McMullen (2003) also note that attentional focus is key; to the extent that context focuses one on the standard itself, reflection is likely, but to the extent the focus is on the *comparison* between the self and standard, evaluation is likely (see McMullen, 1997).

A key feature of the REM that distinguishes it from other models is its functional orientation. Specifically, the REM suggests that motivation

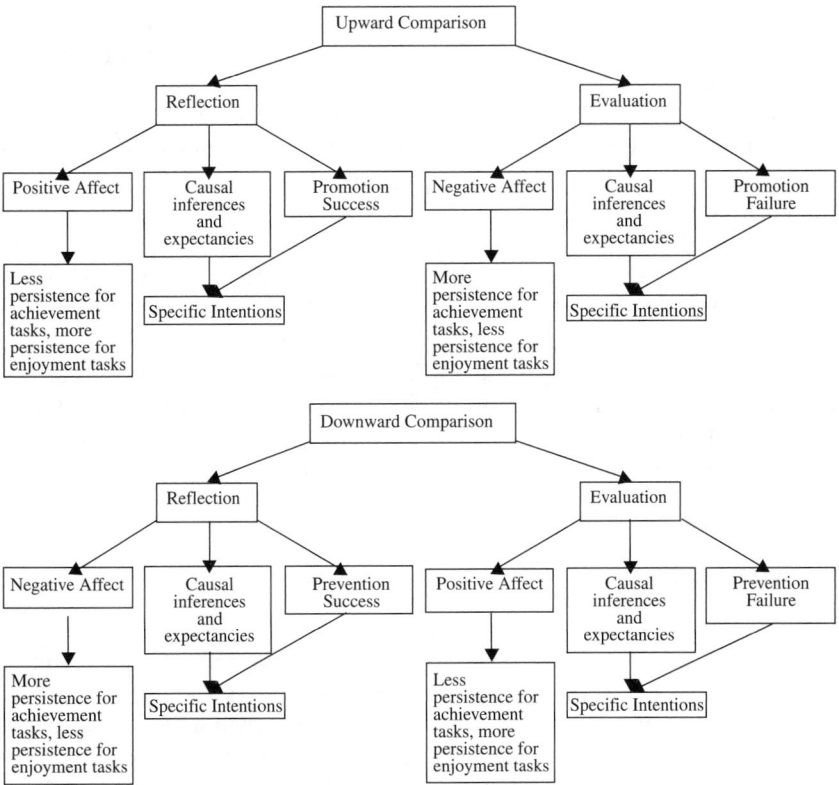

FIGURE 3.4. Consequences of comparative thinking in the Reflection–Evaluation Model (REM). (From Markman, K. D., & McMullen, M. N. [2003]. *Personality and Social Psychology Review, 7,* 244–267. With permission.)

and behavior are affected via the affective consequences of comparisons. For example, if one compares the self to a distinct, upward target, this might put one in "evaluation" mode and generate negative affect. In turn, and based on the concept of "feelings as information" (Martin et al., 1993; Schwarz, 1990), this negative affect may produce persistence on achievement tasks but less persistence on enjoyment tasks (see Figure 3.4). Some studies have shown links among comparison direction, affect, and behavior that provide at least a hint of support for these suggestions. For example, Roese (1994, Study 3) gave failure feedback to individuals on an anagrams task and then induced some to engage in upward counterfactual thinking (e.g., "list some specific actions that could have been taken to improve your score"). Compared to those who imagined downward counterfactuals, the "upward" participants improved their scores on a subsequent anagrams task. Solving anagrams is an achievement task, and thus these results are consistent with the prediction that the negative affect caused by upward comparisons (contrast) may enhance persistence on achievement tasks. In an unpublished study cited in Markman and McMullen (2003), an *enjoyment* task ("have fun and stop when you're not having fun") showed the opposite pattern: Those who engaged in upward evaluation (and presumably experienced negative affect) persisted *less* than downward-evaluation or upward-reflection participants.

In general, then, the REM can be thought of as a "hybrid" of the inclusion-exclusion model (Schwarz and Bless, 1992a) and SAM (Mussweiler, 2003a, b), with a hint of expectation-contrast thrown in (Manis & Paskewitz, 1984a, b). The authors suggest that contextual factors affecting inclusion/exclusion (see Chapter 2) set the processes of reflection and evaluation in motion. These processes make different kinds of information accessible and result in assimilation or contrast, which, in turn, prompts particular patterns of motivation and behavior.

☐ Summary

The models reviewed in this chapter have in common the idea that a contextual cue can function either as an interpretive framework or as a reference point. Factors that make the context less distinct from the target (i.e., allow for "inclusion" of the target in the context) facilitate the *interpretation* framework, whereas those that make the context distinct (allow for "exclusion") generally facilitate the use of context as a *reference point* that prompts contrast. The models are largely cognitive in nature, and most of them underemphasize how motivational variables may contribute to judgment outcomes. They also differ in important ways—in terms of the assumed default process (assimilation or contrast), the sequential versus simultaneous nature of the process, the assumed degree of effort involved in contrast (i.e., is it a basic, even automatic, effect or part of an effortful "correction" process?), and the extent to which process variables are articulated (e.g., similarity–dissimilarity testing in the SAM; as-if thinking in the REM). Assimilation and contrast effects both occur under different conditions, and the models described here have been able to predict and explain a large array of findings.

The eight models described in this chapter may not seem to provide much more parsimony than the ten factors outlined in Chapter 2. And integrating the models fully would be an arduous task, particularly as each model may have its own special sphere of relevance. What seems more important is that these models offer a general framework for predicting and understanding why and how the factors outlined in Chapter 2 may operate to produce assimilation or contrast effects. Some factors contribute to the inclusion or joint categorization of context and target; some contribute to exclusion. These factors may also affect judges' naïve theories about the impact of context, which in turn may affect both the default contextual outcome and the direction of any corrective processes brought to hand. My own view, borrowing heavily from a number of these models, is that neither assimilation nor contrast is the default, that both assimilation and contrast may be automatic or effortful, that context may set into motion parallel and independent processes (interpretation versus comparison, expectation versus contrast, incorporation versus anchoring, reflection versus evaluation), and that knowledge made accessible by the comparison process is the proximal predictor of the direction of context effects.

☐ Notes

1. If you are like me, your intuition about prime extremity may be contrary to that of Moskowitz and Skurnik (1999). That is, extreme primes seem more likely than moderate primes to be perceived as biasing, thereby triggering correction and contrast. (This led me to reread Moskowitz and Skurnik, 1989 an embarrassing number of times!) The resolution seems to lie in applicability as it relates to the "setting" stage of the model—extreme primes simply may not "set" the target because of the lack of overlap (lack of applicability), and therefore resetting becomes irrelevant. These authors do point out, however, that extreme *exemplar* primes do produce contrast effects, but not through a correction process. Rather, this may occur through the use of the extreme exemplar as a standard of comparison (i.e., comparison contrast).
2. Recently, in discussing the ICM in the context of social comparison in particular, Stapel and Suls (2004) suggested the *simultaneous* operation of interpretation and comparison: "social comparison may instigate two processing mechanisms that have opposing effects" (p. 861).
3. A related view of this oppositional influence of context appears in another stage model—Trope's (1986) two-stage model of dispositional attribution. In Trope's model,

the current situation in which one views an actor can have an *assimilative* influence on action identification. For example, the observation of someone crying at a funeral will likely prompt an identification of the crying behavior as "sadness" or "grief." At the second stage of dispositional inference, however, the same contextual cue (the funeral) will exert a subtractive or *contrastive* influence: The crying actor will *not* be viewed as dispositionally sad, as the situation provides a very plausible explanation for the behavior.

CHAPTER 4

Self and Other Exemplars as Standards for Judging Others

The previous two chapters emphasized general principles and models regarding how contextual information affects social judgments. In this chapter, the initial focus is more specifically on the role of *self* in judging other people. That the self can be used as a referent for evaluating others is a theme that appears in a number of research literatures. Even Helson (1964), whose work emphasized sensory contributions to judgment, suggested that an individual's attitudes and beliefs can be included in her or his general "adaptation level," affecting subsequent experience and judgment. Psychologists interested in attitudes and attitude scaling have also argued that one's own attitudes serve as anchors in the evaluation and perception of other attitude stances—a view expressed most clearly in Hovland and Sherif's (1952) social judgment theory (Hovland, Harvey, & Sherif, 1957; Sherif & Hovland, 1961) and in other judgment models (Eiser & Mower White, 1974; Eiser & Stroebe, 1972; Insko, Murashima, & Saiyadain, 1966; Judd & Harackiewicz, 1980; Lord, Ross, & Lepper, 1979; Upshaw, 1962, 1969; Zavalloni & Cook, 1965; see Eiser, 1990, for a review).

Other research more particularly emphasizes the role of self in evaluating people and groups; indeed, the self is often viewed as playing a unique role in processing the social environment (Rogers, 1981; Rogers, Kuiper, & Rogers, 1979). This chapter will offer a taste of just some of this work by describing research on (1) the role of self as a "habitual reference point" in similarity judgments (Holyoak & Gordon, 1983), (2) the tendency to use our own attributes to describe specific others, and (3) false consensus and false uniqueness effects. Finally, the chapter will consider the role of other exemplars (besides the self) in making judgments of others.

☐ The Self in Similarity Judgments

When judging the similarity between two objects (e.g., "how similar is A to B?"), B serves as the referent and A is the subject of the comparison. The roles of A and B could, of course, be reversed by a simple transformation or "reframing" of the question ("how similar is B to A?"). Researchers have documented a pattern of asymmetry in similarity judgments of this type, whereby the object that is "more of a habitual reference point—i.e., more familiar, salient, or prototypical—than the other" is viewed as *less* similar to the other object than vice versa (Holyoak & Gordon, 1983, p. 881). For example, among Americans, Australia is likely to be perceived as more similar to the U.S. than the U.S. is to Australia. Judging Australia as similar to the U.S. reflects a form of *assimilation*; judging the U.S. as dissimilar to Australia reflects *contrast.*

The comparison processes involved in similarity judgments of this sort were delineated in Tversky's (1977) contrast model, which focuses on the roles of shared and unique (noncommon) features of the subject of the comparison in rendering similarity estimates. Specifically, if more information (and therefore more unique and distinct information) is known about A than B, comparing A to B will produce lower similarity judgments than will comparing B to A. Tversky's (1977) theoretical work focused on perceived similarity between countries, but others have used the similarity asymmetry effect to document that the *self* is used as a habitual point of reference in social judgment (Holyoak & Gordon, 1983; Karylowski, 1990; Karylowski & Skarzynska, 1992; Srull & Gaelick, 1983). For example, when participants in one study were asked to rate "how similar is your friend to you?" versus "how similar are you to your friend?" on ten social and physical dimensions, mean similarity was consistently higher in the former case (Holyoak & Gordon, 1983, Study 1; see Holyoak & Mah, 1982; Rosch, 1975; Tversky & Gati, 1978; Sadalla, Burroughs, & Staplin, 1980, for examples in nonsocial domains). That is, friends were judged more similar to the self (assimilation) than the self was to friends (contrast). This effect seems to be particularly strong when self-knowledge is primed prior to the judgment of similarity (Karylowski & Skarzynska, 1992).

However, it is probably not surprising that the *unique* role of the self in this regard has been questioned. Just as the self-referent effect in *memory* has been shown to be due less to the uniqueness of the self-concept than to its cognitive organization, richness, and familiarity (see Greenwald & Banaji, 1989; Kihlstrom & Klein, 1994), asymmetrical similarity judgments may also be due to these features, especially familiarity (Catrambone, Beike, & Niedenthal, 1996). Other familiar constructs may operate like the self in producing similarity asymmetries. For example, in the second study of their paper, Holyoak and Gordon (1983) examined the perceived similarity between self and nine different social stereotypes (e.g., "how similar is the typical vegetarian to you?") or vice versa. Significant asymmetries were found for some groups but not others, and the size of the effect could be accounted for by the degree of knowledge participants had about the stereotyped group (operationalized as the number of attributes listed as descriptive of the group). Specifically, the more attributes listed, the less asymmetry in self–other similarity judgments. The authors write, "The self appears to function as a habitual reference point with respect to stereotypes about which little is known. However, stereotypes about which a great deal is known are at least as prominent as reference points as is the self" (Holyoak & Gordon, 1983, p. 886).

Nonetheless, some researchers have emphasized that motivational factors such as a desire to see the self as unique may account for asymmetries in self–other judgments. For example, based on studies on similarity judgments as well as estimates of physical distance ("how far are you from others?" versus "how far are others from you?"), Codol and his colleagues have argued that asymmetry effects can be interpreted as a "sign of personal identity affirmation and defence" (Codol, Jarymowicz, Kaminska-Feldman, & Szuster-Zbrojewicz, 1989, p. 12; see also Codol, 1990). In a series of studies on perceived interpersonal distance, participants were asked to estimate (either from a graphical depiction or from actual standing in a room) how far they were from specific others or how far the others were from them. Participants consistently *underestimated* the distance others were from the self relative to self from others: "It looks as though subjects feel that others occupy their own space, even though they do not think they occupy the space of others" (Codol et al., 1989, p. 12). This asymmetry was found to increase as the density of people in the space increased and as actual distance of others from the self decreased— supporting the likely role of *defensiveness* in this process (Codol, 1985 [described in English in Codol, 1990]).

Further supporting the role of identity defense, other studies documented that "I"–"other" asymmetries of this sort are stronger than "we" (in-group members)–"other" asymmetries and that such asymmetries increase (1) as the self is viewed as more distinct from others, (2) among those who are "endocentric" in nature (i.e., unable to take the perspective of others), and (3) among participants led to feel deindividuated in high-density spaces (Codol et al., 1989). With regard to this latter finding, deindividuated participants (who were referred to only by a number and addressed as part of a group) likely felt some identity threat that was enhanced when their personal space was occupied by others. That they then showed high levels of asymmetry ("others are a lot closer to me than I am to them") supports the notion that motivational factors may be implicated in self–other physical distance asymmetries.[1]

Still, it may be difficult to fully tease apart the influence of Tversky's (1977) feature-matching process and the motivational alternative. However, most researchers would agree that the self is a commonly used and well-known reference point relative to most subjects of comparison. When others are compared to this construct, perceived similarity (in both direct similarity judgments and self-versus-other probability estimates) is heightened. In other words, assimilation of others to the self occurs. Codol (1990) describes this as a "self-centered assimilation process" that occurs because people "generally tend to perceive others as belonging to the same 'category' as themselves" (p. 391). When the self is compared to others, however, contrast (reduced similarity, increased physical distance, increased optimism) is more likely: people "do not perceive themselves as belonging to the same category as others" (Codol, 1990, p. 391). Interestingly then, Codol bases his motivational account on a categorization process and echoes themes introduced in Schwarz and Bless's (1992a) inclusion–exclusion model (see Chapter 3). Categorization of others with self produces assimilation; exclusion of others from the self (which occurs when the self is the subject of comparison) produces contrast.

☐ Using Our Own Attributes in Judgments of Others

The research reviewed in the previous section implicates the self in judgments of others when that judgment is *directed* explicitly (i.e., "compare self and other"). Perhaps more telling about the role of self in other judgments is research focusing on other judgments in which no direct mention of the self is made. One such line of research has documented a positive relationship between one's standing on a given trait and judgments of that trait in others. For example, self-relevant attributes appear in the free description of others more often than do non-self-relevant attributes (e.g., Dornbush, Hastorf, Richardson, Muzzy, & Vreeland, 1965; Lemon & Warren, 1976; Shrauger & Patterson, 1976), and individuals who judge themselves extremely on attributes tend to rate ambiguous or attribute-consistent targets more highly on those traits than do individuals for whom the attribute is less relevant (e.g., Carpenter, 1988; Catrambone & Markus, 1987; Lambert & Wedell, 1991; Lewicki, 1983; Markus, Crane, Bernstein, & Siladi, 1982; Markus & Smith, 1981; Markus, Smith, & Moreland, 1985).[2] Recently, it has been shown that we may also assume that fictional others will approach learning situations in the same way we do (Kawada, Oettingen, Gollwitzer, & Bargh, 2004).

Lambert and Wedell (1991) further documented that this positive relationship between one's own and an other's standing on a trait (at least when the other's attributes are ambiguous with regard to the trait) holds even after controlling for the rated importance of the trait and affective reactions to the other's behaviors. For example, self-described "sociable" participants judged an ambiguously sociable actor (who "installed a telephone answering machine in his/her apartment" and "decided to join the Peace Corps") to be more sociable than did self-described nonsociable participants—an effect that did not dissipate after factoring out the importance of sociability and evaluative extremity in reactions to the target behaviors (Lambert & Wedell, 1991, Study 1).

These results indicate assimilation: Judgments of others are drawn toward the self. However, some of this same literature points to circumstances under which differentiation or *contrast* of others from the self is more likely to occur. One condition for contrast seems to be that the target other is unambiguously low on the self-relevant trait (see entry 9 in Table 2.1). For example, Markus and Fong (1979 [cited in Markus & Smith, 1981]) reported that "independent schematics" judged an actor who never behaved independently as less independent (i.e., more dependent) than did aschematic participants. Somewhat different interpretations have been advanced for these sorts of contrast effects. Markus and Smith (1981) interpret them in social judgment theory terms (Sherif & Hovland, 1961). To the extent that a target's actions fall outside an individual's latitude of acceptance (as do very dependent actions when one is an independent person), those actions are seen as distinctive and therefore contrasted from one's own position. However, Lambert and Wedell's (1991) more recent research suggests that participants' judgments of *un*ambiguous behaviors (e.g., both those clearly high and low in sociability) are not directly mediated by self-standing on the trait in question but by the extremity in one's evaluative reactions to the target behaviors. This explanation is more consistent with accentuation theory, which posits that reactions to stimuli (in this case, targets who behave sociably versus not) are polarized in accordance with value connotations of those behaviors (Eiser, 1990; Eiser & Stroebe, 1972; Judd & Harackiewicz, 1980; Tajfel, 1957).

A somewhat different form of contrast effect is also evident in research on "egocentric definitions" of trait concepts (Dunning, 1993; Dunning & Cohen, 1992; Dunning, Meyerowitz, & Holzberg, 1989). In a series of studies, Dunning and his colleagues have consistently reported *negative* relationships between participants' objective standing on an attribute (e.g., SAT scores) and their subjective judgments of a target person (whose SAT scores are known) on that same attribute (e.g., intelligence; Beauregard & Dunning, 1998; Dunning, 1993; Dunning & Cohen, 1992; Dunning & Hayes, 1996; Dunning & McElwee, 1995; Dunning et al., 1989; Dunning, Perie, & Story, 1991; see also Felson, 1990). For example, Dunning and Cohen (1992, Study 4) found that the more hours of athletic activity participants engaged in per week, the less athletic they judged targets who were described as engaging in various hours of athletic activity themselves. This general contrast effect was strongest for low-athletic targets (those described as spending just one hour per week in athletic pursuits). That is, low-athletic participants tended to judge these targets favorably on the athletic dimension, whereas high-athletic participants judged them unfavorably (see comparable findings in Lambert & Wedell, 1991; Markus & Smith, 1981).

The type of contrast effect demonstrated by Dunning (1993) appears to be self-serving in nature: Individuals will define traits in ways that "reflect back favorably on themselves" (Beauregard & Dunning, 1998, p. 608). The high-performing individual—for example, one who scores 780 on the math SAT—will set high standards for math performance, thereby distinguishing among targets with lower scores and successively denigrating these targets as their scores decrease. The result is that one's own performance and underlying ability are favorably distinguished from others, presumably increasing one's sense of self-worth. The low-performing individual—e.g., one who scores 500 on the math SAT—will set lower standards for math performance such that he or she can be included among those "qualifying" for the trait (i.e., having math ability), with some regard for "reality constraints" (Kunda, 1990). The result is that few distinctions are made among targets with higher scores; all are viewed as relatively high in math ability, including the self (see similar themes in research on the "genius effect" by Alicke, LoSchiavo, Zerbst, & Zhang, 1997).

Additional research has demonstrated that this "egocentric contrast effect" is strongest among those participants who explicitly mention comparing the target to themselves (Dunning & Hayes, 1996), among those dispositionally high in self-esteem (who presumably have a positive self-image to protect; Dunning & Beauregard, 2000), and under conditions when self-esteem is threatened (e.g., as a result of failure on a task; Beauregard & Dunning, 1998). Interestingly, Beauregard and Dunning

(1998, Study 3) demonstrated this latter pattern using a classic paradigm from the attitudes literature: Participants who were strongly pro-choice on the issue of abortion were asked to evaluate a target who voiced a moderately pro-choice opinion. The tendency to denigrate this opposing view and contrast it from one's own (i.e., to view it as unreasonable, biased, closed-minded, and pro-life) was enhanced after a failure experience. Dunning and his colleagues acknowledge that contrast effects of this sort may be affected by cognitive factors (e.g., the anchoring of a response scale, accessibility of the self as standard) but that motivational factors such as esteem enhancement/protection may "begin to assert themselves" "when the domain in question is important or self-defining to the individual" (Beauregard & Dunning, 1998, p. 618).

Before leaving this overview of research on self-attributes in judgments of others, it is important to note an important distinction between the work of Dunning and his colleagues and that of Markus, Lambert and Wedell, and others. As indicated above, these latter researchers have primarily documented assimilative effects of self on judgments of others, whereas Dunning and his colleagues report contrastive results. A key difference seems to be that the self attributes Dunning assesses are participants' specific performances or behaviors on the dimensions of interest (e.g., SAT scores, hours of athletic activity, times per week being late to class) rather than the more typically used global trait ratings (e.g., intelligence, athleticism, punctuality). Consistent with the notion that *distinct* contexts trigger contrast (see Chapter 2), others may more easily be contrasted from *specific* self-referential standards but assimilated to *abstract* self-views. Indeed, in one study from Dunning's lab that relied on less-distinct self-ratings (e.g., to what extent do you "make friends easily"?), judgments of others on the related trait (e.g., sociability) were assimilated to self-ratings (Beauregard & Dunning, 2001).

☐ False Consensus and False Uniqueness

This discussion of self-as-standard for judging others has thus far skirted around two large[3] relevant literatures: one on the false consensus effect (the tendency to overestimate the likelihood that others will act or feel as we do) (e.g., Alicke & Largo, 1995; Marks & Miller, 1987; Mullen, Atkins, Champion, Edwards, Hardy, Story, & Vanderklok, 1985; Mullen & Hu, 1988; Nisbett & Kunda, 1985; Orive, 1988; Ross, Greene, & House, 1977; Sherman, Presson, & Chassin, 1984) and one on the false uniqueness effect (the tendency to underestimate the commonality of our self-attributes) (Campbell, 1986; Goethals et al., 1991; Marks, 1984; McFarland & Miller,

1990; Miller & McFarland, 1987; Perloff & Brickman, 1982; Suls & Wan, 1987; Suls, Wan, Barlow, & Heimberg, 1990; Suls, Wan, & Sanders, 1988). In general terms, these two phenomena represent assimilation and contrast effects, respectively. Although they are clearly relevant to our previous discussion of the role of self in judging others, they have one distinction: False consensus and false uniqueness effects involve making predictions regarding the attitudes and behaviors of a target population or group rather than judging a specific individual about whom some descriptive information has been provided. Thus, these effects are more predictive than evaluative, and more general (group-related) than particular (person-related).

False Consensus—Description and Accounts

Operationally, the false consensus effect is said to have occurred "when a person engaging in a given behavior estimates that behavior to be shared by a larger proportion of some reference group than would be estimated by a person engaging in an alternative behavior" (Mullen, Driskell, & Smith, 1989, p. 84). In other words, false consensus is not about deviations from *actual* consensus (see Gross & Miller, 1997, for some discussion of this type of error) but rather deviations between individuals who differ in their self-reported attributes in terms of their predictions and expectations regarding others' standing on those attributes. The effect has been reported in such domains as behaviors, traits, preferences, beliefs, and personal problems (see Marks & Miller, 1987; see Wallen, 1943, for an earlier attitudinal example). For example, people who indicate that they would wear a sandwich board sign saying "Eat at Joe's" assume that 65% of others would do the same (compared to a 31% estimate among those who would not wear the sign themselves; Ross et al., 1977); similarly, people who prefer music from the 1960s to that of the 1980s assume that 67% of others feel the same (compared to a 33% estimate by 1980s music lovers; Gilovich, 1990), and people who take showers during a shower ban assume 63% of others do as well (compared to a 39% estimate by non-bathers; Monin & Norton, 2003). The false consensus effect—again, an assimilative tendency—is conceptually linked to the phenomenon of social projection (Allport, 1924), attributive or assimilative projection (Berkowitz, 1960; Holmes, 1968, 1978; Murstein & Pryer, 1959), and assumed similarity (Cronbach, 1955). One meta-analysis based on 23 studies indicated a reliable, moderate false consensus effect size ($R = .31$; Mullen et al., 1985; see also Krueger, 2000).

As is true of other self-as-standard phenomena, explanations for the false consensus effect have focused on both cognitive and motivational factors. These will be examined below, but the bottom-line conclusion reached in a meta-analysis covering ten years of research on the FCE was that the FCE is "influenced by a host of variables …; no single explanation can account for the range of data" (Marks & Miller, 1987, p. 72).

The most common cognitive account emphasizes selective exposure and/or cognitive availability and accessibility—people normally associate with (and therefore have available in memory) others who are similar to themselves (Bosveld, Koomen, & van der Pligt, 1994; Goethals, Allison, & Frost, 1979; Manstead, 1982; Mullen et al., 1985; Ross et al., 1977; Sherman, Presson, Chassin, Corty, & Olshavsky, 1983). Dawes's (1989) cognitive/statistical *induction* account further suggests that one's own behavior may be the only available information regarding prevalence; if the self is akin to a randomly drawn individual from the population of interest, it may be reasonable to assume that one's own behavior is the majority position.[4] It is also the case that individuals are more likely to project onto ingroup than outgroup members, suggesting that the assumption of similarity may drive this process (Bosveld, Koomen, & van der Plight, 1996; Bramel, 1963; Messe & Sivacek, 1979; Mullen, Donidio, Johnson, & Copper, 1992; Spears & Manstead, 1990).

In addition to these cognitive factors, false consensus may also be motivated by the need to validate the correctness of a position, maintain or protect self-esteem, promote smooth interaction, and so on (Agostinelli, Sherman, Presson, & Chassin, 1992; Sherman et al., 1984; see also Holmes, 1968, and Marks & Miller, 1987, for reviews). In one set of studies, for example, participants given failure feedback (about their ability to discriminate among fake and real suicide notes) showed a strong false consensus effect (relative to success–feedback individuals) in their estimates of the performance of other undergraduates on the same task (Sherman et al., 1984). Importantly, in the success conditions, participants were just as likely to "project" from their own behavior as from an available other individual's behavior in their estimates of group performance, but in the failure condition, projection was greatest when the self rather than another available individual was involved. The authors write, "When self is threatened, perceptions of consensus may be increased by a motivation to seek normalization and support for one's own behavior" (Sherman et al., 1984, p. 127). Interestingly, in their work showing greater projection from self to ingroup than from other (one's roomate) to ingroup, Krueger and Stanke (2001) offer a cognitive account based on accessibility of knowledge and categorization effects. That this tendency is enhanced following a failure experience nonetheless throws the issue back into the "motivation" court.

It also appears that opinion extremity, certainty, and relevance are positively correlated with false consensus tendencies (Crano, 1983; Marks &

Miller, 1985; van der Pligt, Ester, & van der Linden, 1983). For example, Crano (1983) found that participants who had a vested interest in an issue (a tuition surcharge that would affect them personally) showed stronger false consensus effects in their estimates of other students' opinions relative to those for whom the issue was not personally relevant. Interestingly, these projection effects did not extend to a different group (faculty) and held even when controlling for attitude extremity. When we feel strongly about issues or preferences, we may be blind to the possibility that others could have a different view (see also Gilovich, 1990).

This latter account, however, need not imply motivation *or* cognition directly. Instead, it may represent something akin to what Krueger (1998) has claimed is an egocentric *perceptual* process. That is, "the perception of consensus is assumed to be part of the initial encoding of the stimulus rather than the outcome of subsequent higher level processes" (Krueger, 1998, p. 202). As support for this view of false consensus (or projection more generally) as automatic, Krueger (1998) notes that many of the factors shown to increase false consensus effects may be sufficient but not necessary causes (see also Clement & Krueger, 2000). For example, FCE effects may be reduced by some manipulations (such as increasing the salience of a rejected alternative), but the FCE does not disappear entirely in these cases (e.g., Marks & Duval, 1991). Furthermore, (a) perceivers tend to be unaware of the association between their own responses and their predictions about the responses of others (Krueger, 1998), (b) their own responses facilitate consensus estimates (more so than vice versa; Clement & Krueger, 2000; Krueger & Stanke, 2001), and (c) the FCE is typically not diminished by attempts at control and appears to be unintentional (Krueger & Zeiger, 1993; Krueger & Clement, 1994). Projection may occur because people "grant privileged status to their own endorsments ... presumably because each endorsement tends to be rooted in converging layers of experience" (Clement & Krueger, 2000, p. 288).

False Uniqueness

The false uniqueness effect is a complementary pattern indicating contrast of others from the self. With false uniqueness, the prevalence of one's own attributes in a given population is underestimated. This result tends to appear in judgments of talent, ability, or other desirable characteristics, (or on internal traits; see McFarland & Miller, 1990), such that one's virtues are perceived as rare (Suls et al., 1990).[5] Mullen, Dovidio, Johnson, and Copper (1992) have noted that the term "false uniqueness" has been inappropriately applied to the phenomenon of underestimating *actual* consensus, rather than the underestimation of the prevalence of attribute A by individuals who have attribute A relative to those who have attribute B. In some cases, the former effect— underestimating *actual consensus*—is labeled "uniqueness bias" rather than "false uniqueness" (e.g., see Monin & Norton, 2003). For the present purposes, however, these two phenomena will not be distinguished, as they both reflect contrastive tendencies.

In general, false uniqueness effects are rarer than false consensus effects—as a count of relevant published articles attests. Moreover, researchers creating situations favorable to both phenomena seem more likely to find evidence for consensus (e.g., Campbell, 1986; Sherman et al., 1984; Agostinelli et al., 1992). Citing "rare reversals of the FCE," Krueger (1998) has gone so far as to deny that the false uniqueness phenomenon exists at all. He notes, "It is important to realize that a few reversals of the FCE can be expected by chance alone" (p. 168).

Whether this suggests the dominance of assimilation over contrast is not clear; perhaps instead it indicates the cumulative effect of perceptual, cognitive, and motivational forces in the false consensus effect. That is, the dominant cognitive account for false consensus effects— cognitive availability and accessibility—cannot explain false uniqueness effects, nor can Krueger's "perceptual" account. Perhaps this leaves self-enhancement as the primary contributor to (the more rare) false uniqueness effect.

However, recent research suggests that evidence of both false consensus and uniqueness can be apparent in a single judgment context. One example can be found in work on "myopic social prediction"—the tendency for individuals to base comparative predictions (e.g., how likely am I to beat an opponent on a quiz?) on the focal actor (e.g., the self) rather than others in the context (Moore & Kim, 2003). In these studies, individuals are asked to make bets on their likelihood of beating an opponent on a simple or difficult quiz. The key finding is that more money is bet on winning the simple rather than difficult contest, even though one's probability of winning does not change across these contests—the difficulty of the quiz affects both self and opponent (Moore & Kim, 2003). On its face, this appears to indicate a lack of false consensus—individuals do *not* assume that the opponent is similarly affected by task difficulty. But as Moore and Kim (2003) note, predictions of one's own scores do correlate with predictions about the performance of others—consistent with false consensus. At the same time, predictions about others' scores are regressive—less extreme than predictions about own performance (e.g., less good on the simple quiz and less bad on the difficult quiz)—consistent with false uniqueness. Moore and Kim (2003) write that individuals tend to expect that "others will behave like me, only less so" (p. 1132). Interestingly Moore and Kim (2003) favor an explanation based on focus of attention rather than egocentric bias, in that they find evidence that any focal actor (not just the self) produces a pattern of myopic prediction (see also Eiser, Pahl, & Prins, 2001; Windschitl, Kruger, & Simms, 2003). That both false consensus and uniqueness effects may be moderated by attentional focus brings us back to cold rather than hot determinants of both effects. But as with so many psychological phenomena, it is probably the case that both motivated egocentrism and attentional focus contribute (Windschitl et al., 2003).

Moderators of False Consensus and False Uniqueness Effects

A number of researchers have asked the important question, "Under what conditions will assimilation (false consensus) versus contrast (false uniqueness) occur?" For example, studies have documented assimilative effects on some dimensions (e.g., attitudes) and contrast on others (e.g. abilities; Marks, 1984). Valence of the dimension may play a role as well—we may underestimate the percentage of others who perform "moral" acts such as giving blood but overestimate the prevalence of "selfish" acts (Allison, Messick, & Goethals, 1989; Goethals, 1986; Mullen & Goethals, 1990). These findings further point to the important role of self-enhancement and protection motives (we want our attitudes and inadequacies validated by others; our competencies to be rare). Furthermore, a meta-analysis indicated that independent of this valence effect, false consensus reduces as the *actual* consensus regarding an attribute increases. That is, when perceivers are *actually in the majority*, the tendency to overestimate this consensus is reduced (Mullen & Goethals, 1990; see also Krueger, 1998).

Additional studies have demonstrated that the effect which is observed depends on an individual's standing on the dimension (Campbell, 1986; Goethals, 1986; Sigelman, 1991). For example, Campbell (1986) found that those *low* in self-rated ability showed stronger false consensus effects (especially when the abilities were self-relevant) than those *high* in ability (though the latter did not show reliable false uniqueness effects). And in a study focusing on own attitudes toward stigmatized groups and perceptions of the attitudes of others, those *low in tolerance* showed strong false consensus effects, whereas those *high in tolerance* showed strong false uniqueness effects (Sigelman, 1991).

Still others have found evidence for both effects in a single judgment context but on different sets or types of questions. For example, in one study, false consensus was found on a measure of choice between two unpleasant situations, whereas false uniqueness was found on a measure of emotional reactions in the least-preferred-choice situation (McFarland and Miller, 1990). In a series of studies, my colleagues and I further suggested that the form of judgment (whether objective or subjective in nature) as well as judgment order (self versus other) determines whether others are contrasted from or assimilated to the self (Biernat, Manis, & Kobrynowicz, 1997). In that research, false consensus effects were evident overall—e.g., those who voted Republican in a presidential election were more likely than Democratic voters to assume others voted Republican as well. However, when self-ratings *on subjective response scales* were made first, such that the self served as the comparison standard, they were negatively correlated with participants' judgments of the *objective standing* of other college students. For example, participants who judged themselves subjectively religious made lower estimates of the *objective religiosity* of other college students (as indicated by a behavioral checklist). But when judgments of other college students' religiosity were made first, the *self-rating* in *objective* (behavioral) units was contrasted from it. We concluded: "Initial judgments appeared to set the anchor for future judgments on a given dimension. When the self was salient, by virtue of being judged first, objective judgments of others were contrasted from the 'self' anchor. When others' standing on the judgment dimension was similarly made salient, objective judgments of self were contrasted from the 'other' anchor" (Biernat et al., 1997, p. 265).

Other research suggests that false consensus and false uniqueness effects depend on the extent to which the construal of a category being judged (e.g., in positive or negative terms, or in broad or narrow terms) matches expectations associated with the population whose opinions are being estimated (Bosveld et al., 1996; Bosveld, Koomen, van der Pligt, & Plaisier, 1995). For example, in one study, highly involved Christians (compared to less involved Christians and "nonbelievers") showed a false uniqueness effect when estimating the percentage of Christians in the Netherlands, and this effect was based in part on their construal of the category "Christian" in narrow terms (Bosveld et al., 1996). That is, a narrow and *distinct* construct was more likely to produce contrast than a broadly construed one (see Chapter 2).

In general, false uniqueness effects *and* false consensus effects may be more likely when there is a mismatch between one's own construal and one's beliefs about the construals of the population being judged. Gilovich (1990) has argued that false consensus effects are stronger on items or issues that allow a great deal of "subjective construal" of their meaning. For example, false consensus is greater when individuals make self–other judgments of "competitiveness" (a highly subjective, multiply construed attribute) compared to self–other judgments of being a "first-born child" (a more "objective" attribute). In general, perceivers may assume that others construe an attribute in the same way they do, when this may not be the case. Thus, fans of recent as opposed to older films may call to mind positive exemplars of the category "recent films" and assume others do as well; on these grounds, they estimate high consensus for "recent film fan-ship" (Gilovich, 1990; see also Bosveld, Koomen, & Vogelaar, 1995). To the extent that construals are the same, accuracy should be the more likely outcome.

Another moderator of false consensus and uniqueness effects is also hinted at in Mullen and Hu's (1988) meta-analytic review. These researchers found that people who hold a minority position tend to overestimate actual support for their position, whereas people in the majority tend to underestimate actual consensus (Gross & Miller, 1997; Krueger & Zeiger, 1993). These effects reflect *true* overestimation and underestimation rather than traditionally defined false consensus and false uniqueness, respectively, but the phenomena are certainly related (Gross & Miller, 1997). More importantly, these findings indicate another potential motivational contributor to the use of self-standing in predicting the attributes of others. Using Brewer's (1991) optimal distinctiveness model as a framework, Gross, Holtz, and Miller (1995) suggested that majorities, relatively secure in the acceptability of their positions, may seek individual distinctiveness as opposed to social validation. However, minority members may already feel sufficiently unique and thus desire certainty about the correctness of their views. This suggests the very interesting hypothesis that others will be assimilated to the self (false consensus) when one is feeling too individuated (and therefore in need of "belonging") but contrasted from the self (false uniqueness) when one is feeling too included (and therefore in need of "differentiation"). However, feeling individuated or unusual may also contribute to the belief that others will not share our preferences, potentially reducing false consensus effects (see Frable, 1993).

Again, the literature indicates that false consensus effects are more common than false uniqueness effects overall. We may frequently desire belonging and validation, self-knowledge is likely to be highly accessible and we may assume we are in the majority (Krueger & Clement, 1997)—that our own characteristics are normal—thereby prompting assimilation. However, when the population of others being judged is distinct from the self (e.g., an out-group), self-standing may be more likely to serve as a standard of comparison, prompting differentiation, contrast, and uniqueness effects.

Interestingly, Karniol (2003) has pointed out an apparent paradox in the false consensus literature: False consensus effects are *weaker* (though not indicative of false uniqueness) when self-standing is salient. For example, when participants first indicate their choices or attitudes and then estimate those of others, the projection effect is reduced relative to conditions where estimates of others are made first (see meta-analyses by

Fabrigar & Krosnick, 1995; Mullen et al., 1985; Mullen & Hu, 1988). This suggests that individuals may not assume similarity between self and other when self is salient. In fact, as reviewed earlier in this chapter, the self is typically viewed as fairly distinct from others (Codol, 1987; Holyoak & Gordon, 1983), a feature that typically gives rise to contrast (Stapel & Koomen, 1998). From my perspective, however, this suggests that all the perceptual, cognitive, and motivational forces that typically push toward assimilation, toward projecting the self onto others, may be dampened, though not entirely reversed, when the self is a distinct, salient standard.

A Sidebar: Sometimes the Self Appears Not to Be Considered in Judgments of Others

Pluralistic ignorance is a term coined by Katz and Allport (1928) which describes a phenomenon in which "virtually all members of a group privately reject group norms yet believe that virtually all other group members accept them" (Miller & Prentice, 1996, p. 804). Despite a person's knowledge of his or her own views—for example, that s/he is uninterested in drinking alcohol—s/he may believe that "everyone else" feels differently, that heavy drinking is the norm (Prentice & Miller, 1993, 1996). This presumably occurs because individuals are guided by what they see other people doing (e.g., Princeton students drink a lot), and then they assume that this behavior is based on corresponding underlying (e.g., pro-alcohol) attitudes. This correspondent inference occurs even though the individual knows, from his or her own experience, that others may not be acting in concert with his/her "true" feelings. Thus, Latané and Darley's (1970) bystanders personally feel upset and concerned in the face of an emergency but take the apparently calm and collected faces of those around them to mean that other bystanders *truly* feel calm; the result is a failure to interpret events as emergencies and subsequently to offer assistance. And those who comply with a shower ban because of the normative pressure to do so may mistakenly assume that other non-bathers are more intrinsically community-minded (i.e., less affected by social pressure) than they are (Monin & Norton, 2003; for a review, see Miller & Prentice, 1996).

Interestingly, Miller and McFarland (1987) offer an account of this apparent inability to recognize that others' social behavior is just as motivated by social pressures as our own that takes us back to false uniqueness. People tend to believe that they possess stronger levels of "internal" or private traits than do others (a contrastive effect)—for example, they believe that relative to others, they are more sensitive, hesitant, and self-conscious (Miller & McFarland, 1987, Study 1) and are more uncomfortable in nonpreferred situations (McFarland & Miller, 1990). Because these states are internal, we have more evidence for them in ourselves than in others. This uniqueness effect may contribute to pluralistic ignorance: We fail to recognize that others have the same level of discomfort, hesitation, and fear of embarrassment that we do, and therefore we take their observable public behavior at face value. Indirectly then, self-standing is implicated in the (mis)perception of group norms.

☐ Judging Others Based on Representations of Specific Other Exemplars

In addition to the self, our representations of *individual* people we know may also be used as reference points in evaluating or responding to others. In other words, "a new person may be experienced in terms of previous experiences with a known person or an individual person exemplar" (Andersen, Reznik, & Manzella, 1996). This indicates an *assimilative* pattern, in that target others are judged consistently with previously encountered exemplars. However, I will later return to a topic discussed in Chapter 2 that exemplars may also serve as standards of comparison that produce *contrast* effects in judgment.

A number of researchers in the social cognition tradition have suggested that people may base their judgments in a given situation on a single, previously encountered similar situation or event (Abelson, 1976; Nisbett & Ross, 1980; Schank & Abelson, 1977; Read, 1983, 1984; Wyer & Carlston, 1979). That is, single exemplars, such as individual targets, may function like categories in that they contain descriptive knowledge and experiences (Higgins & King, 1981; Smith & Zárate, 1992). This activated knowledge is then used to interpret a new target person, through the detection of *similarity*. Gilovich (1981) argues, for example, that people engage in a sort of reasoning by analogy, whereby they "see a little of the past in many present situations and base their decisions on what they believe to be the implications of these past events" (p. 798). Thus, when sportswriters were asked to rate profiles of hypothetical college football players, these players were judged more favorably if they shared some similarity with a well-known professional player. Interestingly, this occurred whether the similarity was relevant to football success and explicit (e.g., played the same position as a named player), relevant and implicit (e.g., was a linebacker from Penn State, a school that turned out good linebackers at the time of the study), or irrelevant to football success and explicit (e.g., was from the same hometown as a named player). Others have made the case for analogy-based models of this sort as well (Read & Cessa, 1991; Spellman & Holyoak, 1992).

In another illustrative study, Read (1983) initially exposed participants to behavioral descriptions of six members of a tribe in Northern Australia, half of whom engaged in a behavior of interest (e.g., performing a ritual that involved cutting one's finger and writing with the blood) and half of whom did not. Participants were then exposed to new individuals and asked if these targets would perform the ritual or not. Judgments of likelihood of engaging in the ritual were affected by the target's similarity to one of the initial set of actors—if the initial exemplar performed the ritual, the new similar target was predicted to do so as well. Follow-up research indicated that this tendency was enhanced when the target shared features with the initial exemplar that were *causally relevant* to the behavior (e.g., the actor had "violated a taboo" before engaging in the ritual as opposed to "spent the day harvesting"; Read, 1984).

One could argue that this *assimilative* pattern—new target judged consistently with the initial actor—is due to demand effects: With little else to go on, and with the exposure to initial cases being so explicit, participants may have used the only information available to them to make a judgment. However, other research has documented a similar pattern of assimilation when the initial exemplar exposure is less obvious or explicit. A clever study by Lewicki (1985) is a case in point. Participants first took part in a study during which they were treated in a warm and friendly manner by a female experimenter. After this experience, participants were shown two photos of other women and asked to choose "the one who, according to their feelings, was kinder and friendlier" (Lewicki, 1985, p. 569). One of the photographed new targets was very similar to the friendly experimenter—e.g., like the experimenter, she wore glasses and had short hair. The other was dissimilar in appearance (long hair, no glasses). Thirty-four of forty participants (85%) chose the similar new target as the more kind and friendly. This figure can be compared to a condition in which the choice between two targets was made *prior to* any interaction with a kind and friendly experimenter: 24 of 40 (60%) chose the short-haired, glasses-wearing target in this baseline condition. Another intriguing study demonstrated that racial similarity alone may create conditions for assimilation. White students who encountered a black confederate behaving rudely later terminated an interview with *another* black individual more quickly than was the case after an encounter with a rude white confederate or no earlier encounter (Henderson-King & Nisbett, 1996, Study 2; see also White & Shapiro, 1987).

It may be the case that much information about the social world is represented in terms of specific individuals or exemplars (in addition to abstract schemas) and that these representations influence judgments about newly encountered, similar individuals and groups (Smith & Zárate, 1992). For Smith and Zárate (1992), "similarity is not taken to be a fixed, context-independent property of stimuli, but is modulated by the perceiver's relative allocation of attention to stimulus dimensions" (p. 4). Thus, if perceivers' motives and goals lead them to attend to a particular feature of a target person, they will likely recruit from memory exemplars who are similar on that feature, "allowing information sorted with the exemplars ... to be accessed and applied to the current target" (Smith & Zárate, 1992, p. 6). For example, if an instructor is disturbed by a student who routinely falls asleep during lectures, this event likely recruits previously experienced examples of students who have done the same. The attributes of these retrieved exemplars (e.g., "not very bright," "partyer") are likely to be ascribed to the newly encountered student. However, less salient attributes of the sleeping student (manner of dress, hair color) are unlikely to be used as a basis for exemplar retrieval.

Transference

Perhaps the most striking evidence of the impact of representations of specific individuals on judgments of new targets comes from the work of Andersen and her colleagues on "transference," the phenomenon in which beliefs and feelings about *significant others* are "transferred" to other people (Andersen & Baum, 1994; Andersen & Cole, 1990; Andersen, Glassman, Chen, & Cole, 1995; Andersen, Reznik, & Manzella, 1996). Rather than viewing transference in Freudian terms, Andersen and her colleagues describe an information-processing model whereby transference is conceptualized as "going beyond the information given" about a target (Bruner, 1957) and applying a representation of a significant other (including its overall evaluative tone) onto him or her (Andersen & Baum, 1994; Andersen et al., 1996). For example, using idiographic methods, Andersen et al. (1995, Study 1) found that participants made more false-positive memory errors about targets who resembled their significant others than they did about targets who resembled nonsignificant others or yoked participants' significant others and nonsignificant others. For example, if one's significant other "sings in the shower, reads mysteries, and is socially skilled," a target person described as a socially skilled mystery reader is likely to be remembered as singing in the shower as well. This suggests that perceivers "fill in the blanks" about a newly encountered person with information that the similar significant other possesses.

Other research has documented that similarity to social stereotypes and trait categories can also produce false-positive memory errors (Andersen

& Cole, 1990), but that representations of specific, significant others have a stronger impact in this regard. Furthermore, attributes of the significant other may be mistakenly attributed to targets who share *no* features of the significant other (Andersen et al., 1995, Study 2). These effects suggest that representations of significant others may be chronically accessible (e.g., Higgins & King, 1981)—ready to be applied to new targets even in the absence of direct feature overlap or similarity—though and priming nonetheless enhance transference tendencies. Recent work has also documented that transference effects in impressions of a fictitious "game partner" can occur even when the significant-other representation is triggered subliminally (Glassman & Andersen, 1999). And in one interesting extension, perceivers' *behavioral* responses to a new target who resembled a liked or disliked significant other were consistent with the affective tone of that other (e.g., as evidenced in naïve judges' ratings of conversation friendliness; Berk & Andersen, 2000).

Clear in all of this research is that representations of specific individuals seem to affect memory for and evaluations of others in an *assimilative* fashion. Comparing the effects of positive and negative significant others perhaps shows this pattern most strongly, in that facial affect, target evaluations, expectancies regarding the degree to which the target person might like the self, and motivations to approach the target all tend to assimilate toward the overall valence of the significant-other representation (Andersen et al., 1996).

Contrast?

In this chapter, I have considered the role of both self and significant other exemplars in judgments of others. These two types of representations share some features (e.g., see Hinkley & Andersen, 1996; Prentice, 1990), but to my knowledge, occasional findings that others are contrasted from the self (as in false uniqueness effects or Dunning's research on egocentric trait biases) have no counterpart in the literature on significant-other representations. Perhaps, then, significant others are not used as standards of comparison but rather solely as interpretive frameworks (Stapel & Koomen, 2000), triggering affect and associated cognitive links at the time of encountering and encoding a target's attributes (Andersen et al., 1996). Note, however, that significant others (and exemplars more generally) have some features that, according to the research reviewed in Chapter 2, should produce contrast effects. Exemplars are *distinct* and *narrow* versus wide and are *unambiguous* (perhaps *extreme*); these conditions might be expected to lead to their use as standards of comparison.

Indeed, it is worth remembering that the literature on priming effects using person exemplars (e.g., Adolph Hitler, Gandhi) does suggest that contrast effects can be observed with such extreme contextual primes (Herr, 1986; Herr et al., 1983; Stapel & Koomen, 1996). Two features of significant-other representations may make them immune to this contrastive pattern. First, significant others are *entitative*, such that consistency is expected and perceived. As was reviewed in Chapter 2, entitative primes tend to produce assimilation effects for this reason (Hilton & von Hippel, 1990). In transference, the new similar other and significant other may be perceived as an entity, creating assimilative judgment, memory, and behavioral tendencies. Second, Andersen and her colleagues suggest that transference effects generally occur without conscious awareness of resemblance to the significant other on the part of perceivers. Much research suggests that awareness of a prime prompts contrast—perhaps due to an active correction process (Lombardi et al., 1987; Martin, 1986; Strack et al., 1993; Wegener & Petty, 1997). To the extent that awareness of the resemblance between a new other and the significant other was enhanced, contrast effects (e.g., judging a similar target as less likeable than and more distinct from a significant other) might be expected.

☐ Summary

The research reviewed in this chapter suggests a variety of ways in which the self and other exemplars can be used as standards to judge other individuals and groups. The outcome of self-as-standard can be either assimilation or contrast, depending on a number of features of the judgment setting. I have tried to outline some of these in Table 4.1. Many should be familiar by now; factors that make it likely the other will be included in the self, including similarity, ambiguity of target, and broad versus distinct self-aspects, increase the likelihood of assimilation. Additionally, the most common cognitive account of these assimilation effects involves *knowledge accessibility*; the self and significant-other exemplars are highly available constructs that may function as an interpretive framework for judging others. Motivational factors including esteem protection and needs for belongingness, differentiation, or social validation may also contribute to either assimilation effects (as when one projects one's own important attitudes onto others) or contrast effects (as when one's attributes are perceived to be unique). Both cold and hot factors are likely to matter when the self is involved—self is a highly familiar, accessible, salient, and *emotionally charged* standard that leads us to judge individual others and groups as both like us and not.

TABLE 4.1. Summary of Phenomena Involving Self/Exemplars as Standards for Judging Others

Phenomenon	Assimilative Pattern	Factors/Processes Responsible	Contrastive Pattern	Factors/Process Responsible
Asymmetry in self–other similarity judgments	Others judged similar to the self	• Feature overlap • Inclusion	Self is judged distinct from (dissimilar to) others	• Unique features • Exclusion • Identity affirmation/ defense
Own attributes used to judge individual others	Self–other trait judgments similar, positively correlated	• Accessible self-information (e.g., schematicity) • Abstractness of self-concepts (broad traits) • Ambiguous targets	Self–other trait judgments dissimilar, negatively correlated	• Distinct/ specific self-attributes • Extreme/ unambiguous targets • Ego defense
Own attributes to judge groups of others: False consensus and uniqueness	False consensus: Others assumed to be like the self	• Selective exposure (to similar others) • Availability/ accessibility of self-standing; induction • Basic perceptual/ encoding process • Broad judgment dimensions; open to construal • Validation-seeking • Self-esteem protection • Need for belonging	False uniqueness: Others assumed to be unlike the self	• Positive judgment attributes • Private as opposed to more public/ observable attributes • Narrow/ distinct constructs • Self-esteem protection • Need for differentiation
Non-self exemplars to judge others	Projection/ transference of exemplar attributes onto other	• Reasoning by analogy • Going beyond the information given • Similarity detection/inclusion	Explicitly primed exemplars produce contrast in judgments of ambiguous targets	• Distinct/ narrow standard • Awareness of standard • Exclusion

☐ Notes

1. A related finding—though not relevant to asymmetries in similarity or distance judgments—comes from the literature on optimism in probability judgments. Hoorens and Buunk (1993) found that people were particularly likely to be optimistic–to estimate lower health risk for themselves than others–when they first judged a comparsion target's health risk. Presumably, "individuals may not like the idea of seeing their own future as similar to that of others. Indeed the best way of being different is being better" (Hoorens & Buunk, 1993, p. 299; see also Codol, 1987; Codol,

Jarymowicz, Kaminska-Feldman, & Szuster-Zbrojewicz, 1989; Klein & Weinstein, 1997; Otten and van der Pligt, 1996).

2. The tendency to judge all others comparably to the self might also be viewed as a general "perceiver" effect in interpersonal perception (see Kenny, 1994).

3. The body of publications on false consensus is much larger than that on false uniqueness. At this writing, a PsycInfo search revealed 146 references to false consensus and 16 to false uniqueness.

4. However, Krueger and Clement (1994) have demonstrated that the false consensus bias remains even after providing participants with other statistical information and educating them about the bias (see also Alicke & Largo, 1995).

5. However, a few findings suggest that those with *un*desirable attributes may perceive those attributes as (relatively) unique (Nisbett & Valins, 1972). For example, Suls et al. (1990) found a false uniqueness effect for the attribute "being diagnosed with an anxiety disorder," and van den Eijnden, Buunk, and Bosveld (2000) found that women (but not men) showed false uniqueness in their prevalence estimates of extra-dyadic and unsafe sex. The latter authors suggest that these findings may be due to stigmatization—feelings of deviance based on the socially disapproved (especially for women) yet not publicly visible pattern of behavior.

Stereotypes and Stereotyping of Others

The study of group stereotypes and their effects on judgments of individuals is a long-standing and still very active tradition in the field. The main theme of this body of work is that to the extent that we possess stereotypes, which I will define as sets of "beliefs about the personal attributes of a group of people" (Ashmore & Del Boca, 1981, p. 16), we use them to structure our impressions of individual members of those groups. In fact, some evidence suggests that stereotypes may be activated automatically, upon merely encountering an individual who belongs to a relevant social category (e.g., Augoustinos, Ahrens, & Innes, 1994; Devine, 1989; Perdue & Gurtman, 1990; cf. Blair & Banaji, 1996; Gilbert & Hixon, 1991; Lepore & Brown, 1997; Locke, MacLeod, & Walker, 1994). In this sense, they are highly available standards or expectations, ready for use in evaluating others. Stereotypes are generally assumed to function as expectations or interpretive frames toward which judgments of individual targets are drawn (assimilated). For example, we tend to perceive and judge individual women, blacks, soccer hooligans, and hairdressers in accordance with our group stereotypes (see Brewer, 1996; Fiske, 1998; Hamilton & Sherman, 1994; Hilton & von Hippel, 1996; Stangor & Lange, 1994; von Hippel, Sekaquaptewa, & Vargas, 1995, for recent reviews), particularly when category information is available prior to encoding of other information about the target (Bodenhausen, 1988; Park & Hastie, 1987).

☐ Stereotyping Models

Dual-Process Models

Several models of the stereotyping process have been offered, and the most prominent of these are Brewer's (1988) dual-process model and Fiske and Neuberg's (1990) continuum model of impression formation. Both assume that upon encountering a stimulus person, an automatic identification or categorization process occurs (e.g., a target is identified as a Black, elderly female). Assuming at least some minimal relevance, this is followed by additional processing that generally takes the form of confirmatory categorization (unless self-involvement is high, in which case Brewer suggests that a bottom-up "personalization" route to impression formation is taken). At this categorization stage, the fit of the target person to the category is considered; in other words, the target is compared to the expectation or standard of the social category (e.g., to what extent does this individual match the features of the category "female"?). If fit is good (and it frequently will be, for "once a particular category has been activated, the threshold for identifying a match between the category prototype and incoming stimulus information is lowered"; Brewer, 1988, p. 18; see also Higgins & King, 1981), perceptions and judgments of the target will be category based, or assimilated to the group stereotype.

If fit is not good, the person is recategorized (in Fiske & Neuberg's model) or individuated (in Brewer's model). Both processes involve seeking a better category or subtype with which to characterize the target (for Fiske & Neuberg, 1990, an exemplar or even the self-concept can serve as a category at this stage). It is only after failure at the recategorization stage that perceivers turn to individuated or piecemeal processing of the target in Fiske and Neuberg's (1990) model; in this sense, "perceivers give priority to category-based processes" (p. 13). In Brewer's model, "individuation" is still category-based, as "the distinguishing features (of a target) are defined with reference to the more general category or person type" (Brewer, 1988, p. 21). Only "personalization," triggered by "affective investment" on the part of the perceiver, involves a direct focus on the individual, with category information about him or her stored as just one feature. Brewer offers the example of Janet, a nurse. In category-based representation, Janet is subordinate to the overall category "nurses," but in personalization, the nurse feature is subordinate to Janet. Again, both Brewer's model and Fiske and Neuberg's model suggest that categories often dominate impressions and do so in an assimilative fashion.

Evidence for the "fit testing" stage of both models comes from research by Erber and Fiske (1984), who found that perceivers' comments during a "think-aloud" procedure suggested they were spontaneously testing the extent to which a target's attributes fit the category label. Perceivers also reinterpreted information that was potentially inconsistent with the label as consistent. For example, the attribute "strong" was assumed to imply physical strength when the actor was a construction worker and mental strength when the actor was a professor (Fiske, Neuberg, Beattie, & Milberg, 1987; see also Kunda, Sinclair, & Griffin, 1997).

And other evidence suggests that when category confirmation becomes more difficult—often because the target just does not fit the category—recategorization (at the middle of Fiske and Neuberg's continuum) or individuation (at the opposite end from categorization) becomes more likely. For example, in one study, men described as primary caregivers of children or women described as financial providers (both inconsistent with the gender category labels) were judged more likely to be homosexual than those behaving consistently with gender roles (Deaux & Lewis, 1984). This finding suggests recategorization, in that gender was not rejected as a basis of judgment but rather was combined with the individuating information into a category subtype. Much other research documents that judgmental assimilation to stereotypes is also *less* likely when a category label is weak (as in occupational stereotypes, which are less well-established than, say, gender and racial stereotypes) and combined with nondiagnostic attribute information (see Nisbett, Zukier, & Lemley, 1981), or when category labels are combined with clearly inconsistent individuating information (e.g., Jussim, Nelson, Manis, & Soffin, 1995; Krueger & Rothbart, 1988; Locksley, Borgida, Brekke, & Hepburn, 1980).

Other important work has documented that motivational factors can lead to individuated processing as opposed to category-based processing. For example, *outcome dependency* may motivate individuated processing (or personalization, in Brewer's model), in that we desire to accurately predict and control the target's behavior. This should prompt attention to the target's individuating features. Neuberg and Fiske (1987) found that participants were less affected by stereotypes about schizophrenia (i.e., they made more positive judgments) when their outcomes were affected by a (supposed) schizophrenic target compared to conditions when they were not outcome dependent (see also Erber & Fiske, 1984). Other motives or need states, such as expected competition or powerlessness, may also prompt enhanced attention to and use of individuating as opposed to categorical information (Fiske, 1993; Goodwin, Gubin, Fiske, & Yzerbyt, 2000; Ruscher & Fiske, 1990; see also Vescio, Snyder, & Butz, 2003). In short, evidence does suggest that judgments of stereotyped group members may be driven primarily by either the stereotype itself or individuating attributes of the target, depending on the motivations of the perceiver (see Fiske, Lin, & Neuberg, 1999).

The Brewer (1988) and Fiske and Neuberg (1990) models obviously share some important features. Both models suggest that impression formation begins with categories—we attempt to fit new people into existing schemas. When fit is not possible, attempts to find alternative fits commence. Both models also indicate that motivations can prompt relatively less reliance on category labels and more attention to and use of individuating attributes in the impression formed. Differences between these models include Brewer's contention that categorization is a controlled process—that perceivers choose to use category-based or personalized processing—and that different stages involve different mental representations and modes of processing (e.g., categorization relies on prototypical images, individuation on subtypes or exemplars). For our purposes, however, the important prediction of both models is that impression formation will sometimes show assimilation to stereotypes and sometimes *limited* or *no* effects of stereotypes. Contrast effects, however, are not reflected in either model (more on this below).

A Parallel Process/Connectionist Alternative

The models of Brewer (1988) and Fiske and Neuberg (1990) are serial in nature—information processing proceeds through stages and if/then decision trees. In contrast to this sequential view, Kunda and Thagard (1996) offer a "parallel constraint satisfaction" model of impression formation. This model relies on principles of connectionism, which proposes that bits of information are represented as units in a neural network, along with weights that indicate the strength of the connections between units. Connected units are activated (or inhibited) simultaneously until the system "settles" on some output. Applied to impression formation, Kunda and Thagard's model suggests that category information and associated stereotypes comprise one set of nodes in a network of information that perceivers may possess about a target person. Other nodes, for example, may include observed behavior or attributes of the target as well as myriad associations to those attributes. The nodes of the network are activated and adjusted in parallel, constraining each other's meaning, until the network settles on an overall impression of the target. This model gives no special status to categorical information—it comprises just one of many nodes in the network—a point of key contrast to the other models.

One advantage of this perspective is that it avoids some of the confusion surrounding the precise distinction between categorical and individuating information. For example, is "nurse" a category or an individuating attribute of the fictitious Janet? For Brewer, as noted above, its status can vary depending on the type of processing (and resulting mental representation) formed of the person. But for both Brewer's and Fiske and Neuberg's models, it seems important to *conceptually* distinguish the constructs. This turns out to be difficult to do; instead, categorical and individuating information are often *operationally* distinguished by the order of presentation of information. For example, in one illustrative study, Fiske et al. (1987, Study 2) presented perceivers with target descriptions of this sort: "Professor: Intellectual, productive, pre-occupied, self-regulated, hard-working" (p. 409). Under such conditions, think-aloud protocols revealed relatively less attention to the attributes and more to the category label (compared to conditions when attributes were inconsistent with the label or the label was not informative [e.g., "person"]). But had the word "intellectual" appeared first in the list, "professor" might have become one of the individuating attributes. Fiske et al. (1987) acknowledge this point when they write, "The relatively heavy use of the category label, compared to the average attribute, supports the current view that the category label has special status. Of course, this conclusion is not explicitly tested here, because the category label always came first" (p. 417).

At any rate, Kunda and Thagard's perspective, in which stereotypes are just one piece of the "mix" that drives impression formation, avoids the difficulties described above and perhaps has the advantage of allowing multiple categories to be represented simultaneously. And this model has been used to account for a number of findings supporting the notion that judgments are often assimilated to social stereotypes. For example, the fact that a construction worker who "hit someone" is judged to be more aggressive than a housewife who "hit someone" may derive from the fact that the construction worker node has stronger links to the trait "aggressive" or the behavior of "punching" than does the housewife node (which, in fact, may have inhibitory links to those other constructs; Krueger & Rothbart, 1988; Kunda & Sherman-Williams, 1993). The network describing this situation is depicted in Figure 5.1, in which observed behavioral information (hitting) and categorical information (housewife versus construction worker) ultimately produce heightened aggressiveness ratings of the construction worker (assimilation). In this example and others, stereotypes may also constrain the meaning of other trait and behavior terms. Thus, participants believed the construction worker who "hit someone" had "punched" the person while the housewife who "hit someone" had "spanked a child." In another study, the trait description "very extraverted" was construed in unpleasant and pushy behavioral terms when applied to a car salesman (e.g., "talks too much") but in pleasant and skilled behavioral terms when applied to an actor (e.g., "makes others feel comfortable"; Kunda et al., 1997, Study 1a).[1]

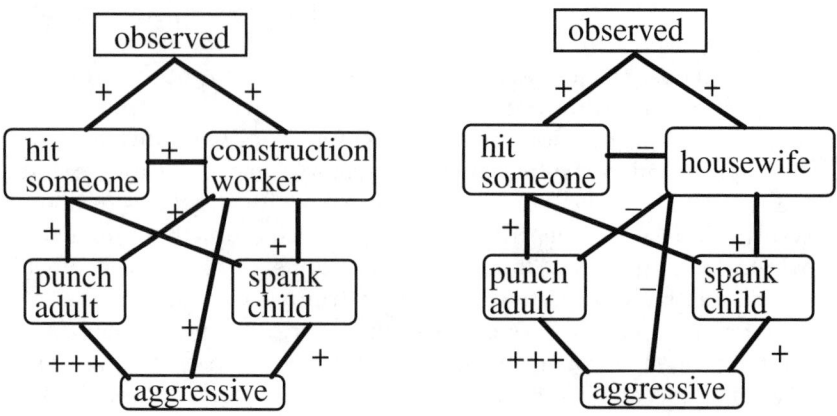

FIGURE 5.1.   The parallel constraint satisfaction model, depicting network activation when participants judge the aggressiveness of a construction worker or housewife who "hit someone." (From Kunda, Z., & Thagard, P. [1996]. *Psychological Review, 103,* Figure 5. With permission.)

Kunda and Thagard's (1996) model may also explain a common finding in the stereotyping literature—that stereotypes dominate impressions *less* when clearly diagnostic individuating information is also available. Take, for example, a famous study by Linville and Jones (1980). These researchers found that when evaluating Black and White law school applicants, evidence of weak academic credentials produced negative judgments, but race did not moderate this effect.[2] Kunda and Thagard (1996) argue that this is the case because the behavior "weak credentials" and traits such as "incompetent" and "unintelligent" are likely to be more strongly associated in the network activated during the judgment task than the association between the category label (Black vs. White) and those traits. In other words, the behavioral information swamps the impact of the category and its associates. Note that Fiske and Neuberg would refer to this judgment outcome as evidence of individuation (or at least recategorization), perhaps prompted by the lack of fit between "White law school applicant" and "weak credentials" (for Brewer, this might reflect personalization, or at least individuation).

The Kunda and Thagard (1996) parallel constraint satisfaction model seems to offer a more parsimonious account, though it too has its shortcomings. One is that it may be difficult, *a priori*, to predict the relative strength of association between nodes in the network. For example, to what extent can we be sure that the "weak credentials–unintelligent" link is stronger than the "African-American target–unintelligent" link? Of course methods of measuring associative strength (such as reaction times) are available, but it then becomes a complex task to estimate, in any given laboratory study or real-world impression-formation experience, the relevant parameters and subsequent judgment predictions. A second shortcoming and distinction from the serial models of Fiske and Neuberg and Brewer is that motivational factors are not incorporated or considered (except in passing, as something that prompts more controlled processing of information). Indeed, for Kunda and Thagard, the processing of information about a target other is assumed to take place largely outside of awareness, relatively automatically.

Facilitation and Inhibition in Stereotyping

In an approach informed by the dual-process models reviewed above, Bodenhausen and Macrae (1998) proposed a model of facilitatory and inhibitory factors relevant to "stereotype-based perceptions, judgments, and behaviors" (p. 4). As its core psychological processes, the model begins with categorization and stereotype activation, which may produce biased interpretation and, in turn, discriminatory responses to individual targets. But at each stage, some factors *facilitate* the assimilative influence of stereotypes, and some *inhibit* that influence (resulting in null effects and occasional contrast effects).

In the initial processing phase, stereotypes may be activated if a category membership of a target individual is primed but actively inhibited if not primed. For example, in one well-known study, participants viewed a videotape of a Chinese woman (Macrae, Bodenhausen, & Milne, 1995, Study 1). For some participants, this woman's "Chinese" identity was initially activated through a parafoveal priming task in which the category word "Chinese" was presented; for others the task presented the category word "woman," and for others, control words appeared. Participants' reaction times to "Chinese" and "woman" traits that appeared in a subsequent lexical decision task were then assessed. Relative to the control condition, activated primes facilitated responses to the primed category— those exposed to "woman" primes responded more quickly to gender stereotypical words and those exposed to "Chinese" primes responded more quickly to Asian stereotypical words. Importantly too, relative to the control condition, nonprimed categories were inhibited—Chinese traits were responded to more slowly in the "woman" prime condition and "woman" traits were responded to more slowly in the Chinese prime condition. More recently, Hugenberg and Bodenhausen (2004) have documented similar patterns with regard to *self*-categorization. In general, the model suggests that though individuals belong to multiple categories, one is likely to dominate the impression formation process and others are not just ignored but also automatically inhibited.

Once a stereotype is activated, it may produce an assimilative effect on judgments of the target person either through a direct path—in which the stereotypical beliefs are "added (or averaged) into one's general impression of the target" (Bodenhausen & Macrae, 1998, p. 6)—or through an indirect path of biased selection and interpretation. Specifically, stereotype-consistent information may be attended to more closely than counterstereotypical information, and stereotypes may guide the construal of information about the individual. In describing the mechanisms that contribute to facilitation or assimilation, Bodenhausen and Macrae (1998) distinguish between a sort of automatic "default assimilation," whereby activated constructs directly affect subsequent behavior processing, and a more motivated process whereby one desires to use stereotypes in impressions of others and therefore actively construes information in a manner that supports stereotypical preconceptions. The construal theme is quite consistent with the work of Kunda and her colleagues described above and with general principles of motivated reasoning (Kunda, 1990; Kruglanski & Webster, 1996).

However, it is also possible for individuals who personally reject activated stereotypes to work against these assimilative tendencies and attempt to suppress stereotypes. Much recent research on stereotyping has taken up this theme, noting that perceivers may be reluctant to use their stereotypes to judge others—either because they worry about appearing prejudiced or because they have internalized norms suggesting that prejudice and stereotyping are wrong (Crandall & Eshleman, 2003; Crandall, Eshleman, & O'Brien, 2002; Gordijn, Hindriks, Koomen, Dijksterhuis, & van Knippenberg, 2004; Plant & Devine, 1998). In their model, Bodenhausen and Macrae (1998) describe work on stereotype suppression by Devine and Monteith and their colleagues (Devine, Monteith, Zuwerink, & Elliot, 1991; Monteith, 1993), who consider suppression in self-regulatory terms. More detail on this research will appear in Chapter 7 of this book, but for now I will note the basic idea that such self-regulation may be difficult, in part because "attempts to squelch stereotypic responses are working against" spontaneous assimilative tendencies (Bodenhausen & Macrae, 1998, p. 23).

In Chapter 2, I discussed *prime awareness* as a factor that promoted contrast effects, presumably because perceivers actively correct their judgments in a direction opposite to the implication of the primed context. It is not much of a stretch to suggest that stereotypes may operate in this same manner. That is, to the extent that I know a stereotype may bias my judgment (I am "aware" of the lurking stereotype), I may correct (or overcorrect) and avoid assimilation to the stereotype (cf., Wegener & Petty, 1997;

Wilson & Brekke, 1994). Indeed, research has shown that stereotypes can be successfully suppressed, at least under explicit instructions to do so, resulting in null and occasional contrast effects in judgments of stereotyped targets (Macrae, Bodenhausen, Milne, & Jetten, 1994). In one study, for example, when participants were explicitly asked *not* to use their stereotypes of skinheads as they formed an impression of a skinhead, they were able to form less stereotypical impressions (relative to participants in a control condition; Macrae et al., 1994, Study 1). At the same time, however, this reduction of stereotyping for one target made subsequent stereotyping more likely—when writing about a second skinhead target, participants in the "do not stereotype" condition formed more stereotypical impressions than control participants. This tendency has been termed the "stereotype rebound" effect (Liberman & Förster, 2000; Macrae et al., 1994; Monteith, Sherman, & Devine, 1998; Wyer, Sherman, & Stroessner, 2000), and it has been documented even when the goal of not stereotyping is introduced more subtly, at least among those whose personal standards are against stereotyping (Macrae, Bodenhausen, & Milne, 1998).

What is most interesting to me about stereotype rebound is that it suggests that initial contrast from the stereotype (not applying the stereotype to an individual) may ultimately produce greater assimilation to it (increased stereotyping of a subsequent category member). This idea also appears in interesting research on "compensatory stereotyping," which suggests that when stereotyped expectations are violated, perceivers predict that another group member will compensate for the violation— behave more stereotypically—in the future (Seta & Seta, 1993). For example, after learning about a minister who had an affair with a married woman and molested a 7-year-old child (presumably leading to a contrast effect in perceptions of that target), judges predicted that *another minister* would be extremely likely (relative to nonviolating or moderately violating conditions) to "donate one third of his income tax refund to charity even though he was not asked to do so and no one would know about his donation" (Seta & Seta, 1993, p. 725). The initial contrastive response prompted by the expectancy violation led to a heightened assimilative response—expecting another group member to behave consistently with the stereotype. Rebound and compensation may operate through different mechanisms, but both function to maintain stereotypes.

But back to Bodenhausen and Macrae's (1998) model: The final step is the expression of a discriminatory response. That this is a separate step from impression formation builds on the idea that there may be a dissociation between the impression we form and how we behave toward a given individual. It is in this stage that social norms come into play. These norms can either facilitate discriminatory responding (as when one senses the local environment is supportive of prejudice expression) or inhibit such responding (as when the opposite is true). In both cases, some awareness of norms is necessary—the individual must be "familiar with expectations and standards for acceptable and unacceptable behavior" (Bodenhausen & Macrae, 1998, p. 35). Several lines of research indicate that individuals' expressions of stereotypes and prejudice are affected by perceived norms in the situation (Blanchard, Lilly, & Vaughn, 1991; Sechrist & Stangor, 2001; Wittenbrink & Henly, 1996). In short, another form of assimilation—to social norms rather than stereotypes per se—is outlined in this perspective.

Interestingly, however, Bodenhausen and Macrae (1998) describe at least the potential for a phenomenon they call "norm rebound." That is, "the social processes that normally regulate public behavior [may] fail to function effectively and even backfire" (p. 39). In a process akin to psychological reactance (Brehm, 1966), individuals may feel that norms constrain their freedom to behave as they like—say, to express their prejudices— and they may respond in a direction counter to norms but consistent with their personal beliefs. Recently, Plant and Devine (2001) documented such a pattern—resistance to "political correctness" norms—among individuals who were low in internal and high in external motivation to suppress their prejudices (e.g., those who did not feel any personal motivation to appear unprejudiced but who did feel concerned that others would react negatively to them if they expressed prejudice). To my knowledge, however, no research has examined whether those whose *personal beliefs* dictate nonprejudicial responding, when placed in a normative situation that condones prejudice, experience reactance. Norm rebound ultimately describes assimilation to personal beliefs, and in many cases, those personal beliefs are in a stereotype-supportive direction.

This model of activation and inhibition shares much with the previously described models of stereotyping. Along with Brewer (1988) and Fiske and Neuberg (1990), this model highlights the importance of categorization and of general assimilative tendencies in the impressions formed of individual targets (the model assumes some ambiguity or minimal "fit" to activated stereotypes). It also considers motivational factors that contribute to stereotyping effects. And along with Kunda and Thagard (1996), Bodenhausen and Macrae (1998) recognize the importance of construal processes in the interpretation of information about targets. The main distinction of this model is its focus on both facilitative and inhibitory mechanisms that operate on the stereotyping process, and its link to self-regulatory principles. Although some aspects of the model suggest contrastive processes (e.g., inhibition of categories, stereotype suppression), it can still be conceptualized as largely *assimilative* in nature. That is, even when inhibition works momentarily, rebound—often to the default stereotype-assimilative outcome—occurs.

☐ The Ubiquity of Assimilation Effects?

Extended discussion of the relative merits of the models described here is not my purpose. I wish to note, instead, their utility in accounting for (1) the assimilative influence of stereotypes, particularly when little, ambiguous, or irrelevant individuating information is available about a target person (such that the fit of a target to the category is facilitated), (2) the relatively lesser impact of stereotypes when unambiguous, diagnostic information is available (such that the target may not fit the category, or the clarity of the behavior gives it greater weight; see Kunda & Thagard, 1996 for a review), and (3) the potential for motivation, in addition to cognitive factors such as knowledge accessibility, to guide the stereotyping process. Furthermore, these models highlight the fact that stereotypes, in their role as interpretive frameworks, can affect the *meaning* or construal of other information (behaviors, traits) about a target person. "Aggressiveness" may be construed as "arguing and complaining" if the target is a lawyer but as "punching and yelling insults" if the target is a construction worker (Kunda et al., 1997); similarly, the behavior of "terminating a few employees" may be encoded as "firing a few people" if the actor heads a computer software company but as "killing a few people" if he is a drug dealer (Dunning & Sherman, 1997; see also Kobrynowicz & Biernat, 1997). All of these findings suggest assimilation—stereotypes serve as expectations toward which perceptions of others are drawn (see also von Hippel, Sekaquaptewa, & Vargas, 1995).

Stereotypes as Standards

Another view suggests that in addition to serving as interpretive frameworks, stereotypes also function as comparison standards for judging individual group members on stereotype-relevant dimensions (Biernat, Manis, & Nelson, 1991; Biernat & Kobrynowicz, 1997; Biernat & Manis, 1994; Biernat, Vescio, & Manis, 1998). For example, the stereotype that women are more verbally able than men may not only lead perceivers to expect that a given woman will have higher verbal skill than a given man but also prompt them to compare the woman's skill to the expected (high) skill level of women and to compare the man's skill to the expected (lower) skill level of men. Because women are compared to women and men to men, standards can be thought of as "shifting" with category membership. The result in this example is that women are held to a higher standard than men are, with the potentially paradoxical consequence that a given woman may be judged as *less* verbally skilled than a comparable man—a contrast effect (see Biernat & Manis, 1994; Biernat & Kobrynowicz, 1997).[3]

In a series of studies, my colleagues and I have noted that such contrastive patterns are more likely to result when judges use "subjective" evaluative language (labels such as "high" or "low," "good" or "bad") rather than "objective" or common-rule assessments (e.g., estimates of verbal SAT scores). This is the case because subjective language is slippery—there is no inherent, stable, agreed-upon meaning of the label "good"—and therefore it can be used and interpreted in a within-category fashion. "Good verbal skill" for a woman may mean something quite different (objectively better) than "good verbal skill" for a man. By definition, objective units of evaluation cannot shift in meaning as one moves from one category to another; for example, an SAT score retains the same meaning regardless of the category membership of the target to whom it is applied. In the gender and verbal skill example, objective estimates of verbal skill (SAT scores, grades) tend to reveal higher estimates for female than male targets, even when subjective evaluations for the sexes are identical (Biernat & Manis, 1994). Indeed, the signature finding of my research on the "shifting standards model" is that stereotype-assimilative findings tend to emerge when target judgments are made in objective units, but reductions or reversals (contrast) appear when subjective evaluations are rendered (see Biernat, 2003; Biernat et al., 1998, for reviews).

This point about subjective versus objective judgment has an important analog in Kunda and Thagard's (1996) distinction between trait judgments and behavioral predictions. Specifically, Kunda and Thagard (1996) provide evidence that in situations where diagnostic individuating information overrides the influence of stereotypes on trait ratings of targets, stereotypes may nonetheless continue to influence *behavioral predictions* relevant to the trait. This argument echoes back to the notion that a given trait or category has many associates. Not only do construction workers and accountants differ with respect to aggression, but they also differ with respect to social class; furthermore, there are different expectations or associates of aggression for different social classes. For example, although a construction worker and an accountant were judged equally unaggressive after "failing to react to an insult," judges nonetheless assumed that the construction worker was more likely than the accountant to engage in aggressive behaviors such as "punching" and "cursing" (Kunda et al., 1997). This finding parallels the subjective–objective difference that emerges in much of my own shifting standards research, suggesting that behavioral predictions function in much the same manner as objective judgments.

For Kunda and Thagard (1996), behavioral predictions continue to be influenced by stereotypes because individuating information about a trait (e.g., knowledge that a construction worker has walked away from a fight) does not override any number of other associates to the category label. These other associates (such as "working-class" or "unrefined" in the case of the construction worker) can have connections to other stereotype-consistent behaviors (e.g., "punches people"). Thus, activation of an expected behavior can still occur even in the face of behavioral evidence or individuating information that is nonstereotypical. In the shifting standards model, objective judgments are influenced by stereotypes because they invite a cross-category perspective that better taps into available stereotyped mental representations of targets. The comparison standard makes a given behavior more likely for a target from one group versus the other. These explanations obviously differ in a number of ways, but they are similar in suggesting that stereotyped expectations may combine with other information or cues to produce assimilative judgments in one format (judgments on common-rule scales, behavioral prediction) and null or contrastive judgments in another (subjective trait ratings).

The shifting standards model also shares some features with the impression formation models of Fiske and Neuberg (1990) and Brewer (1988). Specifically, all of these perspectives suggest that there is some assessment of fit (some comparison) between category expectations and target features and that discrepancy from expectations will prompt different processes or outcomes. In the impression formation models, discrepancy leads to recategorization (called "individuation" in Brewer's model) until an appropriate relevant category is found. Even in Kunda and Thagard's (1996) parallel constraint satisfaction model (which does not incorporate comparative processes), counterstereotypical targets are assumed to activate subtypes of the broader category. The shifting standards model assumes that the global category remains activated in these cases but that stereotype-discrepant targets are judgmentally contrasted from the group standard ("he has good verbal skills ... for a man").

This contrastive judgment pattern is also described in the literature on "expectancy violation theory" (Bettencourt, Dill, Greathouse, Charlton, & Mulholland, 1997; Biernat, Vescio, & Billings, 1999; Jackson, Sullivan, & Hodge, 1993; Jussim, Coleman, & Lerch, 1987). According to this perspective, when information about a target violates stereotype-based expectations, evaluations are extremitized in the direction of that violation. Thus, Blacks with strong academic credentials may be judged as more competent than Whites with comparable credentials (Jackson et al., 1993; Linville & Jones, 1980), female employees may be judged more agentic than male employees (Eagly & Steffen, 1984), Whites who speak nonstandard English may be viewed more negatively than Blacks who do the same (Jussim et al., 1987), and baby-faced children who commit serious misbehavior may receive harsher punishment than their mature-faced peers (Zebrowitz, Kendall-Tackett, & Fafel, 1991; see also Zebrowitz & Lee, 1999). An important distinguishing characteristic of the shifting standards model, however, is its contention that these contrastive patterns may be more apparent than real, in that they tend to diminish when targets are judged along a common continuum (i.e., in objective units).

For example, an employer may hold a stereotype that women are less competent than men are in a particular position. Because of this relatively low expectation for women, any given female applicant will have a better chance than a male applicant of surpassing within-category standards. Thus, paradoxically, the employer may be more impressed with a strong female applicant than with a male applicant with comparable credentials ("wow, she's really good!"). My colleagues and I (see Biernat & Kobrynowicz, 1997) found just such a pattern of low expectations and relatively high subjective evaluations of women in an applicant evaluation setting of this sort. However, the same study revealed that when other judgments and decisions were made about the applicants—e.g., objective performance estimates, decision rules to be certain of the applicant's ability—women were judged more negatively than men (lower "objective" performance appraisals were given; harsher decision rules for diagnosing ability were applied). In other words, these objective judgments showed assimilation to stereotypes (see also Foschi, 1998; Foddy & Smithson, 1989; Foschi, 1992).

A very similar pattern emerged in a study of expectations and stereotypes based on baby-facedness. Berry and Zebrowitz-McArthur (1988) found that baby-faced defendants who committed intentional offenses were sentenced more severely than were analogous mature-faced defendants. However, this contrast effect appeared only on the subjective sentencing decision (rated from "minimum" to "maximum"). In forced-choice judgments of *guilt* (yes or no), baby-faced defendants received the benefits of the benign stereotype associated with their group: They were less likely than mature-faced defendants to be found guilty of intentional crimes.

Research on expectancy-violation nonetheless highlights the dual role that stereotypes and expectations may play in social judgment: They tell us what we are likely to see (and thereby influence our perceptions in the process), and they serve as benchmarks against which deviations from expectation can be noted. This echoes themes introduced in Chapter 3 of this volume, and perhaps most particularly the expectation–contrast model of Manis and Paskewitz (1984a,b). The outcomes of these two processes seem to depend, in part, on the form that judgments take.

An additional avenue that should be pursued in research on expectancy-based judgment concerns the role of affect. The broader psychological literature suggests that met expectations generate positive affect (Mandler,

1975) and that violations of expectancies may lead to arousal (Bobes, Valdes-Sosa, & Olivares, 1994; Clary & Tesser, 1983; House & Perney, 1974; Orive, 1988), emotion intensification (Burgoon, 1993; Clore, Schwarz, & Conway, 1994), and negative emotionality (Fagen & Ohr, 1985; Murray & Jackson, 1982–83; Olson et al., 1996; Rosen, Mickler, & Collins, 1987). This suggests that extremitized subjective judgments of expectancy-violating targets may be mediated by emotional response (Biernat et al., 1999). The more objective judgments we have described—verdicts, decision rules for diagnosing ability—may be less driven by the immediate emotional reaction to a perceived violation and subject instead to the assimilative influence of stereotypes/expectations.

Related Issues

Echoing a persistent theme of this volume, it is clear that perceptions and judgments of others may be either assimilated to or contrasted from social stereotypes, depending on features of the target person and the nature and form of the judgment. Abele and Petzold (1998) have offered an additional and intriguing perspective on this issue that focuses on perceivers' ability to use category information about target persons in "flexible and pragmatical" ways. These researchers compare the role of stereotypes as expectations (which can produce assimilation effects, in that assumptions about the "typical case" are integrated into judgments of the target; Anderson, 1981) and stereotypes as frames of reference or "perspectives" (which can produce contrast in that the target is judged relative to the category range or boundaries; Biernat et al., 1991; Eiser & van der Pligt, 1982; Ostrom & Upshaw, 1968; Parducci, 1965; Upshaw, 1962).

The consequence of using stereotypes as expectations is that the distinction *between* categories is enhanced, and differentiation within categories is reduced. When stereotypes are used as frames of reference, however, greater within-category distinction relative to between-category differentiation results. Abele and Petzold (1998) argue that "if the differentiation within categories is more important than the differentiation between them, then the reliance on the category boundaries (frame of reference) ... is the pragmatically adequate psychological mechanism" (p. 349). Thus, this perspective suggests that assimilative effects will be observed whenever conditions are present that emphasize the need for between-category differentiation. These may include motivational factors such as social identity concerns (Hogg and Abrams, 1988; Tajfel 1957; Turner, Hogg, Oakes, Reicher, & Wetherall, 1987) or position in a high-power role (Fiske, 1993), as well as explicitly stated task purposes or "metainformational cues" (Leyens, Yzerbyt, & Schadron, 1994; Yzerbyt, Schadron, Leyens, & Rocher, 1994).

In their research, Abele and Petzold (1998) documented that a mixed presentation of information about targets (e.g., learning about the helpfulness of both nurses and stockbrokers in a series of trials) cued perceivers that differentiation between categories was important. In this condition, assimilation to stereotypes occurred (nurses were judged more helpful than stockbrokers; see also Manis et al., 1986; Seta et al., 1979; Martin & Seta, 1983; Tajfel & Wilkes, 1963). When targets were presented in blocks (nurses separated from stockbrokers), this apparently cued perceivers that within-category differentiation was critical: In blocked conditions, stockbrokers were judged more helpful than nurses (a contrast effect). This work emphasizes that stereotypes can be applied to the judgment of individual group members in varied, flexible, and functional ways (for a related view in the social identity theory tradition, see Oakes, Haslam, & Turner, 1994).

☐ Summary

Few would deny that stereotypes play an important role in the judgments we make about other people. And most of the literature on stereotyping concerns itself with *assimilation* effects—the tendency for individual members of stereotyped groups to be judged consistently with the group stereotype. However, assimilation is less likely to occur when target attributes are inconsistent with the category label, and more generally, when clearly diagnostic individuating information is available (see Kunda & Thagard, 1996, for a review). Assimilation to stereotypes is also less likely when judgments are assessed in subjective as opposed to common-rule units.

A number of these features (and others) map onto the factors affecting assimilation and contrast effects that were outlined in Chapter 2. For example, target inconsistency and diagnosticity of target features are relevant to the *target ambiguity/extremity* factor. Ambiguous features of targets are likely to prompt assimilation, as the information can readily be drawn to and interpreted in light of the stereotype. But extreme targets (who presumably have features that are diagnostic of the judgment at hand) will not be assimilated and may in fact be contrasted from the stereotype (as in expectancy violation effects). Furthermore, *context/target overlap* may be reframed in terms of "fit" between category and individuating information—when fit occurs, judgments of others are category-based. Chapter 2 also introduced the idea that *judgment language or form* may affect assimilation effects, such that they are more likely on common-rule response scales.

It is also worth noting that when stereotypes are thought of as "contextual" factors, they can be conceptualized as *wide* or *indistinct*, as well as *entitative*—all features that promote assimilation (see Chapter 2). And the serial models of stereotyping described here—Fiske and Neuberg's (1990) model as well as Brewer's (1988) and Bodenhausen and Macrae's (1998)—highlight the importance of *processing goals*: Motivational factors such as accuracy and interdependence or the desire not to use stereotypes may make assimilation to stereotypes less likely.

☐ Notes

1. Note that Fiske and Neuberg (1990) also discuss this phenomenon of differential construal but frame it as a reinterpretation of behavior that helps resolve fit issues (e.g., as when strength refers to mental abilities of the professor but physical attributes of the construction worker; Fiske et al., 1987).
2. This study was more complicated than described here; for example, race did matter when evaluating applicants with strong credentials, with Black applicants being evaluated more favorably than White applicants—a contrast effect. More on this appears later in this chapter.
3. The idea that perceivers routinely make within-group comparisons also appears in McGill's (1993) research on causal explanation, based in part on Kahneman and Miller's (1986) norm theory. In McGill's (1993) research, participants were asked to explain the failure of a male or female actor on either a masculine (e.g., shooting pool) or feminine (e.g., sewing) task (Study 1). Men's failure was explained by comparison to males who succeeded, regardless of type of task. This suggests that "male failure mutates readily to male success" (p. 704); i.e., men were always compared to other men. Women's failure on feminine tasks was explained by reference to women (another within-sex comparison), but failure at masculine tasks was explained by reference to men. This work suggests that the tendency to make within-category comparisons may be muted to the extent that the context cues a different referent—in this case, women's performance on a masculine task cued the gender category linked to the task as the comparison standard rather than the gender category of the actor.

Beyond Assimilation: Toward a Broader View of Stereotyping Effects[1]

The previous chapter reviewed models and research on social stereotyping and touched briefly on a perspective that has guided much of my own research—the shifting standards model. In this chapter, I attempt a broader overview of my own work in this area. The general theme, reflected in the title, is that stereotyping effects should be thought of as more than assimilation effects.

When researchers describe a "stereotyping effect," they are typically referring to a case in which a member of a stereotyped group is judged to have more of a stereotypical attribute than a member of some contrasting group. For example, a man is judged to be a better leader than a woman with the same credentials; a physician is judged more intelligent than a hairdresser, etc. (for reviews, see Brewer, 1996; Fiske, 1998; Fiske & Neuberg, 1990; Kunda & Thagard, 1996; Schneider, 2004; Stangor & Lange, 1994). These types of effects certainly indicate that stereotypes have been used to judge individuals and that the outcome is assimilation (individuals judged in a direction consistent with the stereotype). However, less well recognized is the fact that stereotyping can also be manifested in other ways, most notably in counterstereotypical or contrast effects. The goal of this chapter is to take a broader view of stereotyping effects by examining how different forms of judgment, decision making, and behavior may document substantially different patterns of stereotype influence.

This review is guided by research my colleagues and I have conducted over the past dozen years or so on how stereotypes may function as judgment standards against which individual members of stereotyped groups are judged (e.g., Biernat & Kobrynowicz, 1997; Biernat & Manis, 1994; Biernat et al., 1991; Biernat & Thompson, 2002). Some of this work was reviewed in Chapter 5, but here I hope to illustrate more extensively that stereotyping effects are varied, complex, and highly dependent on the form of judgment—from the scientists' perspective, the dependent variables—being assessed.

☐ Stereotypes as Standards: The Shifting Standards Model

The basic premise of the shifting standards model is this: When we judge individual members of stereotyped groups on stereotype-relevant dimensions, we do so with reference to *within-category* judgment standards. For example, given stereotypes that men are more athletic than women are, the athleticism of a particular woman is likely to be judged relative to the (low) *female* standard, and the athleticism of a particular man relative to the (high) *male* standard. The result is that evaluations of men and women on athleticism may not be directly comparable, as their meaning is tied to different contexts: "Very athletic" for a woman does not mean the same thing as "very athletic" for a man.

A standard incorporates the mean and range that is expected from members of a group on a particular dimension and aids the judge in anchoring the endpoints of a subjective rating scale (e.g., "high" to "low" athleticism). Rating points are defined to reflect the expected distribution of category members on the dimension, with high numbers reserved for targets with the highest expected level of the attribute. When groups are expected to differ, endpoints are anchored differently for the contrasting groups; in this sense, standards shift depending on the target being evaluated (for related themes, see Parducci, 1963; Postman & Miller, 1945; Upshaw, 1962; Volkmann, 1951).

Implications for Judgment

Implicit in the preceding statements is the idea that these sorts of standard shifts are possible because of the subjectivity of judgment. When asked to rate how competent, aggressive, or emotional an individual is, we typically respond (in real life and in the laboratory) with subjective language—"he's very aggressive," "she's reasonably competent," "he's not very emotional," etc. The slipperiness of subjective language is what allows us to label a man and a woman equivalently despite having very different underlying representations of them. I can declare that a man and a woman are both "fairly aggressive," in the same way I may claim that my 5-year-old daughter and Albert Einstein are both "brilliant." But if pushed, I might admit that *in absolute terms*, I view the fairly aggressive woman as *objectively* less aggressive than the fairly aggressive man, and Einstein as *objectively* smarter than my daughter.

This distinction between *subjective* and *objective* (or "common-rule") language has played a central role in the development of the shifting standards model. Specifically, evidence supporting the operation of stereotype-based standard shifts can be gleaned from comparisons between judgments that are made on *subjective* rating scales and those made on *objective* scales (externally anchored, "common-rule" scales whose judgment units maintain a constant meaning across contexts and types of targets). Likert-type scales, semantic differentials, and many instruments that display trait judgments as continua (e.g., "very unathletic" to "very athletic") are subjective in the sense that their rating points can be differentially defined and adjusted (e.g., across time, across perceivers, and across targets). In evaluating people, common-rule scales may include such judgments as estimated standardized test scores or grades (to assess competence stereotypes), monetary or time judgments (to assess salary, effort, ability, or worth), and rank orderings (which fit our conception of objectivity in that the meaning of a ranking unit is clear—it places a target individual in a readily interpretable position relative to a given frame of reference; see Biernat & Manis, 1994; Biernat, Crandall, Young, Kobrynowicz, & Halpin, 1998). A key prediction of the shifting standards model, noted in Chapter 5, is that common-rule judgments are more likely than subjective judgments to reveal the influence of stereotypes—to show a classic "stereotyping effect." On the other hand, because subjective scales can be differentially adjusted for different target categories, they may mask this influence.

This idea is schematically presented in Figure 6.1. We begin with the assumption that the perceiver holds a stereotype that men are more athletic than are women. This perceiver is presented with information about a specific man or woman (Mary or Mark) along with some individuating information about him or her (that s/he went for a jog) and is asked to rate the target on an *unathletic* to *athletic* response scale. Because of the stereotype, Mark is cognitively represented as more athletic than Mary is. But also because of the stereotype, the perceiver defines the subjective

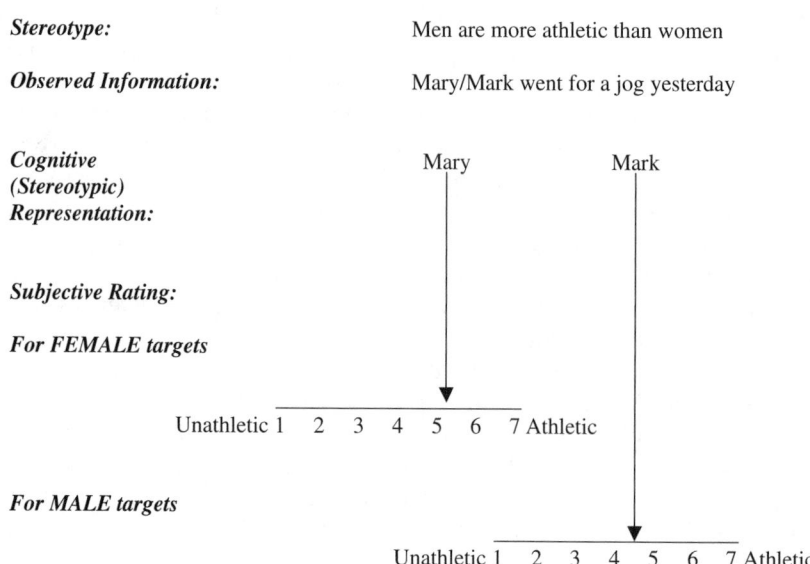

Stereotype: Men are more athletic than women

Observed Information: Mary/Mark went for a jog yesterday

*Cognitive   Mary   Mark
(Stereotypic)
Representation:*

Subjective Rating:

For FEMALE targets

　　　　　　　　Unathletic 1   2   3   4   5   6   7 Athletic

For MALE targets

　　　　　　　　Unathletic 1   2   3   4   5   6   7 Athletic

FIGURE 6.1. Schematic depiction of how stereotypes may lead to contrast effects. (From Biernat, M. [2003]. *American Psychologist, 58,* 1019–1027. With permission.)

rating scale in a category-specific manner. When judging a female target, the scale endpoints are shifted to the left, consistent with expectations about lower levels of athleticism. When judging a male target, the entire scale is shifted to the right, overlapping only minimally with the expected distribution of female athleticism.[2] As a result of these shifts, the judgment that follows from the representation suggests that Mary is slightly more athletic than Mark. In other words, this pattern suggests a null effect, or perhaps a slight contrast effect, relative to the gender stereotype.

Important to the shifting standards model, however, is that such an effect does not represent the dilution of stereotypical influence but rather occurs precisely because the stereotype is operative. Indeed, if the perceiver were asked to judge Mary's or Mark's athleticism on a more "objective" response scale—one that did not allow for within-category adjustment of meaning—the cognitive representation of Mark as more athletic than Mary would likely be revealed. For example, if one were asked to rank order jogging Mary and jogging Mark, Figure 6.1 suggests that Mark would be chosen as the more athletic of the pair. Or if one were asked to estimate the speed at which Mark and Mary run, or the time it would take each to run a mile, or some other judgment that relied on stable, common-rule response units, the model again predicts that Mark would be perceived as speedier than Mary.

Following the logic laid out in Figure 6.1, evidence of shifting standards can be seen when assimilative stereotyping effects are stronger on common-rule response scales than on subjective response scales. This pattern has, indeed, been documented in a variety of judgment domains. For example, with regard to the athleticism example outlined above, two studies found that male targets were ranked more athletic than female targets and judged to run faster than female targets at the same time that subjective ratings showed substantially smaller male–female differences (Biernat, Kobrynowicz, & Weber, 2003). In another study, predictions about the batting averages of coed softball players gave an advantage to men, whereas subjective judgments of batting quality significantly reduced this effect (Biernat & Vescio, 2002).

This pattern has been documented with respect to a wide variety of other stereotyped dimensions as well: Judgments of male and female targets' heights in feet and inches versus *short* to *tall* rating units show comparable patterns (Biernat et al., 1991), as do judgments of weight, verbal ability (with the stereotype favoring women in this case), writing quality, and leadership competence (Biernat et al., 1991; Biernat & Manis, 1994; Biernat et al., 1998). Similarly, judgments of Black and White targets have revealed stronger evidence of assimilative racial stereotyping in objective than subjective units in the domains of verbal and math ability, athleticism, and job-related competence (Biernat & Manis, 1994; Biernat & Kobrynowicz, 1997; Kobrynowicz & Biernat, 1997).

Occasionally, studies have revealed reliable *contrast* effects on subjective rating scales. For example, in one study participants judged the financial success of female and male targets depicted in photographs. Some judges made these estimates in objective units (dollars earned per year) and others in subjective units (*financially unsuccessful* to *financially successful* ratings). The income estimates clearly revealed that men were seen as more financially successful than women, but the subjective judgments produced a significant reversal of this effect. Women who were judged to earn, on average, $9,000 less per year than target men were *subjectively* seen as *more* financially successful than these men (Biernat et al., 1991 Study 2). In another study, participants reviewed the resume of either a female or a male applicant for a "masculine" (executive chief of staff) or "feminine" (executive secretary) job.[3] Judgments of applicant quality in objective units (e.g., predicted percentile scores on standardized tests) revealed preference for the gender that fit the job—female applicants for the secretarial position were judged better than male applicants; male applicants for the chief of staff position were judged better than female applicants. However, subjective judgments revealed reversals of these patterns. Participants seem to be reporting that the male applicant for the feminine job is "very good, *for a man*," and the female applicant for the masculine job is "very good, *for a woman*." A variety of other studies have also documented contrast effects of this sort on subjective response scales (e.g., Abramson, Goldberg, Greenberg, & Abramson, 1977; Branscombe & Smith, 1990; Costrich, Feinstein, Kidder, Marecek, & Pascale, 1975; Deaux & Taynor, 1973; Dipboye & Wiley, 1977; Eagly & Steffen, 1984; Jackson, Sullivan, & Hodge, 1993; Jussim, Coleman, & Lerch, 1987; Linville & Jones, 1980; Pratto & Bargh, 1991; Taynor & Deaux, 1973; Zebrowitz & Lee, 1999).

In short, consistent with the shifting standards model, subjective judgments are more likely than objective judgments to reveal reductions or reversals of traditional (assimilative) stereotyping effects. Thus, the direction of stereotyping effects will differ depending on the type of response language available to participants. This dual influence of stereotypes on judgment is summarized in the "Judgment" portion of Table 6.1.

Subjective judgments are by far the most commonly used in the stereotyping literature and in applied settings, such as employee evaluations (Murphy & Cleveland, 1995). Yet research from the shifting standards tradition suggests that interpreting these ratings at face value—e.g., by making comparisons across targets of varying social category membership—may be misleading. Assimilative effects that *do* emerge may underestimate judges' actual perceptions of targets. Null effects do not necessarily mean that stereotypes are inoperative. And contrast effects do not necessarily mean that "reverse stereotyping" is occurring or that perceivers are somehow "correcting" for perceived bias (Wilson & Brekke, 1994). Instead, patterns that emerge on subjective response scales may indicate that stereotypes are operating *via their instantiation of different judgment standards*.

A Closer Look at Judgment Standards

In the research discussed thus far, there was no direct measurement of the standards perceivers used when asked to evaluate members of different social groups. But the assumption is that evidentiary standards are *lower* for members of the group stereotyped as deficient on an attribute. For example, consistent with stereotypes, standards for women's athleticism and aggression are lower than those for men; standards for men's verbal ability and emotionality are lower than those for women. It is these differing standards that presumably produce the judgment effects described previously.

In two studies on gender and work-related competence, my colleagues and I assessed standards by asking participants to indicate what level of performance, or how much evidence of work-related skills, targets would need to provide to meet *minimum* standards for a job. These studies

TABLE 6.1. Examples of How Judgment, Standard Setting, and Behavior Differ Depending on Form or Type of Response

Outcome and Stereotype Example	Assimilation	Contrast or Null Effect
JUDGMENT	*Common-rule*: A judged > B	*Subjective*: A judged < or = B
Gender and competence	Man judged more competent than woman	Woman judged subjectively more competent than man
Gender and nurturance	Woman judged more nurturing than man	Man judged subjectively more nurturing than woman
Race and athleticism	Black man judged more athletic than White man	White man judged more athletic than Black man
STANDARD SETTING	*Confirmatory*: A held to lower standards than B	*Minimum*: B held to lower standards than A
Gender and competence	Man can achieve lower score than a woman to be considered competent	Woman can achieve lower score than man to reach minimum standards
Gender and nurturance	Woman can perform fewer nurturing behaviors to be considered nurturing	Man is suspected of being nurturing based on fewer nurturing behaviors
Race and athleticism	Black man can perform fewer athletic behaviors than White man to be considered athletic	White man can perform fewer athletic behaviors than Black to suspect he might be athletic
BEHAVIOR	*Zero-sum*: Behavior is stereotype consistent	*Non-zero-sum*: Behavior is in reverse direction of stereotype
Gender and competence	Man hired over woman for "masculine/agentic" job	Woman receives more positive feedback than man
Gender and nurturance	Woman hired over man for "feminine/communal" job	Father gets more approving looks when caring for baby than mother
Race and athleticism	Black man more likely than White man to be chosen for team; assigned to key positions	White man cheered more than Black man for same performance

Note: A = member of group stereotyped as having an attribute (e.g., women are nurturing); B = member of contrast group (e.g., men are less nurturing).
Source: Based on Biernat, M. (2003). *American Psychologist, 58,* 1019–1027.

demonstrated that women were held to lower minimum standards than men, and Black men were held to lower minimum standards than White men. That is, the bar was set lower—women and Black men needed to provide less evidence of competence—to meet perceivers' low-competence expectations (Biernat & Kobrynowicz, 1997). Other research from our lab on the diagnosis of a variety of traits further indicates that minimum standards (i.e., expectations) are lower for members of groups stereotypically depicted as deficient on the trait. For example, when assessed in terms of the number of behaviors that would be required to suspect that a person has a trait, minimum standards were lower for men than for women in the domain of emotionality and were lower for women than for men in the domains of aggression and competitiveness (Biernat, Ma, & Nario-Redmond, 2005). That is, perceivers indicated they began to "suspect" that a man might be emotional on the basis of fewer behaviors than were necessary to suspect emotionality in a woman.

However, given low expectations, we seem to require *more* evidence to be *certain* that an individual possesses an unexpected attribute (e.g., see Olson, Roese, & Zanna, 1996). Sentiments that women or African-Americans need to work "twice as hard to be perceived as half as good" as White men are consistent with this notion (Carter, 1993). And indeed, this is a key prediction derived from the sociological literature on expectation states theory—that a stricter inference standard is introduced for those about whom low expectations exist (see Foddy & Smithson, 1989; Foschi, 2000; Foschi & Foddy, 1988). Do perceivers hold devalued group members to both low minimum standards and high standards to *diagnose* unexpected traits?

To try to capture this possibility, the studies described above on minimum standards also included conditions requiring judges to report their *confirmatory* standards: How much, or how high in quality, must the evidence for an attribute be to be certain that an individual possesses that attribute? We found that women and Black men were required to obtain higher test scores and to provide more evidence of job-related skills (relative to White men) for judges to feel confident that they were truly competent (Biernat & Kobrynowicz, 1997). Similarly, standards to *confirm* that a man was emotional, or that a woman was aggressive or competitive, were high relative to standards for the opposing gender group (Biernat et al., 2005). And in a study that examined race-based standards of trait confirmation across a set of 180 traits, trait stereotypicality predicted a lower number of behaviors required to confirm and a greater number needed to disconfirm those traits in outgroup actors (Biernat & Ma, 2005; see also Maass, Montalcini, and Biciotti, 1998). Overall, these data suggest that minimum standards are lower but confirmatory standards are higher for members of groups stereotyped as deficient on a given attribute.

In keeping with the theme of this book, these findings regarding standard setting suggest that the effects of stereotypes can be revealed in patterns of either assimilation or contrast. When an individual belongs to a group that is stereotyped along some trait dimension, evidentiary standards to diagnose that trait may shift, and this shift can occur in the direction of leniency or stringency, depending on the type of standard called to mind (minimum or confirmatory). When judges are focused on minimum standards, stereotypes are directly used as expectations—less competence and aggressiveness are expected from women, and less emotionality is expected from men, so the evidence required to meet these expectations is minimal. As indicated in the "Standard setting" section of Table 6.1, I characterize the use of minimum standards as a type of *contrast* effect, because it means that a target stereotyped as deficient on an attribute will more readily meet and surpass the minimum standard for that attribute (thus, the greater suspicion that a man versus a woman might be emotional based on the same behavioral evidence). Interestingly, these low evidentiary standards (particularly in the domain of competence) may also be interpreted by target group members as patronizing in nature (Foschi, 1992, 2000). Judgmental contrast occurs only because standards are so low, as when one black employee noticed that his white colleagues were "astonished to find that I could write a basic memo. Even the completion of an easy task brought surprised compliments" (Pettigrew & Martin, 1987, p. 55). And again, precisely because of low expectations for members of stereotyped groups—and presumably to overcome them—judges require *more* behavioral evidence to confirm or diagnose those attributes. As indicated in Table 6.1, this represents a form of *assimilation* in that the target stereotyped as having an attribute needs to do less to document that she or he has the attribute (i.e., the stereotyped attribute is more readily diagnosed).

Thus, use of a stereotype can produce seemingly favorable treatment of members of the negatively stereotyped group (e.g., women and black men may initially be held to lower standards in the workplace) but, at the same time, unfavorable treatment as well (more is required of these same individuals to prove their worth). Indeed, in two studies that attempted to map this pattern onto workplace decisions, we found that women were more likely to make "short lists" for masculine-stereotyped jobs but less likely to be hired for those same jobs (Biernat & Fuegen, 2001).[4] From the researcher's perspective, the pattern of stereotype findings is highly dependent on the type of evidentiary standard—minimum or confirmatory— that is referenced in a decision.

From Judgment to Behavior

Much of the literature described above has considered judgment effects— how perceivers evaluate individual members of a stereotyped group (on common-rule versus subjective response scales, with regard to minimum versus confirmatory standards). However, the short-listing/hiring studies (Biernat & Fuegen, 2001) begin to look at *behavioral* outcomes for members of stereotyped groups. This is an important step, as most stereotyping researchers are ultimately interested in the behavioral consequences of stereotypes for individual actors. One might assume, generally, that perceivers behave toward individual group members in a manner consistent with their judgments. From the shifting standards perspective, however, this question becomes intriguing because judgment takes different forms depending on the response scale format or the type of question asked. Will perceivers behave in accordance with their *subjective* or with their *common-rule* judgments of individual actors? Will their behaviors follow from consideration of minimum versus confirmatory standards? For example, if a man and woman receive equally laudable subjective evaluations (e.g., both are "very good") but the woman receives more negative common-rule evaluations than the man (e.g., she is predicted to generate less sales revenue), how will an employer behave toward these two targets?

The answer to this question may be, "it depends." As was the case with judgment and standard setting, the pattern of behavioral outcomes may depend on the *type* of behavior being performed and assessed. Recently, my colleagues and I made a distinction between two broad types or forms of behavior—those that involve allocation of limited resources and those that do not (Biernat et al., 1998). Included in the first category are actions characterized by the fact that behaving toward one individual restricts the behavioral options that are available toward another. Thus, behavioral choices (e.g., who gets promoted, who is assigned to the best tasks or positions?) and allocation of "valuable" assets (e.g., money) have a *zero-sum* quality and are highly meaningful to recipients in that tangible resources are at stake. The second class of behaviors has a *non-zero-sum* character, in that the same or similar actions can be bestowed on a limitless number of targets, without resource depletion. Falling under this category are such behaviors as nonverbal acts, verbal praise or punishment, etc. Thus, a hiring decision is a zero-sum behavior: By hiring one individual, others are rejected. In contrast, a pleasant behavioral interaction style (e.g., smiling, making eye contact, etc.) is a non-zero-sum behavior that can be displayed to many individuals without being expended.

As indicated in Table 6.1, I conceptualize these behavior types as paralleling the objective/subjective *judgment* distinction outlined earlier. Zero-sum behaviors, like common-rule or objective judgments, require that one take a "cross-category" or "absolute" perspective on the set of actors being evaluated—each actor's standing can be interpreted unambiguously in the context of the others. This leads to the prediction that zero-sum behaviors will generally coincide with common-rule or objective target judgments. For example, in the hiring study described above (Biernat & Fuegen, 2001), women were less likely to be hired than men, despite their elevated presence on a short list (a situation that presumably resulted because women were held to lower minimum standards and were subjectively appraised as quite good).

On the other hand, non-zero-sum behaviors, like subjective judgments, invoke a "within-category" perspective such that targets are compared to expectations for their group. For example, non-zero-sum behaviors such as cheering or smiling may reflect surprise that an individual has surpassed a low group-based performance standard. Similarly, a very positive subjective evaluation is based on the violation of a negative group expectation (see Biernat, Vescio, & Billings, 1999; Jussim et al., 1987). For this reason, non-zero-sum behaviors should generally be consistent with *subjective* judgments of group members.

To summarize these predictions, stereotypes may guide behavior in different ways depending on the nature of the behavioral act. *Zero-sum* behaviors should follow from stereotypes in an assimilative fashion— e.g., a man should be more likely than a woman to be hired for a masculine job. But *non-zero-sum* behaviors should "favor" members of groups stereotyped as deficient on a relevant attribute—e.g., women may receive more verbal praise for job success than men. Furthermore, objective *judgments* should be better predictors of zero-sum behaviors than subjective judgments, whereas subjective judgments should be better predictors of non-zero-sum behaviors than objective judgments.

Empirical evidence regarding these predictions is scanty but supportive. In two studies that invited participants to role-play being the manager of a coed softball team, we found that zero-sum behaviors—team member selections, assignments to fielding positions and slots in the batting order— favored men over women (when these targets were matched for moderate perceived athleticism). That is, men were more likely than comparable women were to be selected for the team, to play key infield positions, to bat early in the lineup, and to avoid being benched. At the same time, non-zero-sum behavior—a hypothetical report of how the "manager" would react if the player hit a single—favored women over men. Managers were more likely to respond favorably, to provide positive feedback and nonverbal responses, to a successful performance by a woman than to a successful performance by a man. It was also the case that objective estimates of batting ability (seasonal batting averages) better predicted zero-sum behaviors such as team selection than subjective estimates of the same ("poor" to "good" hitter) but that the subjective batting estimates better predicted the non-zero-sum behavior (Biernat & Vescio, 2002).

In another relevant study, male participants placed in leadership roles were significantly less likely to assign valued tasks to female subordinates than to male subordinates, particularly when the leaders were oriented toward the weaknesses of those subordinates (Vescio, Gervais,

Snyder, & Hoover, 2005, Study 1). That is, female subordinates were less likely to be assigned as captain or to the first string of a team competing in an "academic challenge" contest. These zero-sum behaviors indicated preference for males over females—an assimilation effect. At the same time, male leaders *praised* female subordinates more than they praised male subordinates for their work (e.g., offering such comments as "Your answers during the first phase of the experiment were excellent!"). Consistent with Biernat and Vescio (2002), non-zero-sum behaviors favored women over men—a contrast effect.

Other studies in the literature, though not designed with these predictions in mind, also support the distinction between zero-sum and non-zero-sum behaviors. In a field study that examined gender effects on subordinate and supervisor cross-evaluations, Gupta, Jenkins, and Beehr (1983) found an overall tendency for females (both supervisors and subordinates) to be *subjectively* evaluated more positively than males. At the same time, however, the *behavior* of employers toward the employees seemed more consistent with a stereotype-consistent *objective* representation of males as better than females—male subordinates were awarded more promotions and pay raises than the same females who were subjectively evaluated so positively. As the authors write about employers' treatment of women, "While opinions (evaluations) may be positive, actions (promotions) still follow tradition" (p. 183).

Similarly, in a study on race, Weitz (1972) examined the behavioral choices of White participants who were led to believe that they would be interacting with either a Black or a White partner. She found that although some Whites reported extremely positive subjective feelings of "friendliness" toward their Black partners, these same individuals engaged in the most negative behavioral responses to the partner—e.g., they were less likely to choose to wait with the partner during a break in the experiment, and they chose to interact with the partner in only the least intimate of experimental tasks. These can be conceptualized as zero-sum behaviors in that they involved choices between limited alternatives that gave a resource to the target or did not. Again, behavior followed not from the subjective sense of friendliness but rather from the stereotypical representation of Blacks as less desirable partners than Whites.

Finally, in a study relevant to non-zero-sum behavior, Harber (1998) examined the written feedback that White judges offered to either Black or White authors of poorly written essays. Comments on essay content (a non-zero-sum behavior) were more favorable and supportive for Black authors than for White authors, as were subjective evaluations. For example, Black writers were told how much "potential" was in the essay; White writers were told, "When I read college work this bad I just want to lay my head down on the table and cry" (Harber, 1998, p. 625). This behavioral outcome appears to be positive for black individuals, but it follows nonetheless from negative stereotypes about blacks' competence. Such favorable comments, like the cheering that female batters receive following a hit, might even be seen as patronizing in nature (see Foschi, 1992, 2000) in that the positivity does not reflect sincere judgment of quality (see also Jackman, 1994; Pettigrew & Martin, 1987).

In short, zero-sum behaviors reflect an assimilative influence of stereotypes. Non-zero-sum behaviors, on the other hand, may indicate contrast from those stereotypes, in that members of negatively stereotyped groups are treated more favorably (e.g., they receive more favorable comments and figurative pats on the back). The point, however, is that both of these patterns reflect stereotyping effects. In one case, the stereotype is directly reflected in a behavioral choice; in the other, it activates low (patronizing) minimum standards that are more readily surpassed, producing a subjective sense of positivity—a "wow" effect. That this positivity is not borne out in outcomes that matter for the target (getting the job or the key fielding position) suggests that the favorable treatment is more apparent, fleeting, and ephemeral than real.

It is worth noting that other stereotyping and prejudice researchers have made distinctions between types of behavioral response to stereotyped group members. For example, Dovidio and his colleagues have distinguished between spontaneous and deliberative behaviors (Dovidio, Brigham, Johnson, & Gaertner, 1996; Dovidio, Kawakami, Johnson, Johnson, & Howard, 1997), suggesting that the former are better predicted by implicit measures of out-group attitudes and the latter by more direct self-report measures (see also Dovidio & Fazio, 1992; Fazio, Jackson, Dunton, & Williams, 1995). There is some overlap between the spontaneous/deliberative distinction and the zero-sum/non-zero-sum distinction. For example, deliberative behaviors are likely to be zero-sum in nature. But one can easily imagine a non-zero-sum behavior that involves deliberation (e.g., should I smile at this person or not? should I laugh at this joke?) or a zero-sum behavior that does not (e.g., I spend more of my available time helping one person rather than another). For our purposes, the zero-sum/non-zero-sum distinction better captures the fact that in a given situation, some behaviors are of limited and some of unlimited supply. This distinction is important in that limited supply (zero-sum) behaviors require consideration across a number of potential targets, whereas unlimited supply (non-zero-sum) behaviors do not. As the shifting standards model suggests, it is when one is making cross-target comparisons that stereotypical between-group differences are likely to be noted and revealed. When behavior toward one target is independent of behavior toward another, however, it may follow from intra- rather than intergroup perceptions of target individuals.

☐ Summary and Conclusions

Table 6.1 provides an overview and examples of the distinctions among measures and outcomes highlighted in this chapter. In general, and as the columns of the table reflect, stereotypes may lead to a class of assimilative effects or to a class of contrast effects, depending on the outcome at hand. Assimilation to stereotypes can be expected when (1) trait-like judgments are made on common-rule or objective response scales, (2) confirmatory standards are assessed, and (3) behavior has a zero-sum quality. Thus, given stereotypes regarding race and athleticism, one might expect an individual Black man to be judged in "objective" units as more athletic than a comparable White man, to be held to lower confirmatory standards (his athleticism is more readily diagnosed), and to be awarded more zero-sum behavioral "goodies" (e.g., valued team assignments).

In contrast, contrast from stereotypes, or null effects of stereotypes, can be expected when (1) trait-like judgments are made on subjective response scales, (2) minimum standards are assessed, and (3) behavior has a non-zero-sum quality. Thus, given stereotypes regarding gender and nurturance, a man might be judged subjectively more nurturant than a comparable woman (e.g., imagine the response to a father versus a mother changing a baby's diaper), he might be held to lower minimum nurturing standards (e.g., one changed diaper might be sufficient for a man to be suspected of nurturance), and he is likely to receive more non-zero-sum praise or approval (e.g., the father picking up his child from day care receives more positive commentary than the mother doing the same). These contrast effects should nonetheless be considered stereotyping effects, as they would not occur in the absence of stereotyped expectations.

Of course, other factors may contribute to when assimilation to versus contrast from stereotypes occurs. Perhaps the most obvious one is the nature of the individuating information known about the target. In general, in both the real world and the laboratory, individual targets may be described in ways that are consistent with, inconsistent with, or neutral regarding the stereotype. To continue with the gender and nurturing example, the male versus female targets might be depicted as highly nurturing (consistent with the female stereotype but inconsistent with the male stereotype), as highly non-nurturing (inconsistent with the female stereotype but consistent with the male stereotype), or as moderate or neutral on this dimension (no information might be provided, nondiagnostic information might be provided, or "average" or "ambiguous" information might be provided; see Kunda & Thagard, 1996, for a review).

Clearly one might expect contrast to be more likely when targets are inconsistent with the stereotype—the highly involved father is *really* nurturing, and the highly uninvolved mother is *really* non-nurturing. In most of the research I have done on the shifting standards model, I have not focused on or manipulated the features of the targets and instead have examined the cases when targets might be best described as having neutral or moderate standing on attributes of interest (e.g., an employee application depicts moderate credentials). I am most interested in these cases for two reasons. First, in many judgment situations in the real world, information is ambiguous or moderate in its connotations. Second, I acknowledge that perceivers are swayed by strong individuating information—the highly competent female, the superstar, will have little trouble succeeding in the workplace (Heilman, 2001), and the obviously incompetent White male will fail. It is in the moderate or ambiguous cases when stereotypes might be expected to have their strongest schematic role—of filling in or going beyond the information given. As Stapel and Winkielman (1998) put it, a construct such as a stereotype "will be a guide to interpretation only when there is something to be interpreted, that is, when the target stimulus is ambiguous rather than unambiguous" (p. 635). The assimilative phenomena outlined in Table 6.1 might best be thought of as applying most readily in those cases when an individual actor is described as or behaves in ways that are ambiguous, moderate, or neutral regarding the stereotype of interest—a theme quite consistent with the discussion of target ambiguity in Chapter 2. And contrastive effects (as opposed to null effects of stereotypes) on subjective measures are most likely when targets disconfirm stereotypes (e.g., see Linville & Jones, 1980).

This chapter has highlighted the shifting standards model as a framework for a broader understanding of stereotyping effects. How stereotypes affect judgment, decision making, and behavior directed toward members of stereotyped groups is highly dependent on the nature and format of the outcomes being assessed (i.e., the dependent variables). Assimilation, contrast, and null effects are all possible, and they all reflect the operation of stereotypes. A critical point to be taken from the research reviewed here is that any one outcome or type of measure cannot provide a complete picture of how global stereotypes affect the perception and treatment of individual group members.

For example, the fact that a woman is subjectively evaluated more favorably than a comparable man for a "masculine" job, or that this woman is more likely than the man to be placed on a short list, does not mean that gender stereotypes regarding workplace competence have been eschewed. Instead, these patterns—which reflect the use of stereotypes as judgment standards—are likely to be reversed when more "objective" evaluations are considered or confirmatory standards and zero-sum behavioral decisions are assessed. In the case of our softball studies (Biernat & Vescio, 2002), we found that female players were evaluated against lower standards than were male players, such that they were less likely to receive valuable resource allocation but more likely to receive positive nonverbal feedback for good performance. This is surely likely to be a confusing situation for both male and female athletes. Back in the workplace, women and Blacks may also face situations in which scarce resources and choice assignments are not forthcoming, but nonverbal feedback may be overly favorable or unrealistic (Harber, 1998; Massey, Scott, & Dornbusch, 1975; Pettigrew & Martin, 1987; Steele, 1992). How both evaluators and evaluatees respond to the sometimes conflicting judgments and behaviors that stereotypes evoke remains an important research question. In one telling study, female subordinates who received conflicting feedback— they received high praise for their work but were nonetheless assigned to devalued team positions—subsequently expressed more anger and performed more poorly than others on a test of reasoning and logic (Vescio et al., 2005).

Although I am obviously quite biased, I believe the shifting standards model can provide an organizing framework for recognizing the complex ways in which stereotypes affect the evaluations, performance standards, and behavioral outcomes experienced by members of stereotyped groups. These outcomes are not independent: Standards presumably affect evaluations and behavioral choices; behaviors may be guided by evaluations as well. But these outcomes may also be contradictory, depending on the frame of reference used by the perceiver at a given point in time. The employer's "wow" response when a minority employee surpasses a low standard for his or her group is not likely to be parlayed into a large merit raise once the employer takes a cross- rather than within-category perspective. And despite my beliefs in my 5-year-old daughter's brilliance, I have thus far refrained from phoning Yale to inquire about early admission. Stereotyping effects are varied and complex. This has implications for researchers, who are best served by taking into account the context in which a specific judgment occurs, and also for stereotyped individuals who may need to negotiate situations characterized by conflicting feedback.

☐ Notes

1. This chapter is based on Biernat, M. (2003). Toward a broader view of social stereotyping. *American Psychologist, 58,* 1019–1027.
2. The placement of and range depicted in these response scales is hypothetical. Obviously it is possible that the expected distributions of male and female athleticism differ in any number of ways—e.g., in terms of variability, degree of overlap, endpoint placement,

etc. Nonetheless, this particular example illustrates the basic point that subjective response scales allow for shifts that reflect the perceiver's stereotypical expectations.

3. The job descriptions were identical for these positions, but the title was changed. This manipulation resulted in the chief of staff job being perceived as higher in status, worth more money, and more masculine than the secretary job (see Biernat & Kobrynowicz, 1997).

4. This pattern was limited to certain conditions—e.g., it was true only of female respondents, and particularly when the experimenter was female or participants were being held accountable for their decisions.

7

Internalized Guides as Standards for Judging the Self

Just as there are numerous standards by which we judge others, sources of standards for self-judgment and evaluation also abound. In judging others, standards and expectancies tend to function as reference points, providing information useful for interpreting and evaluating data about a given target. In judging the self, this informational function is also relevant, but standards can additionally serve as regulatory criteria (see Carver & Scheier, 1981, 2002; Duval & Wicklund, 1972). That is, standards provide information about "valued end states" according to which we appraise ourselves and our progress toward goals (Higgins, 1990, 1996; Higgins et al., 1986).

This and the following two chapters will focus on three general sources of standards according to which we evaluate, appraise, and regulate the self: (1) internally represented "guides," (2) social stereotypes (i.e., self-stereotyping), and (3) other people. In this chapter, I will focus on internalized guides, emphasizing both self-generated or -imposed standards and those conveyed by important others or reference groups. These internalized guides generally refer to "criteria of excellence or acceptability" that ultimately function as guides for behavior and performance (Higgins et al., 1986, p. 30).

That we evaluate ourselves relative to personal standards is clear in much theoretical work on the self (e.g., Cooley, 1902/1964; Kelley, 1952;

Lewin, 1935). For example, Lewin (1951) noted that the experience and judgments of success and failure are based on some frame of reference, such as internalized norms and values of the culture or one's own level of aspiration (see also Sherif, 1936). That such standards are important for self-evaluation can be seen in the case of an objectively "successful" person who, by virtue of setting high standards for performance, may have a relatively lower self-appraisal than someone with low standards or with worse objective performance (see Felson, 1993). The use of internal evaluative standards may "increase the number of failures who are happy with themselves and successful people who are unhappy" (Felson, 1993, p. 16; see Brickman, Coates, & Janoff-Bulman, 1978). In this chapter, I will consider the extent to which the effects of internalized guides on self-judgment and behavior can be conceptualized in terms of assimilation and contrast effects.

☐ Personal Standards and Objective Self-Awareness

One theoretical perspective that has highlighted the tendency to compare the self to internal standards or guides is objective self-awareness (OSA) theory (Duval & Wicklund, 1972). OSA occurs "when attention is directed inward and the individual ... is the object of his [sic] own consciousness" (p. 2). In this theoretical model, OSA is hypothesized to initiate, automatically or spontaneously, a comparison of the self against standards, where standards are defined as "mental representations of correct behavior, attitudes and traits" (Duval & Wicklund, 1972, p. 3). To the extent that comparison to standards reveals discrepancies, negative affect should result, along with motivation to restore consistency. Consistency can be restored either by *changing* the discrepant attribute (typically, the behavior, attitude, or trait, or perhaps even the standard; Batson, Thompson, Seuferling, Whitney, & Strongman, 1999; Duval & Lalwani, 1999) or by *avoiding* self-focus—getting out of the business of comparison to standards and self-evaluation.

In the original theoretical formulation, self-awareness was hypothesized to be aversive, based on the assumption that discrepancies relative to standards are likely to be the norm. That is, because most of the time we do not live up to our standards, self-awareness is likely to be painful, producing an affective *contrast* effect—"I am bad relative to my high standard." However, this was revised with evidence that self-awareness is pleasant if *congruency* with standards is noted by virtue of the comparison (see Gibbons, 1990, for a review). For example, in one study, men who received (fictitious) negative feedback about their personalities showed reduced self-esteem under conditions of self-awareness (listening to their own voices). This is a form of contrast effect, assuming people generally hold themselves to favorable personality standards. But self-aware men who had received positive feedback showed increased self-esteem, relative to the other conditions (Ickes, Wicklund, & Ferris, 1973). Presumably because these men had evidence that they met their favorable personality standards, their self-evaluations *assimilated* to that standard when they were made self-aware.

In general then, OSA theory suggests that comparison to standards will produce *contrast* effects when discrepancies are noted—e.g., negative self-evaluation relative to a (positive) standard. But *assimilation*—favorable self-views, consistent with the standard—can also result when the standard is met (and relative to conditions when the comparison did not occur—e.g., when one was not self-aware). Extensions of the theory suggested that *behaviorally*, self-awareness may prompt movement toward the standard, another kind of assimilation effect. In their test-operate-test-exit (TOTE) feedback model of OSA, Carver, Blaney, and Scheier (1979) posited that self-standard discrepancies also produce an implicit appraisal of the likelihood of reducing the discrepancy. To the extent that expectations of reducing the discrepancy are high, individuals work to meet the standard. But if expectations of meeting the standard are low, avoidance of self-focus is the result. Others have suggested that it is not expectations per se that are key but rather the individual's sense that his or her rate of progress in meeting the standard is sufficient relative to the size of the discrepancy (Duval, Duval, & Mulilis, 1992; Silvia & Duval, 2001). In any case, movement toward the standard reflects an assimilative process. Interestingly, the assimilative tendency may be prompted by the initial *contrastive* emotional reaction. That is, the negative affect produced by becoming aware of a self-standard discrepancy has a motivational quality geared toward assimilative change—typically, moving the self toward the standard (see Silvia & Duval, 2001).

And as noted above, the inconsistency produced by awareness of discrepancy with a standard can also lead to avoidance of self-awareness entirely. That is, rather than behavioral assimilation geared toward meeting the standard, one can ignore the discrepancy altogether. In one illustrative study, Greenberg and Musham (1981) led participants to read aloud statements about women that were either discrepant from, consistent with, or neutral with respect to their own gender attitudes. Participants were then given the choice of waiting in front of a mirror or a nonreflecting wall for a subsequent phase of the study. Those engaging in attitudinally discrepant behavior were likely to avoid self-awareness by choosing to wait in front of the nonreflecting wall, but those who engaged in attitudinally consistent behavior actively sought self-awareness, choosing the mirror over the wall (the neutral condition produced preferences between these two). Interestingly then, self-awareness avoidance may allow the individual to escape the affective contrast that may emerge from self-standard discrepancies; it may also simply make them less concerned about meeting their standards (Silvia & Gendolla, 2001). Self-awareness seeking, on the other hand, heightens not only self-standard comparison but also the experience of affective assimilation to a favorable standard.

Finally, high self-awareness may also affect the attributions people make for successes and failures. In a series of studies, self-awareness was induced in some participants by aiming a video camera at them as they performed and received feedback about an intellectual abilities test (Duval & Silvia, 2002). Self-awareness enhanced the tendency for successful individuals to attribute their success to internal causes (Study 3; see also Federoff & Harvey, 1976). Additionally and perhaps more interestingly, self-awareness increased the tendency to make internal attributions for *failure* if there was evidence one was likely to improve on a subsequent test but increased the tendency to make *external* attributions for failure if there was little likelihood of subsequent improvement (Duval & Silvia, 2002, Studies 1–3). That is, "when highly self-focused people feel that failure can be rapidly remedied, they will attribute failure to the self; when the likelihood of improvement seems low, however, failure will be attributed externally" (p. 58). This is a self-serving pattern, but it reflects an avoidance of responsibility for failure only when there is no chance of meeting the standard at hand. As noted above, if progress toward meeting a standard is good, or in these studies, if the probability of later meeting the standard is high, self-aware individuals are likely to feel responsible for and remain motivated toward resolving self-standard discrepancies—toward behavioral assimilation to the standard.

☐ Self-Discrepancy

The phenomenon of self-evaluation and -regulation relative to internalized standards is also discussed in theoretical work by Higgins (1987, 1990, 1996). In his perspective on the "self as digest," an important component of self-knowledge is the "monitored self": a representation of "how a person is doing in relation to some desired (or undesired) end state" (Higgins, 1996, p. 1070). According to this model, the self is monitored and therefore regulated by means of comparison between various *domains* of and *standpoints* on the self. More specifically, Higgins' (1987) self-discrepancy theory posits that we represent both (1) our own and (2) important others' views of ourselves in three distinct domains: (1) "actual" selves (the collection of attributes we are believed to possess), (2) "ideal" selves (the attributes and outcomes it is hoped we will possess), and (3) "ought" selves (the attributes we ought to or should possess).[1] Each of these standpoint/domain combinations can be thought of as a standard or reference point against which any other "self" is assessed. It is by virtue of comparing these various selves (e.g., comparing the actual/own self to the ought/own self) and noting discrepancies between them that we experience affect (e.g., guilt) and, potentially, engage or redirect our behavioral efforts.

In this model, different types of emotion result from comparison of the actual/own self to the various other self-relevant standards (Higgins, 1987, 1996). (In fact, this assumption of *specific* types of standards and specific emotional reactions is what most distinguishes self-discrepancy theory from the theory of objective self-awareness.) Assuming that discrepancies from standards become apparent by virtue of comparison, the use of an ideal/own standard will likely lead to disappointment and dissatisfaction (due to the failure to attain one's hopes and desires), the use of an ideal/other standard will likely lead to shame or embarrassment (because others are dissatisfied with us), the use of an ought/own standard will likely produce guilt, uneasiness, and self-contempt (because a moral standard has been transgressed), and the use of an ought/other standard will likely activate feelings of fear, threat, or resentment (as we may anticipate sanctions from others). All forms of self-discrepancy are available to us to the extent that relevant aspects and perspectives on the self diverge; the greater the mismatch, the more intense the specific type of emotional discomfort, assuming that the discrepancy is *accessible*. Accessibility is achieved by virtue of recency and frequency of activation, and applicability or relevance of the discrepancy in a given setting (Higgins, 1987).

For example, in an early study on self-discrepancy theory, undergraduates were asked to complete measures of their self-discrepancies (using the Selves questionnaire) and their chronic emotional symptoms (e.g., the Beck Depression inventory along with a number of other scales; Higgins, Klein, & Strauman, 1985; see additional analyses of these data in Higgins, 1987). They also indicated which standpoint (e.g., self, parent) and which domain of self (actual, ideal, or ought) was most meaningful to them. Focusing only on meaningful standards, Higgins et al. found that actual–own/ideal–own discrepancies uniquely predicted disappointment (with other discrepancies partialled out), actual–own/ideal–other discrepancies uniquely predicted "lack of pride" and "loneliness," actual–own/ought–other discrepancies predicted "spells of terror or panic," and actual–own/ought–own discrepancies predicted irritation and *lack* of guilt. The latter relationship was predicted to be positive—more discrepancy, more guilt—but Higgins (1987) suggests the negative relationship reflects denial of the very state being experienced.

Key to self-discrepancy theory is the prediction of *unique* emotional responses to different types of discrepancies. Over the years, the theory has highlighted two particular emotional patterns caused by discrepancies: (1) actual–ideal discrepancies uniquely predict dejection-related emotions (e.g., sadness), and (2) actual–ought discrepancies uniquely produce agitation-related emotions (e.g., tension). This pattern has been supported in studies using participants preselected for their extreme self-discrepancy scores, whose emotions are then assessed (Houston, 1990), or for their extreme anxiety and depression scores, whose self-discrepancies are then assessed (Strauman, 1992). Priming procedures that activate self-discrepancies also produce the unique emotional patterns predicted by the theory. For example, when asked the question "Why is it important to be X?" (where X is an attribute on which a discrepancy exists) agitation increased for social phobics (who have high actual–ought discrepancies) but dejection increased for depressives (who have high actual–ideal discrepancies; Strauman, 1989; Strauman & Higgins, 1987).

Others have found comparable effects but not necessarily *unique* effects of a particular self–other discrepancy on emotional states (see Tangney, Niedenthal, Covert, & Barlow, 1998). This prompted Higgins (1999) to ask, "When do self-discrepancies have specific relations to emotions?" He outlined four moderators of self-discrepancy effects: (1) magnitude/ extremity of discrepancies—unique emotional consequences of discrepancies are found when the discrepancies are large; (2) accessibility of discrepancies—effects are stronger when the self-discrepancy is accessible (acutely, through priming, or chronically, via individual differences); (3) applicability/relevance—effects are stronger when discrepancies are relevant in a given context (e.g., they are more relevant when imagining negative rather than positive events [Higgins, 1989] or when self-as-student discrepancies are assessed in a university versus home context [Boldero & Francis, 2000]); and (4) importance—effects are stronger when individuals believe that possessing the discrepancies has important self-regulatory consequences (Higgins, 1989).

Most of these moderators will sound familiar to careful readers of Chapter 2 of this book. Extremity, accessibility, and applicability were all described there as factors determining whether assimilation or contrast effect emerge in social judgment. To what extent, then, can self-discrepancy effects be conceptualized in assimilation-contrast terms? In general, as was the case with objective self-awareness theory, the emotion patterns described above reflect a type of *contrast* effect—by comparing the actual self to ideal or ought standards, we may accentuate our differences from the desired state and feel worse than we would had the comparison not occurred. From this perspective, it makes sense that extreme, accessible, and applicable discrepancies will prompt the most emotional contrast. Of course, sometimes we meet standards, and research suggests that lack of (or weak) discrepancies tend to produce null effects on emotion (relative to control). To my knowledge, self-discrepancy theorists have not found evidence of assimilative effects in the case of matches between actual self and standards, but perhaps this is because the focus has been on *discrepancies* and largely on *negative* emotions (cf. Higgins, Shah, & Friedman, 1997, Study 3; Idson, Liberman, & Higgins, 2000).

□ Other Perspectives on Discrepancies and Goals

Standards of Non-prejudice

Research on prejudice and prejudice expression represents an important area in which the issue of self-guides and self-regulation have been considered. Devine and Monteith and their colleagues have focused considerable attention on ought–actual discrepancies (or "should–would" discrepancies) in their research on this topic (Devine, Monteith, Zuwerink, & Elliot, 1991; Monteith, 1996; Monteith, Devine, & Zuwerink, 1993; Monteith & Walters, 1998; Plant & Devine, 2001; Zuwerink, Devine, Monteith, & Cook, 1996). In general, this research indicates that individuals tend to respond to prejudice-relevant settings (e.g., "a Black person sits next to you on the bus") in ways that are more prejudiced than their standards suggest they should be. That is, people note failures to live up to internalized standards regarding inter-race relations. As might be expected, those high in prejudice report both more prejudiced "would" reactions and more lenient standards ("shoulds"). Furthermore, should–would discrepancies are associated with self-dissatisfaction, guilt, and discomfort among low-prejudice individuals more so than among high-prejudice individuals, though guilt can be intensified for both groups if standards are initially made salient (Monteith, 1996).

More recently, Plant and Devine (1998) have drawn an even closer connection to Higgins' (1987) self-discrepancy theory by distinguishing between internal ("own") and external ("other") standards regarding appropriate responding in intergroup settings ("oughts"). Consistent with Higgins' predictions, Plant and Devine (1998) found that discrepancy relative to one's *own* "should" standards was associated with guilt-related feelings but that discrepancy relative to *others'* standards was unrelated to guilt. Instead, self–*other* discrepancy (but not self–own discrepancy) was associated with increased threat/fear—presumably because of the potential for punishment that deviation from others' standards brings (see also Baldwin & Holmes, 1987, on the effects of important others as standards). As a whole, these findings suggest that individuals can and do compare their "actual" selves to internally represented standards of various kinds, that awareness of discrepancies from these standards is a likely consequence of comparison, and that unique patterns of affect corresponding to different types of discrepancies may result. As noted earlier, this general pattern can be viewed as a type of contrast effect—comparison to standards typically reveal discrepancies, and these prompt more extreme emotional reactions than occur in the absence of the comparison.

Interestingly, it is also possible that comparison to internalized standards may produce a kind of *behavioral* assimilation effect—moving toward the standard—similar to that posited in the theory of objective self-awareness. For example, Monteith (1993) found that among low-prejudiced individuals, should–would discrepancies activated self-regulatory processes that could lead to increased control of prejudicial responses in the future. Specifically, low-prejudiced participants who had recommended rejecting a gay male law school applicant subsequently *slowed down* their processing of information about how to reduce prejudiced responding and engaged in more *self-focused* thought about their interactions with and treatment of gay men (Monteith, 1993, Study 1). Both responses are geared toward changing behavior so that it approaches (assimilates to) the nonprejudiced standard.

More generally, Monteith and her colleagues have posited that awareness of a discrepancy—as when a low-prejudiced individual fears that she has shown negative arousal in response to a photo of an interracial couple—prompts three responses: behavioral inhibition (slowing down), negative self-directed affect, and retrospective reflection (Monteith, Ashburn-Nardo, Voils, & Czopp, 2002). The latter refers to "investigative behavior to identify indicators of the discrepant response" (p. 1031). These responses are ultimately geared toward establishing "cues for control" that can aid the individual in inhibiting prejudiced responses in the future. These cues can be any feature of the situation that was present when a discrepant response was originally noted. For example, after inappropriately denying admission to a gay male applicant, the presence of another application from a gay male becomes a cue for control. This cue itself should slow down responding (more behavioral inhibition) and produce "prospective reflection"—a careful, controlled, planned consideration of how to respond—and, presumably, nonprejudiced behavior that meets the standard. Again, the consequence of noticing a discrepancy (and experiencing negative affect as a result) prompts behavior designed to move the individual toward the standard.

Possible Selves

The notion of "possible selves" as goal states further suggests that by comparing the current self to a desired future self, activity directed toward that state becomes more energized and organized, with resulting positive effects on performance (Markus & Nurius, 1986; Markus & Wurf, 1987; Ruvolo & Markus, 1992; see also James's 1890/1948 notion of "potential" selves). Possible selves are "the ideal selves that we would very much like to become. They are also the selves we could become, and the selves we are afraid of becoming" (Markus & Nurius, 1986, p. 954). These selves are "the cognitive manifestation of enduring goals, aspirations, motives, fears, and threats" and they "provide the essential link between the self-concept and motivation" (p. 954).

In general, having possible selves should have affective as well as behavioral consequences. Affectively, positive possible selves may create optimism and belief in the mutability of the current self (Markus & Nurius, 1986), thus fulfilling basic needs for self-enhancement. In one study, for example, participants were led to articulate a plan for self-change, and most subsequently reported positive affect for having done so; in another study, those led to articulate a goal showed positive mood, well-being, and optimism about the likelihood of attaining the goal (Gonzales, Burgess, & Mobilio, 2001). Interestingly, however, reports of positive affect and goal energization were strongest among individuals who developed *bad* plans—vague or unstructured rather than detailed and structured. Gonzales et al. (2001) argue that poor-quality plans paradoxically make one feel closer to the possible self and likely to achieve success with greater ease. By virtue of being vague, the possible self seems attainable, and affective *assimilation* occurs. Using the language from Chapter 2 on features that determine whether assimilation or contrast occurs, vague plans are *nondistinct* or *broad* constructs, again contributing to assimilation. But with a well-thought-out, *distinct*, plan, the distance from the possible self appears greater and success seems more distant, resulting in affective *contrast*. Gonzales et al. (2001) write that "poor planning confers the benefit of energization" but "good planning confers the affective liability of anxiety and agitation" (p. 87).

On the behavioral side, possible selves have been predicted to improve self-regulation and to enhance performance precisely because they focus attention on goal-related activity and strategies necessary to achieve goals (Gollwitzer, 1996; Oyserman, 2001). In the absence of these strategies, possible selves may not produce positive outcomes. For example, in a study of low-income eighth graders, academic possible selves predicted improved grades, more time doing homework, more class participation, and less referral to remedial summer school, but only when they were accompanied by "roadmaps" or strategies for achieving positive outcomes (Oyserman, Bybee, Terry, & Hart-Johnson, 2004). (A count of possible selves alone—without considering strategies—did predict class participation and grades, but not homework time or summer school referral. Nonetheless, strategies added power to the prediction of grades beyond the count of possible selves.) Thus, a moderator of the behavioral assimilative tendencies produced by possible selves is the extent to which concrete strategies are made accessible by those future selves.

This may seem at odds with the above findings regarding "bad" plans and positive affect (Gonzales et al., 2001). One immediate possibility of reconciliation lies in the fact that Oyserman et al. (2004) did not code for quality of strategies, and perhaps some qualified as bad. But given the specificity of the context (success in school) and the likely availability of many good, concrete strategies for success (studying harder, listening in class, not skipping classes), it seems unlikely that the plans generated by the eighth graders were dominated by bad plans. Another possibility is that bad plans improve affect but not behavioral strivings. For example, Oettingen and Mayer (2002) distinguished between the effects of positive expectations versus positive fantasies on actual success. While positive expectations facilitate performance, fantasies—mental images about the desired future—may hinder performance because they take up energy that would normally be devoted to successful task completion. For example, in a study of patients recovering from hip-replacement surgery, positive expectations of success (e.g., expected likelihood that one would be able to walk without a cane 2 weeks after surgery) predicted achieving goals, as reported by physical therapists. But fantasies about positive outcomes (positive images and thoughts in reaction to scenarios about physical capabilities following the surgery) were negatively predictive of success (Oettingen & Mayer, 2002, Study 4). It is possible, then, that bad plans evoke fantasies—the simulation of the self as like the ideal. And while this makes for positive (assimilative) affect, it harms behavior (contrast).

☐ Behavioral Assimilation to Standards: Self-Regulation

As noted throughout this chapter, self-standards have obvious implications for self-regulation. The perspectives reviewed here along with many others have highlighted the idea that discrepancies between current standing and goal states may prompt negative self-evaluation and motivation to achieve the desired goal state (e.g., Bandura, 1991, 1997; Carver & Scheier,

1998). There is an enormous literature documenting the importance of goal states in mobilizing and organizing behavior (see, for example, Gollwitzer, 1990; Heckhausen, 1991; Kuhl, 1994; Lewin et al., 1944; Pervin, 1982), and taking on a review of the motivation literature is certainly not my intent here. Rather, I will highlight some predictions and findings regarding self-regulation that tie into the theme of assimilation versus contrast as discussed throughout this book.

The overarching theme described in this chapter is that meeting of standards or goals prompts positive self-evaluation, whereas failure to meet standards or goals prompts negative self-evaluation (e.g., Bandura, 1997). Effortful action to meet goals is then prompted by the "pull" of positive self-evaluation and the "push" of negative self-evaluation, or when one notices a discrepancy between reality and the goal. Again, this is a model of affective contrast geared toward behavioral assimilation. For Bandura (1997), the behavioral movement toward the goal will only occur, however, if the individual feels self-efficacious with respect to the action required for goal attainment.

In their model of cybernetic feedback control, Carver and Scheier also posit that a goal is a standard toward which the individual is oriented. Moving toward the goal requires "identifying one's location on the relevant variable ..., determining where that location is with respect to the goal (by means of a comparison between input and goal), and making changes to diminish the gap between present location and goal" (Carver & Scheier, 2002, p. 305). This "discrepancy-reducing feedback loop" operates in an assimilative fashion. That is, discovering the discrepancy ultimately moves the individual toward the goal.

Interestingly, these researchers have also discussed *anti-goals* such as feared possible selves that garner self-regulation geared toward *enhancing* discrepancies or creating behavioral contrast (Carver, 2001; Carver & Scheier, 1998; Carver, Lawrence, & Scheier, 1999). For example, a teenager may want to avoid being like his parents (see Carver, 2001). However, such "discrepancy-enlarging" loops often get taken up in the "orbit" of a discrepancy-reducing loop. Carver (2001) writes, "The rebellious adolescent, trying to be different from his parents, soon finds a group of other adolescents to conform to, all of whom are remaining different from their parents" (p. 310). Thus, the contrastive inclination may be subsumed by an assimilative or discrepancy-reducing mechanism.

It is also the case that in addition to a behavioral loop geared toward reducing discrepancies in the case of goals or enhancing discrepancies in the case of anti-goals, a second *affective* loop may operate simultaneously (Carver & Scheier, 1990, 1998). Affect may arise as a consequence of an automatically operating feedback process that essentially "checks on how well the behavior loop is reducing its discrepancies" (Carver, 2001, p. 311).

This check also involves comparing the rate of progress with some standard (or desired rate of reduction in this case). Note, then, that this model does not suggest that discovery of discrepancies necessarily produces negative affect; rather, the affective response will be based on the *speed* or *rate* of discrepancy reduction. If a discrepancy is noted and progress toward reducing it is too slow, negative affect results (e.g., depression) *and* the behavioral response is to change something—go faster, work harder, choose a different course of action.[2] If no discrepancy is noted (progress is as expected or better than expected), affect is positive (e.g., elation or joy is experienced) and resources may be pulled back. Similar affective principles operate for discrepancy-enlarging loops (anti-goals), but here the particular emotions vary slightly—instead of depression vs. elation, one might experience anxiety if one is doing poorly in avoiding an anti-goal and relief if one is doing well (Carver, 2001).

Ultimately, this affective system is in service of *behavioral* assimilation toward goals. However, as was briefly discussed in the context of self-awareness theory, one can also decide to change one's standards, either downward, such that progress toward goals seems better and positive rather than negative affect results, or upward, such that a greater challenge is experienced (though negative affect may also result). Carver (2001) writes, "As people accumulate experience in a domain, the pacing that's expected adjusts. This shifting of the reference value creates a kind of recentering of the system around the experience" (p. 319). That is, the standard assimilates toward the behavior. These changes in standard are *not* predicted to be a first response. Instead, failures to meet a standard at an appropriate pace are typically initially followed by increased behavioral effort to meet the goal, and overshooting a standard typically promotes "coasting" rather than upping the standard. And since comparisons to standards may sometimes find us wanting and sometimes doing well, we may not feel the need to adjust these standards. Nonetheless, over time, and with "repeated deviations" in one direction or the other, the standard may move.

In a related vein, and building on his theory of self-discrepancy, Higgins (1997, 1998) posited two broad types of self-regulatory goals designed to meet needs for nurturance and accomplishment on the one hand, labeled *promotion goals,* and for security and safety on the other, labeled *prevention goals.* A promotion orientation is focused on advancement or accomplishment—meeting one's goals, becoming one's "ideal self." This is an *approach* strategy, in which one aims for desirable outcomes. Prevention orientation, on the other hand, is failure-avoidant. The individual is focused on "ought selves" and pursues strategies designed to avoid undesirable outcomes. Different regulatory foci can be induced through situational manipulations—e.g., through framing a task in terms of likelihood of gain for good performance versus loss for poor performance (e.g., Föerster, Higgins, & Idson, 1998; Higgins, Shah, & Friedman, 1997; Shah, Brazy, & Higgins, 2004)—or can be measured as individual difference variables (e.g., Shah & Higgins, 2001; Shah, Higgins, & Friedman, 1998).

The basic distinction between promotion and prevention was supported in a study by Higgins, Roney, Crowe, and Hymes (1994, Study 1), who primed "ideals" versus "oughts" and then, several weeks later, examined how participants responded to a "ways of behaving" questionnaire. Specifically, respondents rated how like them it was to complete phrases such as "What really matters to me is to try ..." with options that reflected either promotion focus ("to be X," where X is a desired end state, or "to be not Y," where Y is an undesired end state, both indicating approach) or prevention focus ("to avoid being not X" or "to avoid being Y," both indicating avoidance). Those primed to think of "ideals" were more likely to report approaching matches with desired end states than were those primed to think of "oughts." However, the priming manipulation did not reliably affect reports of avoiding matches with undesired end states. In a second study, however, those primed with ideals recalled more life episodes in which they had approached a desired goal (promotion focus, such as "waking up early to get to a desired class"), whereas those primed with oughts recalled events in which they avoided *not meeting* a desired goal (prevention focus, such as "not registering for a class so that one could take a more desired other class"; Higgins et al., 1994, Study 2).

Furthermore, those with chronically strong "ideal" self-guides performed better on an anagrams task when it was framed in terms of promotion (gaining money for successful task completion) but worse when it was framed in terms of prevention (losing money for not being successful); the converse was true for those with chronically strong "ought" self-guides (Shah et al., 1998). That is, matches between individual orientation and task framing produced the best performance outcomes (see also Föerster et al., 1998).

Promotion and prevention goals have also been linked to different emotional experiences. Specifically, pursuit of promotion has been tied to cheerfulness (in the presence of achievement) or dejection-related emotions (in the absence of achievement), whereas pursuit of prevention goals has been linked to quiescence-related emotions (in the presence of security; avoiding the negative) or agitation-related emotions (in the absence of security; see Higgins et al., 1997). More recently, EEG data have indicated that regulatory foci (measured as a chronic individual difference variable using reaction time techniques) are associated with distinct patterns of cortical activity. Specifically, promotion-focused individuals show elevated left frontal cortical activity whereas prevention-focused individuals show elevated right frontal cortical activity (Amodio, Shah,

Sigelman, Brazy, & Harmon-Jones, 2004). This asymmetrical pattern links prevention and promotion focus to more general psychophysiological findings regarding approach and avoidance tendencies and emotion (e.g., see Carver, 2001; Coan & Allen, 2003).

How is this relevant to assimilation and contrast? At a very general level, promotion goals can be conceptualized in terms of assimilation—one wants to *be* or *achieve* X, and this organizes action in pursuit of that goal. This idea can be linked to general theorizing about self-efficacy expectations (Bandura, 1997), in which optimistic expectations (I can do this task) can produce strong performance (see Bandura, 1977; Mischel, Cantor, & Feldman, 1996). Prevention focus, on the other hand, can be conceptualized in terms of contrast—one wants to avoid being Y or not being X, and thus one's behavior is geared toward contrasting the self from that undesired outcome. That different brain regions are activated and different emotions experienced in these circumstances points to qualitatively different underpinnings of contrast and assimilation processes, a topic that deserves further research attention.

☐ Summary

As Higgins (1996) notes, a desired self (whether in "ought," "ideal," or "possible" form) "functions as both a goal to be attained and a standard for self-evaluation" (p. 1071). Thus, the more important a desired self, the greater its goal strength, and the greater motivation, effort, and energy the individual is likely to direct toward the goal. The result is an increased likelihood that the goal will actually be achieved (assimilation to the standard). At the same time, the more important a desired self, the more significant it is as a standard for self-evaluation, and the more likely that standing relative to the standard will be closely monitored. The result is enhanced attention to discrepancies and intensified distress reactions when discrepancies are noted (a type of contrast; see Newman, Higgins, & Vookles, 1992). In this sense, internalized standards are like many other constructs discussed in this book, in that they both draw in and push away the target of evaluation under different circumstances and on different measures.

In Figure 7.1, I have tried to provide a general model of how comparison of self to an internalized standard ultimately affects emotional and behavioral outcomes. This is a hybrid of a number of the theoretical models discussed in this chapter, though it is not wedded to any particular perspective (and it does not take into account all of the complexities of these other models). This general model begins with an accessible

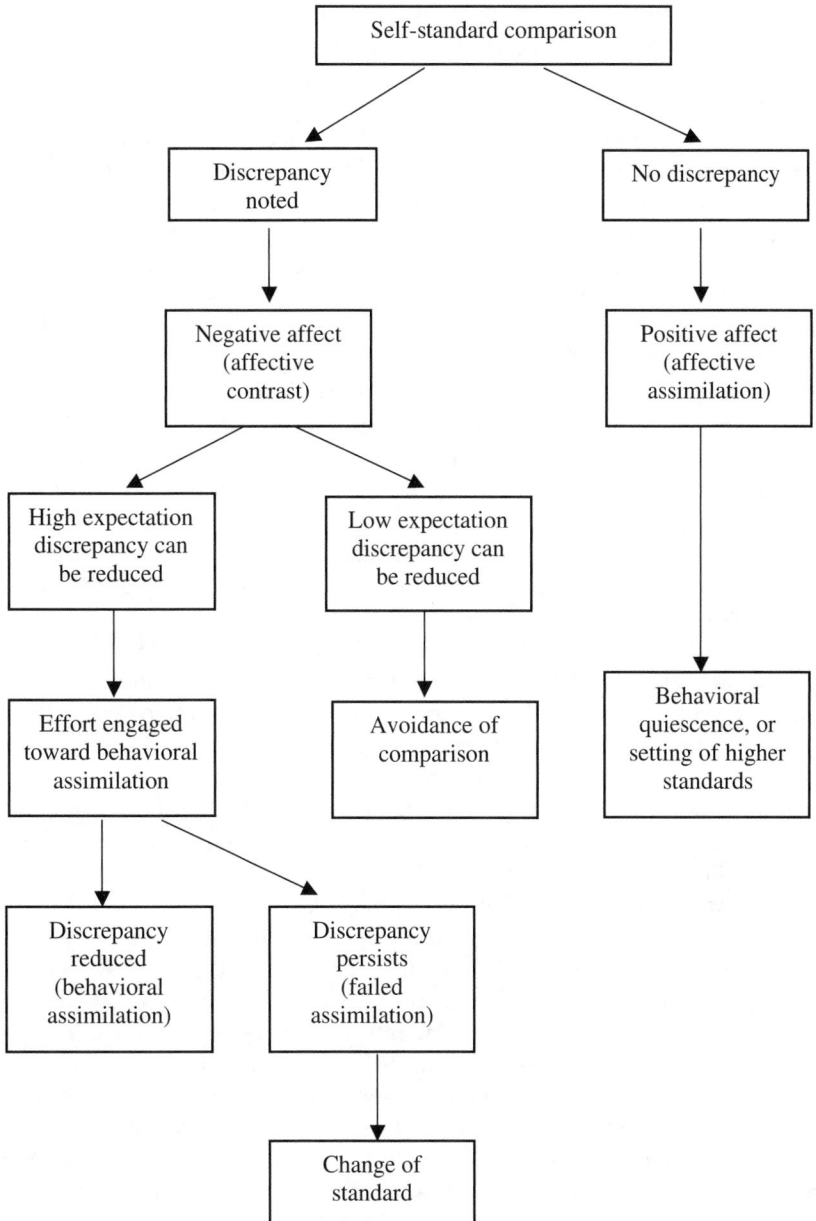

FIGURE 7.1. Generic model for assimilation and contrast effects in comparison of self to internalized standard.

self-standard comparison, which itself may be produced by virtue of an explicit instruction to compare (e.g., "what are your 'ideals'? Are you achieving them?"), a highly salient action (e.g., responding unfavorably to a photo of a mixed-race couple), or manipulations of objective self-awareness. The comparison will produce evidence of either a discrepancy or a consistency between self and standard.[3] To the extent that a discrepancy is noted, affective contrast should occur—that is, negative affect should result because of failure to live up to a desirable standard. Different types of negative affect may be experienced depending on the type of standard invoked (Higgins, 1987), but for my purposes, the negativity of the affective response is key. If no discrepancy between self and standard is noted, affective assimilation—positive affect, consistent with meeting the standard—should occur. This affective assimilation is assumed to produce no further behavioral response—a standard has been met, so quiescence occurs; resources can be pulled back (Carver, 2001). Of course, the individual can then go on to set different, higher standards, which would set the entire process in motion again.

But in the event of self-standard discrepancy and negative affect, a need to resolve the discrepancy is activated. The behavioral response will likely depend on the extent to which individuals expect that they will be able to resolve the discrepancy. Expectations could be high because of self-efficacious beliefs (Bandura, 1977), because the experimenter has indicated one will succeed in the future (Duval & Silvia, 2002), or because of past experiences at making successful progress toward discrepancy reduction (Carver, 2001). If expectations are high, effort will be expended toward behavioral assimilation. Sometimes the individual will be successful, and actual behavioral assimilation to the standard will occur. Sometimes he or she will be unsuccessful; the desire does not produce the desired outcome. Which of these outcomes occurs likely depends on myriad factors, including ability and motivation, but also including some of the factors discussed earlier, such as expending energy in mapping out ways of achieving goals rather than fantasizing (Oettingen & Mayer, 2002). The general point, however, is that the negative affect produced by self-standard discrepancies, in combination with beliefs that something can be done to reduce these discrepancies, prompts attempts (and sometimes success) at behavioral assimilation to the standard. When failure to resolve discrepancies does occur, the individual may simply change the standard—set more realistic goals, soften the "ideals," or hold the self to less stringent standards (Carver, 2001; Duval & Lalwani, 1999). The self-standard comparison process may then begin again.

Finally, this model incorporates the idea that following the awareness of a self-standard discrepancy, individuals may simply avoid the comparison process altogether if their expectations about the likelihood of resolving the discrepancy are low. That is, a discrepancy that one can do little or nothing about may simply be ignored or actively avoided. In the literature on objective self-awareness theory, this is operationalized as the avoidance of self-awareness (Greenberg & Musham, 1981); it can also be achieved through shifts in the focus of attention, distraction, or self-destructive, "escapist" tendencies (e.g., alcohol or drug use, and in extreme cases, suicide; Baumeister, 1990).

The model presented in Figure 7.1 is not meant to be new or comprehensive; rather, I hope that it serves to summarize some key points made by researchers investigating self-standard comparison and self-regulation. At the heart of the model is that affective contrast or assimilation occurs depending on the overlap between self and standard. As outlined in Chapter 2, overlap or "inclusion" of self in the standard prompts assimilation (positive affect); discrepancy or "exclusion" prompts contrast (Schwarz & Bless, 1992). Most interesting to me is that affective *contrast* prompts attempts to behaviorally *assimilate*—to actually reduce the self-standard discrepancy—again when "inclusion" seems possible (expectations for successful discrepancy reduction are high).

☐ Notes

1. Ought selves can also be thought of as negative reference points ("what I should not be") (see Carver & Scheier, 1990; Higgins, 1996; Higgins, Roney, Crowe, & Hymes, 1994).
2. In objective self-awareness theory, this scenario could also prompt avoidance of self-awareness (Silvia & Duval, 2001).
3. This determination may itself be affected by any number of factors, including *reality constraints*—the actual, observable difference between, say, a goal ("getting an A") and an outcome (failing an exam), the vagueness of the standard, the ambiguity of self-standing, etc.

CHAPTER

Stereotypes as Standards for Judging the Self: Self-Stereotyping

The literature on stereotypes and stereotyping has focused primarily on how stereotypes are used to judge *others* (see Chapter 5). But stereotypes are relevant to *self*-judgment as well. We belong to many social groups or categories, and their associated stereotypes are likely to affect how we perceive, think about, and judge ourselves, as well as how we behave. Similar to the effects of stereotypes on judgments of others, the consequences for self-judgment can also be characterized in terms of either assimilation (what researchers typically mean when they use the phrase "self-stereotyping") or contrast (e.g., judging the self as *un*like the group).

☐ Self-Categorization and Self-Stereotyping

A number of studies and approaches predate the event, but the term "self-stereotyping" was formally introduced as part of self-categorization theory and was defined as "the perceptual interchangeability or perceptual identity of oneself and others in the same group on relevant dimensions" (Turner, 1984, p. 528). Turner and his colleagues suggest that the process of self-categorization provides the basis for self-stereotyping: "Self-categorization leads to a stereotypical self-perception and depersonalization, and adherence to and expression of ingroup normative behavior" (Turner, Hogg, Oakes, Reicher, & Wetherell, 1987, p. 102; see also Turner, Oakes, Haslam, & McGarty, 1994; Hogg & Turner, 1987).

This statement clearly describes *assimilation* to the group: To the extent that one categorizes oneself as a member of a group, attributes of the group are taken on as part of the self. This assimilation may be seen in trait ratings, in judgments of similarity and interchangeability with the group, and in behavior that is normative for the group. Thus, with regard to gender, self-stereotyping may be said to occur when women judge themselves more emotional and less aggressive than men judge themselves, when women and men view themselves as highly similar to their respective groups, and when women behave in a more "nurturing" way when interacting with kittens and infants than do men (cf., Bem & Lewis, 1975; Bem, Martyna, & Watson, 1976). Similarly, sorority women may be said to engage in self-stereotyping to the extent that they view themselves as "outgoing" and "materialistic," see themselves as similar to or interchangeable with their sorority sisters, and engage in sorority-normative behavior (such as binge-eating; Crandall, 1988; Biernat, Vescio, & Green, 1996 ; Pickett, Bonner, & Coleman, 2002).[1]

To document a pattern of self-stereotyping requires, of course, comparison with some criterion. With regard to trait ratings, the proper comparison may be the self-judgments of members of a contrasting group (women compared with men) or simply of non-group members (students who are not members of sororities). By this standard, the large literature on sex-typing, which documents the divergent self-views of women and men along dimensions of competence (agency) versus warmth (communion), indicates the prevalence of gender-based self-stereotyping (e.g., Bem, 1981; Cross & Madson, 1997; Martin, 1987; Spence, Helmreich, & Stapp, 1975; Spence & Buckner, 2000). Describing the impact of gender stereotypes on the self, Rosenkrantz, Vogel, Bee, Broverman, and Broverman (1968) suggested that "sex role stereotypes . . . may articulate for the individual the sex-role behaviors that others expect from him and, in that manner, influence his self-concept" (p. 287). Interestingly, one early study that explicitly examined the degree to which endorsement of gender stereotypes predicted self-stereotyping found only weak effects (rs from .00 to .25, across both men and women and different indexes of stereotyping; Spence, Helmreich, & Stapp, 1975), though data are generally lacking on the relation between self- and other-stereotyping.

While the between-group comparison of trait ratings is informative, much research on self-stereotyping has focused instead on comparisons *across situations or motivational states*, examining factors presumed to increase the *degree* of self-stereotyping within a particular group. Some of these factors are considered below.

Category Salience

From a self-categorization theory perspective, the *salience* of a group membership should be key in producing self-stereotyping: "People stereotype themselves and others in terms of salient social categorizations, and this stereotyping leads to an enhanced perceptual identity between self and ingroup members and an enhanced perceptual contrast between ingroup and outgroup members" (Turner & Onorato, 1999, p. 21). The salience of any given self-categorization is based on a "readiness X fit" analysis. Readiness refers to accessibility, needs, goals, etc.—any factor that makes an individual inclined to use a social category. Fit refers to "the match between the category and reality" (p. 22) and has two components— comparative fit and normative fit.

Comparative fit relies on the metacontrast principle, introduced by Turner (1985). Essentially, this principle suggests that comparative fit is high if, in a given social context, a particular categorization maximizes the differences between groups and the similarities within groups. For example, gender is more likely to be a salient category in a mixed-gender group as opposed to a single-gender group. Normative fit refers to whether category members behave in a manner "consistent with normative beliefs about the substantive social meaning of the social category" (Turner & Onorato, 1999, p. 23). Thus, gender would be particularly salient as a category in a mixed-gender group in which women and men behaved consistently with expectations for women and men, respectively. For example, when men and women debate each other in groups where men take the stereotypically "male" position on an issue and women take the "female" position, both comparative and normative fit are high and hence self-categorization, followed by self-stereotyping, should occur.

This latter scenario was tapped in a study by Hogg and Turner (1987). Men and women held discussions in either same-sex dyads or mixed-sex groups (two men and two women). In the dyads, members discussed a topic on which the individuals expressed differing opinions (ascertained in a pretest); in the groups, individuals were told that the discussion topics were "ones established by recent census to differentiate the sexes—male students holding the opposite position to that held by female students" and that they "would be acting as representatives of their own sex" (p. 330). On one measure that assessed the extent to which participants felt they had acted "like a typical man/woman" during the discussion, Hogg and Turner (1987) found that in the gender-salient condition (mixed-sex groups), men judged themselves as more typically male and women judged themselves as more typically female, compared to the nonsalient (same-sex dyads) condition.

On another measure of trait-based self-stereotyping, however, the findings were more complex, in part because the researchers analyzed change scores in gender stereotypical trait descriptions. Specifically, prior to the discussion, Hogg and Turner (1987) asked participants to rate 20 characteristics for the extent to which "you personally feel that a typical person of your own sex" would behave in a situation like the dyad/group discussion that was to follow. In this way, the researchers obtained "individual subjects' situation-specific own sex stereotypes" (p. 329). After the discussion, participants then rated themselves on the same attributes, and differences from the initial ratings served as primary dependent measures. That is, positive numbers would indicate individual movement toward the situation-specific stereotype. One difficulty in interpreting the actual data from this research was that all of the mean change scores were *negative*, indicating that individuals fell short of achieving the behavior they expected of a typical group member in the discussion situation. Overall, though, groups produced less negative scores when judging themselves on *positive attributes* than dyads (−.92 vs. −1.19, collapsing across gender), consistent with the notion that individuals should be *closer* to the group stereotype when gender is salient. But on negative items, men self-stereotyped more but females less in groups relative to dyads, and on neutral items there was no group-dyad difference. In sum, though some of these findings are consistent with the salience–self-stereotyping hypothesis, the overall pattern is a bit murky.

I am aware of very little other evidence that explicitly supports the metacontrast-based salience hypothesis with regard to *self*-stereotyping (e.g., see Lorenzi-Cioldi, 1991, and Eidelman, 2004, for a review).[2] However, salience in the sense of numerical distinctiveness *does* seem to lead to greater awareness of the distinctive social category membership (e.g., McGuire & McGuire, 1988) and to increased self-stereotyping on group-relevant traits (Simon & Hamilton, 1994).

Readiness/Priming

Although data supporting the role of metacontrast in self-stereotyping are relatively rare, there is a large literature on what might be considered an aspect of the "readiness" component of self-categorization theory. Specifically, readiness may be enhanced through manipulations that make a social category accessible in some way—i.e., through *priming*. Postmes and Spears (2002, Study 2), for example, manipulated readiness to use gender categories through a procedure often used in priming research (Srull & Wyer, 1979). Male and female participants unscrambled sentences that contained either sex-stereotyped words (competitive, emotional) or neutral words and then took part in a computer-mediated discussion in mixed-sex groups (two men and two women, maximizing comparative fit). Following this discussion (which focused, in turn, on a masculine topic [a citywide car-free zone policy] and a feminine topic [the importance of physical appearance]), participants rated themselves on a series of masculine traits. Consistent with a priming hypothesis, self-ratings of men and women were more differentiated (men judged themselves more masculine and more experienced with computers than women judged themselves) when gender had been primed.[3]

In another study, gender stereotypes were activated in high school students by exposure to sex-typed photographs from magazines (versus control photographs; Chiu, Hong, Lam, Fu, Tong, & Lee, 1998). Participants then listed ten adjectives they would use to describe themselves to other females (or males) with whom they expected to interact, and the femininity/masculinity of these self-descriptions was later coded by independent judges. Two findings were of interest: Men were more likely to describe themselves "masculinely" and women "femininely" in the sex-typed photographs condition relative to the control condition—priming intensified gender-based self-stereotyping. Additionally, the audience mattered as well—women anticipating interactions with men were more feminine in their self-descriptions than were women anticipating interactions with women (though men's descriptions did not differ based on audience). These findings suggest that priming of gender stereotypes promotes self-stereotyping and that an opposite-sex audience may prompt stereotypical self-presentation, at least in high-school-aged girls. Chiu et al. (1998) refer to their audience manipulation as a manipulation of "gender category salience," following the reasoning of self-categorization theorists and the metacontrast principle: "gender category salience was expected to be high when the gender of the interactants did not match the participant's gender" (p. 89). However, as noted here, it was the priming manipulation that produced cleaner evidence of enhanced self-stereotyping; the salience effect held only for women.

In another set of studies, Shih and her colleagues focused on the fact that individuals belong to multiple categories and that the stereotypical implications of those categories may be in conflict (Shih, Pittinsky, & Ambady, 1999). For example, Asian women are subject to conflicting stereotypes in the domain of math—Asians are stereotyped as good at math, but women as bad at math. These researchers documented that when Asian women were primed with the Asian stereotype (by virtue of indicating their ethnicity on a questionnaire and answering questions relevant to ethnicity—languages spoken, number of generations their family had lived in America), they subsequently performed better on a math test compared to "no-identity-salient" controls. Conversely, when these women's gender identity was primed (by indicating their sex on a questionnaire and answering questions about preference for single-sex or coed living), math performance was lower relative to the control condition. Arguing that these effects were due to the group stereotypes and not to identity per se, Shih et al. (1999) also documented that in a setting where the "Asians excel at math" stereotype was not endorsed as strongly (Vancouver, British Columbia), enhanced performance did *not* occur when ethnicity was primed, but performance continued to be relatively low when gender was primed.

Another interesting example of self-stereotype priming research involved activation of different *aspects* of a single stereotype. Levy (1996) assessed the memory performance of elderly individuals following exposure to subliminal primes that activated the "senile" or "wise" image of old age. On four different measures of visual memory, wisdom primes enhanced performance (relative to baseline) whereas senility primes produced decrements in performance (also relative to baseline). Both patterns reflect *assimilation*—following activation of positive or negative aspects of aging, behavior follows, even when the primes are subliminal in nature. Interestingly, too, follow-up research documented that the primes did not have the same effects on a sample of young respondents to whom the stereotypes did not apply (Levy, 1996, Study 2).

☐ Stereotype Relevance and Self-Stereotyping

Levy's (1996) research suggests that an activated stereotype must be *relevant* to the individual to have an effect (Levy, 1996, uses the terminology "important to one's self-image" p. 1092). However, others have found stereotype priming effects even among individuals who are not members of the stereotyped group. Examples of this appear in an article that is already a modern classic (Bargh et al., 1996). In one study, *college-age* participants were primed with stereotypes of the elderly via a scrambled-sentences task (critical elderly primes included the terms *old, Florida, wise, bingo, forgetful, wrinkle, courteous*—i.e., a combination of positive and negative traits and noun associates). Compared to those primed with neutral words, participants in the elderly prime condition subsequently walked more slowly as they left the experiment (see also Hausdorff, Levy, & Wei, 1999). In another study, non-African-American participants were subliminally primed with faces of either an African-American or a Caucasian male as they worked on a boring computerized visual task. After a staged computer failure and news that the task would have to be redone, those primed with the African-American faces showed more hostile facial expressions than those primed with the Caucasian faces.

Other research has demonstrated that priming of African-American stereotypes—by virtue of writing an essay about an African-American male—led non-African-American participants to perform worse on a GRE math test, relative to those who wrote about a White male (Wheeler, Jarvis, & Petty, 2001). And Dijksterhuis and van Knippenberg (1998) found that individuals performed better at a Trivial Pursuit game following priming of the category "professor" relative to control and "secretary" primes, even though participants themselves were neither professors nor secretaries.[4] Primed stereotypes may also lead individuals who are *not* members of the stereotyped group to adopt the attitudes typical of that group. For example, college students expressed more prejudicial attitudes after thinking about a "skinhead," and more conservative attitudes after thinking about an elderly person, relative to control conditions (Kawakami, Dovidio, & Dijksterhuis, 2003).

This distinction between findings suggesting that the primed stereotype must be self-relevant to affect subsequent behavior and those suggesting it does not is explored in a recent paper by Wheeler and Petty (2001). These authors highlight the fact that these two lines of research and data can be characterized by a theoretical distinction between *hot* and *cold* explanatory principles: *Stereotype threat* theory represents the "hot" approach, which posits that activated stereotypes impact members of stereotyped groups through mechanisms such as anxiety and fear of confirming the negative stereotypes (Steele, 1997; Steele & Aronson, 1995). On the other hand, the *ideomotor processes* approach represents the "cold" view, that activated stereotypes can prime related behavior *in all individuals* who possess the stereotyped mental representation (Dijksterhuis & Bargh, 2001).

Both the stereotype threat and ideomotor action approaches have generated considerable research support demonstrating the basic phenomena, and both lines of research have been the topic of recent comprehensive and interesting reviews (e.g., Dijksterhuis & Bargh, 2001; Steele, Spencer, & Aronson, 2002; Wheeler & Petty, 2001). Important for my perspective is that both approaches generally posit *assimilation* effects when stereotypes have been activated. That is, whether one's own group stereotype or a stereotype of another group is primed, behavioral assimilation may result. It seems likely that both paths may operate in any situation that activates a stereotype. Thus, behavioral effects may be strongest when the primed stereotype applies to one's own group, perhaps because both hot and cold mediational paths operate (Dijksterhuis & Bargh, 2001). For example, Blacks may underperform on an intellectual test when race has been made salient both because stereotype content has been primed and because fears about confirming the negative stereotype are activated.

☐ Contrast Effects in Self-Stereotyping?

Both the ideomotor action and stereotype threat perspectives may have trouble explaining a somewhat different phenomenon that has emerged in the literature as well. I noted above that making race salient prior to an intellectual test may lead to the underachievement of Blacks, due perhaps to both the anxiety induced by stereotype threat and the more basic priming phenomenon. But it is not clear why Whites in this same situation might experience a "stereotype lift"—improvement of performance relative to "non-threat" conditions (Walton & Cohen, 2003). It does not seem to be the case that Whites are simply assimilating to a positive stereotype of *their* group in these situations, for Whites are likely to be *nonstereotyped* in terms of intellectual ability (Aronson, Lustina, Good, Keough, Steele, & Brown, 1999; Walton & Cohen, 2003). In their meta-analysis documenting stereotype lift effects, Walton and Cohen (2003) argue that members of high-status groups (such as men or Whites) "link intellectual tests to negative stereotypes automatically" (p. 464), and this provides a salient downward social comparison target that is motivating for one's own performance: "we think that stereotype lift is driven *not* by positive stereotypes about Whites, men, and wealthy people but by *negative* stereotypes about Blacks, women, and poor people" (p. 464). Interestingly, then, it may be possible to conceptualize stereotype lift effects as *contrast* effects: A negative stereotype (of a group other than one's own) is activated and performance is contrasted from this representation.[5]

Is there other evidence of contrast effects in self-stereotyping? Yes. In an intriguing line of research, Schubert and Häfner (2003) and Spears and colleagues have suggested that behavioral contrast away from an outgroup can occur if an *us–them* comparison is also activated (Spears, Gordijn, Dijksterhuis, & Stapel, 2004). These researchers begin with a consideration of Stapel and Koomen's (2000, 2001b) interpretation/comparison model (see Chapter 3 of this book), which distinguishes between the priming of broad abstract concepts (such as traits or categories) and exemplars (e.g., specific individuals). As noted in Chapters 2 and 3, broad contexts tend to produce assimilation effects whereas narrow or distinct contexts (such as exemplars) tend to produce contrast. Some evidence that the trait–exemplar distinction operates in the realm of stereotype-relevant behavior was demonstrated in a study by Dijksterhuis and colleagues (1998). Specifically, these researchers primed the elderly stereotype in much the same manner as Bargh et al. (1996) in their study demonstrating reduced walking speed following elderly primes. However, in some conditions, an exemplar (the Dutch queen mother) was also activated. Here, rather than move more slowly, participants walked more *quickly* than others—a contrast effect (see also Haddock, Macrae, & Fleck, 2002). The presumed process by which this occurred was an implicit comparison between the primed exemplar (the elderly queen mother) and the self. Some evidence for this process was found in another study assessing the accessibility of self-thoughts following an exemplar prime. In that study, participants were primed with an intelligent exemplar—Albert Einstein— and then completed a lexical decision task in which some words were related to intelligence and some to stupidity. When self-words (such as "I" and "me") appeared at subliminal levels before the target words, reaction times were reliably quicker for terms indicating stupidity. That is, an "Einstein smart, me dumb" comparison may have occurred (Dijksterhuis et al., 1998, Study 3).[6]

In addition to this *interpersonal* comparative process, an *intergroup* comparison may produce behavioral contrast as well (Schubert & Häfner, 2003; Spears et al., 2004). In one study, Schubert and Häfner (2003) found that after forming impressions of out-group targets (based on a minimal groups manipulation) who were elderly, young people responded to a lexical decision task more quickly than those exposed to young exemplars or uncategorized exemplars. That is, categorizing others as out-group members produced behavioral contrast. A second study demonstrated that priming the self (through subliminal "I," "me," "myself" primes) during activation of an out-group stereotype produced the same pattern of behavioral contrast. That is, participants who were led to think of "professors" versus "hussies" *and* who were exposed to the subliminal self-primes subsequently performed *counter* to the stereotype on a multiple choice test: Those in the professor stereotype condition performed more poorly, and those in the hussy stereotype condition performed better compared to participants subliminally primed with "other" rather than "self" primes (Schubert & Häfner, 2003, Study 2).

In a similar vein, Spears et al. (2004) write, "When intergroup comparisons become salient, and particularly when there is a perception of group difference, and/or some degree of antagonism or rivalry between the groups (giving a reason to differentiate in-group from outgroup), there may be an unconscious tendency to "distance" oneself from the outgroup and contrast one's behavior accordingly" (p. 607). In one study, participants were psychology students who first completed a "psychology student" identification questionnaire so as to make this group identity salient. They were then exposed to a scrambled-sentence prime that activated a belief that either psychology students (the in-group) or economics students (the out-group) possessed the trait "neat." The dependent variable was change in the messiness of one's coloring (overshooting the lines) from pre- to post-prime. The key finding was one of contrast—psychology students became messier after exposure to the "outgroup = neat" prime.

A second study demonstrated that *in the same group of participants,* both assimilation and contrast to an activated stereotype may be observed. Spears et al. (2004, Study 2) primed a stereotype of "busy business people" through a story about the lives of four business people; other participants read a control story. The time taken to complete an exit questionnaire indicated that those exposed to the business prime worked more quickly than those who did not. Participants themselves were college students in psychology, not business, so these data provide another example of stereotypes producing assimilative behavior even when they are not self-relevant. After the questionnaire procedure, participants completed another questionnaire designed to increase the salience of the "psychology student" identity. Researchers then timed how long participants waited for the experimenter to show up to give them credit for their participation. Spears et al. suggest that the activation of the "psychology" identity should make the comparison between psychology and business salient, thereby producing a contrast effect. Indeed, this is what was observed—those initially primed with the "busy business people" story waited *longer* than those in the control condition after their psychology identities were made salient.

Overall, then, stereotypes—like most other concepts considered in this book—may lead to either assimilation or contrast in behavior, though assimilation is by far the more common outcome (see Wheeler & Petty, 2001). Interestingly, contrastive patterns are more likely when a *comparison* is invoked between the self and the activated stereotype—as in stereotype lift effects, when majority group members perform better in the condition that is normally threatening for minority group members (Walton & Cohen, 2003), or in situations where an in-group identity is salient and compared to an activated out-group stereotype (Schubert & Häfner, 2003; Spears et al., 2004). The next chapter will take up the issue of social comparison directly, but before doing so, I will give additional consideration to motivational issues relevant to self-stereotyping.

☐ Motivations Affecting Self-Stereotyping

In addition to studying the effects of priming or readiness on self-stereotyping, other researchers have posited that various motivational factors will intensify the extent to which self-stereotyping—more specifically, assimilation to group stereotypes—occurs. I have already briefly mentioned one such motivational factor—stereotype threat. Stereotype threat theory is based on the idea that (at least with regard to negative stereotypes), reminders of the stereotype activate anxiety, vigilance, and arousal that ultimately undermine performance on difficult tasks (Steele, 1997; Steele et al., 2002). Interestingly then, this approach suggests that threat produces a desire *not* to confirm the stereotype but that, behaviorally, assimilation to the stereotype nonetheless occurs.

Other approaches highlight the role of other forms of threat in increasing both desire to assimilate and actual assimilation to group stereotypes. For example, Dion (1975) measured women's self-stereotyping following a manipulation of "interpersonal threat." Specifically, some women received positive and some received negative performance feedback, delivered by either a group of three women or three men. Internal analyses collapsing across the feedback manipulation revealed that *perceived* threat (the extent to which women viewed their co-players as prejudiced versus not) predicted self-stereotyping when the co-players were male. That is, women self-stereotyped—evaluated themselves more strongly on positive female stereotypical traits such as warmth and nurturance—when threatened by males versus not. But degree of self-stereotyping did not differ based on perceived prejudice when the co-players were female. Comparable findings emerged in a sample of Jewish undergraduates, who increasingly self-stereotyped on Jewish stereotypes following a threat of prejudice by Christian evaluators (Dion & Earn, 1975). With both of these studies in mind, Dion (1975) suggested that "perceived prejudice elicits a heightened personal identification with the positive aspects of one's membership group" (p. 305).

The threat of prejudice against one's group is quite different from the threat of confirming a negative group stereotype, and indeed, only the former seems to produce heightened identification with one's group (Branscombe, Schmitt, & Harvey, 1999; Cozzarelli & Karafa, 1998; Crosby, Pufall, Snyder, O'Connell, & Whalen, 1989; Dion, 1975; Simon, Loewy, Sturmer, Weber, Freytag, Habig, Kampmeier, & Spahlinger, 1998). In contrast, stereotype threat researchers have posited that one consequence of stereotype threat is *disidentification* with one's group (Spencer, Steele, & Quinn, 1999; Steele, 1997; Steele & Aronson, 1995). It is interesting nonetheless that both perspectives predict assimilation to group stereotypes— in stereotype threat research, performance assimilates to the stereotype; in the "threat of prejudice" research, self-ratings on traits or identification indicators show this pattern.

Various other forms of "threat" or motivations may increase the tendency to self-stereotype as well. One interesting line of research has developed out of the theory of optimal distinctiveness (Brewer, 1991), which posits that identification with social groups occurs to maximally satisfy two opposing needs—the need for assimilation (in-group inclusion and belonging) and the need for differentiation (distinctiveness from others). Brewer and Pickett and their colleagues have suggested that the arousal of both of these need states may prompt increased self-stereotyping. For example, Pickett, Bonner, and Coleman (2002) aroused assimilation needs by telling group members that they were quite different from their fellow in-group members (on a general self-attributes questionnaire)—thereby "threatening their secure status" as in-group members (Pickett et al., 2002, p. 548). Following this threat, self-stereotyping increased (relative to a no-need arousal control) in samples of three groups—honors students, Ohio State University students, and sorority members.

These studies also included conditions in which differentiation needs were aroused by telling participants that they were very similar to other in-group members and indistinguishable from out-group members. This manipulation was designed to threaten "the distinctiveness of the in-group in relation to the out-group" (Pickett et al., 2002, p. 548). The researchers again predicted and found enhanced self-stereotyping in these conditions relative to control (no need arousal) conditions; levels of self-stereotyping were comparable to those found in the need for assimilation conditions. In other words, aligning oneself with group stereotypes can be a way of both differentiating the self when distinctiveness is low and assimilating the self when distinctiveness is high. The latter pattern makes intuitive sense: For those needing assimilation, taking on the attributes of the group—creating a "perceptual closeness of the self to the in-group"—is a fairly straightforward method of meeting the aroused need (p. 545). But it seems contradictory that the need for *differentiation* can produce the same pattern. Pickett et al. (2002) note, however, that when one needs to be different, self-stereotyping is a means of heightening *intergroup* differentiation, "thereby restoring the distinctiveness of the identity" (p. 545).

At the same time, there may be conditions under which those whose differentiation needs are aroused will *distance* themselves from the group and show less evidence of self-stereotyping. At a very general level, this should occur if the targeted group cannot meet the aroused need—as when the group is too broad to really distinguish the self or too similar to some other group. Under these conditions, individuals may take another route to distinguishing themselves, such as choosing a different, more distinctive group with which to align or by making within-group differentiations. Brewer and Pickett (1999) produced reaction-time evidence supporting the idea that differentiation-need arousal can *reduce* levels of self-stereotyping. In their study, Ohio State students were led to believe they were chosen for the study because of their excessive similarity to other students ("your own personality type was one of those shared by most of the 60,000 students at OSU," p. 80—activation of the need for differentiation) or their excessive distinctiveness (activation of the need for assimilation). Those in the former condition endorsed stereotype-relevant traits as self-descriptive more slowly than need-for-assimilation or control participants (RTs measured for hitting "ME" on the keyboard). Slowness in responding is not the same as literally disavowing the traits, but nonetheless these data suggest that when a group cannot make one feel distinct (as when OSU students already believe they are indistinct and then consider OSU-relevant traits), some form of reluctance to self-stereotype may be found.

It also seems to be the case that preexisting level of identification with a group affects the extent to which self-stereotyping occurs. Those high versus low in identification should—almost by definition—see the group as highly relevant to the self and therefore self-stereotype (Turner et al., 1987). Identification may also function as a kind of "readiness" to use a social category (Doosje & Ellemers, 1997; Turner & Onorato, 1999). And the combination of high identification and threat are particularly likely to produce self-stereotyping (Spears, Doosje, & Ellemers, 1997; Verkuyten & Nekuee, 1999). For example, Spears et al. (1997) introduced psychology students who were low versus high in identification with this group to two types of threats: a status threat (in Studies 1 and 2) and a threat to distinctiveness (in Studies 3 and 4). Specifically, psychology students were threatened by virtue of comparison to higher-status physics students or affirmed by virtue of comparison to lower-status arts students; in the other studies, their distinctiveness was threatened by indicating they were very similar to business students (versus quite different from them). Self-stereotyping was assessed in these studies by two items tapping general perceived similarity with the group (e.g., "I am similar to the average psychology student"). In all four studies, those high in identification self-stereotyped more than those low in identification but did so particularly when under threat (low status or need for differentiation aroused).[7]

That self-stereotyping is a motivated process is also evident in the phenomenon of "selective self-stereotyping," whereby the self is assimilated to *positive* attributes of the group but not to negative ones (Biernat et al., 1996). For example, sorority women may willingly view favorable sorority traits as self-descriptive ("I'm outgoing, philanthropic, and popular") but not the negative ones ("I'm not snobby, materialistic, or promiscuous"). Interestingly, in my own research, it was not the case that these sorority women were denying that the negative traits were stereotypical, for they were willing to characterize "sororities in general" as possessing those traits. But in terms of self-description, assimilation only occurred to the positive traits (Biernat et al., 1996).

Similar patterns have emerged in other studies as well, often focusing on participants who are members of highly stigmatized groups. In one, recently admitted psychiatric patients were found to share a negative stereotype of the mentally ill with psychiatrists and psychiatric nurses, but they did not characterize themselves in relation to it (O'Mahony, 1982). Similarly, Fransella (1968) found that stutterers distanced themselves from negative stereotypes of their group: "We are unlikely to embrace the stereotype to 'us' if it is evaluatively 'bad'" (Fransella, 1968, p. 1532; see also Hoy, 1977, for similar data among alcoholics). However, O'Mahony (1982) also found some evidence of acceptance of the negative "mentally ill" stereotype in that psychiatric patients viewed "myself as I am now" as being much more like the group "mentally ill" than "myself as I usually am." In other words, patients rejected the stereotype as it described the "usual self" but more willingly embraced it as a description of the "present (hospitalized) self." Gibbons and his colleagues also found that as smokers progressed through a smoking cessation program, they began both viewing themselves as less similar to and derogating the "typical smoker" (Gibbons, Gerrard, Lando, & McGovern, 1991; see also Gibbons, 1985).

Writing from the perspective of self-categorization theory, Hogg and Abrams note that individuals may "try to achieve wide acceptance that ingroup/outgroup categorization is correlated with *only* those focal dimensions which reflect well on the ingroup" (Hogg & Abrams, 1988, p. 74; see also Hogg & Turner, 1987). Selective self-stereotyping may be one way of attaining this "wide acceptance." However, some recent research does suggest that this selectivity may be foregone if other motivational concerns are more pressing. Specifically, Pickett et al. (2002) found that even negative stereotypes were accepted as self-descriptive among those highly identified with their groups and in whom needs for assimilation and differentiation were activated. "Increases in the perceived self-descriptiveness of negative stereotype traits suggest a willingness to forego a certain degree of positive self-regard in service of other motivations that may be more situationally urgent" (Pickett et al., 2002, p. 559).

☐ Summary

This chapter has reviewed theory and evidence on the phenomenon of self-stereotyping, which is typically conceptualized as the tendency to *assimilate* the self to group stereotypes. At the same time, I have reviewed evidence suggesting that contrast from stereotypes can also occur. In Figure 8.1, I have attempted to lay out the various pathways through which both assimilative and contrastive influences of stereotypes have been noted in the literature.

With regard to assimilation, one influential line of work emerges from self-categorization theory, depicted in Figure 8.1 as assimilation path A (Turner, 1984; Turner et al., 1987, 1994). From this perspective, self-categorization gives rise to self-stereotyping, defined as the "perceptual identity" between self and other group members—the taking on of group attributes and behaviors. Salience of a category contributes to whether self-categorization occurs, and salience itself is based on a readiness × fit analysis (see Turner, 1984). The figure also identifies readiness alone as a contributor to self-categorization, thus allowing findings on priming effects to be conceptualized as enhancing self-categorization (e.g., Levy, 1996; Shih et al., 1999). Identification with a group may enhance the likelihood of self-categorization as well (perhaps also functioning as a sort of "readiness"). Additionally, this self-categorization path to assimilative self-stereotyping can be moderated by level of identification, by a variety of threats (e.g., threats of prejudice against one's group, threats to distinctiveness or affiliation), and by identification × threat interactions. For example, research by Spears et al. (1997) suggests that self-stereotyping is strongest among highly identified group members whose group distinctiveness is threatened.

The second assimilation path, path B, jointly depicts theorizing from stereotype threat theory and ideomotor action accounts and is based partly on Wheeler and Petty's (2001) analysis. This path indicates that activation of a stereotype can produce anxiety if one is a member of the stereotyped group and activation of a representation of the stereotype-relevant behavior in all individuals. These mediators each prompt behavioral assimilation (see also Dijksterhuis & Bargh, 2001).

Additionally, Figure 8.1 depicts three related, though distinct, stereotype-contrastive paths. Path C begins with the same stereotype activation as depicted in assimilation path B. But what is important here is that an *out-group* stereotype is activated, presumably also activating a representation of the self as *distinct* from this out-group. The distinctiveness may itself give rise to behavioral representations that differ from those stereotypical of the out-group and subsequently to stereotype-contrastive behavior. For example, in the typical case of "stereotype lift" (Walton & Cohen, 2003), activation of the African-American stereotype regarding intelligence may lead *White* actors to differentiate themselves from this (negative) group standing and behave in a direction opposite the stereotype (i.e., perform better on an intellectual task).

Assimilative Paths

a. Self-categorization

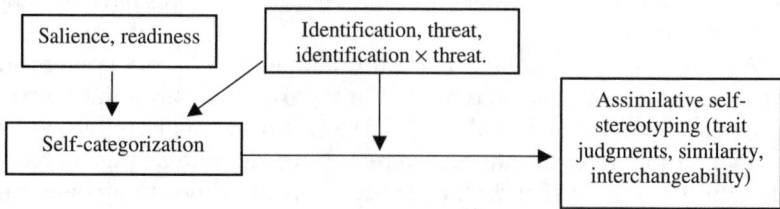

b. Threat and ideomotor paths

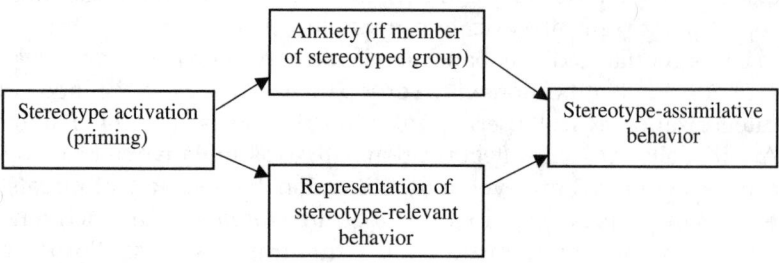

Contrastive Paths

c. Stereotype lift

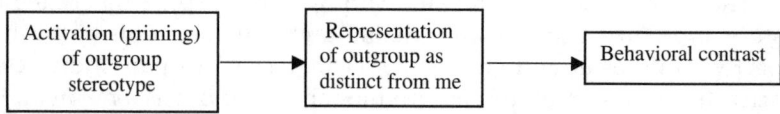

d. Exemplar activation

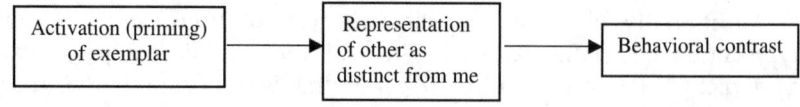

e. Ingroup-outgroup comparison

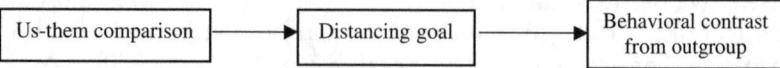

FIGURE 8.1. Assimilative and contrastive pathways in self-stereotyping.

Contrastive path D highlights the finding that exemplar activation—priming of an individual instance of a stereotyped category—also produces behavioral contrast. This general pattern is consistent with much research reviewed earlier in this book indicating that distinct primes are more likely than nondistinct primes to produce contrast (see Chapters 2 and 3). Dijksterhuis and his colleagues (1998) have provided evidence that the availability of self-representations that are distinct from the primed exemplar may mediate this behavioral contrast effect.

Finally, contrastive path E reflects research suggesting that explicit comparisons between in-groups and out-groups can also prompt behavioral distancing from the activated out-group stereotype. Spears et al. (2004) suggest that an "unconscious tendency to distance" the self from the out-group is activated under conditions when the intergroup distinction is salient (especially when there is some antagonism between groups), and behavior follows from this tendency. One might wonder whether this research on contrast from *out-group* stereotypes could be reconceptualized as assimilation to *in-group* stereotypes. In research by Spears et al. (2004), this was not the case, as out-group stereotypes were in focal attention (e.g., among psychology students, the stereotype of "busy business people"; Study 2), and in the one case where an in-group stereotype was primed ("Psychology students are neat"), no behavioral effects were found (Study 1). Nonetheless, it seems possible that an explicit in-group–out-group comparison may activate the desire to distance, and that this distancing may be manifested in enhanced *assimilation* to *in-group* stereotypes.

This set of pathways to assimilation and contrast is not comprehensive, but it provides, I think, a reasonable approximation of current self-stereotyping models in the field. I should note, too, that the paths are not necessarily mutually exclusive, as the same instigator (priming) may set off multiple paths, and key contributors to one path (e.g., self-categorization) are surely implicated in others.

It is worth noting that in terms of stereotype-relevant *behavior*, research has documented both assimilation and contrast effects. But with regard to *self-descriptions*—trait ratings, judgments of similarity between self and other group members—assimilation effects have been the dominant finding in the literature. This may simply reflect the focus of researchers' attention; behavioral findings, whether about performance or walking speed, are often more interesting to pursue than findings regarding self-report ratings. Or perhaps, as Bargh et al. (1996) note, context effects are simply more likely to manifest themselves in behavior than in judgments. But surely there are situations in which needs for differentiation may lead one to disavow a group stereotype (see Pickett et al., 2002), or when reactance about being categorized as a group member leads one to resist group stereotypes as descriptive of the self. Additionally, to the extent that one's in-group stereotypes provide a frame of reference, contrast rather than assimilation to these stereotypes may occur (Biernat, Eidelman, & Fuegen, 2002; Blanton, Christie, & Dye, 2002; Guimond et al., in press).

For example, my colleagues and I found that men who were "solos" in their six-person groups described themselves as more "warm" than women in these groups (Biernat et al., 2002). Presumably, these men judged themselves relative to "low warmth" standards for men (and women relative to "high warmth" standards for women), and contrast from those standards was the result. Thus, an additional contrastive self-stereotyping path may operate such that stereotype activation and/or self-categorization prompts comparison of self to the in-group standard, with judgmental contrast as the result ("compared to women, I'm not very warm and caring!"). Delineating precisely when this will occur remains an important task. Blanton et al. (2002) suggest that this use of the group stereotype as a frame of reference will be more likely when *negative* group stereotypes are activated; the uncertainty or ambiguity of self-standing may play a role as well. This theme of comparison—to individual targets rather than group stereotypes—will be considered more fully in the next chapter.

☐ Notes

1. It is worth noting that assimilative self-stereotyping, which involves the projection of group attributes onto the self, is the converse of social projection, which involves projection of self onto group (see the discussion of false consensus in Chapter 4). It seems likely that group →self assimilation is more likely for well-known groups, whereas self →group projection is more likely for novel or less clearly-defined groups (Otten, 2003; see also Guimond, Chatard, Martinot, Crisp, & Redersdorff, in press; Krueger & Stanke, 2001).
2. There is some support for these ideas, however, in studies examining the perception of *others* in terms of social categories rather than the self (e.g., see Oakes, Turner, & Haslam, 1991).
3. In terms of actual behavior engaged in during the interaction, the authors coded for number of questions asked (a feminine behavior) and degree of autonomy (a masculine behavior) in the communications. Here, the data pattern depended on another manipulated variable, whether participants were depersonalized (anonymous) or not, and the gender-typing of the discussion topic. It was in the depersonalized condition, under gender-priming, when the masculine topic was discussed, that men were particularly likely to write more autonomous communications than women. Also in this condition, women were particularly likely to ask more questions than men. In short, a masculine discussion topic under depersonalized conditions when gender was salient produced the strongest evidence of sex-typing in behavior.
4. Other research suggests that this assimilative pattern can be reduced if other behavioral cues become salient, as when one is made self-aware (Dijksterhuis & van Knippenberg, 2000).
5. Recently, however, Seibt and Förster (2004) have focused on positive group stereotypes as activating a "promotion" focus and negative group stereotypes as activating a

"prevention" focus (Higgins, 1997). In this formulation, stereotype lift effects *are* about assimilation to the in-group stereotype, and that assimilation is achieved through a promotion state of eagerness. Stereotype threat effects are also about assimilation to (negative) in-group stereotypes charged by a failure-oriented or vigilant prevention focus (see Chapter 7).

6. Interestingly, other research by these authors indicates that exposing individuals to five exemplars rather than one again produces behavioral *assimilation*. Presumably, a group of five exemplars operates more like a broad entity, prompting inclusion or assimilation (Dijksterhuis, Spears, & Lépinasse, 2001).

7. However, in the "status threat" studies, the effects were largely due to the tendency for low-identified individuals to self-stereotype *less* under threat; in the "distinctiveness threat" studies, it was high-identified individuals who self-stereotyped *more* under threat.

Other People as Standards: Social Comparison[1]

The previous chapter highlighted the role of groups and group stereotypes in evaluating the self. In this chapter, I will focus on a related, but distinct, standard against which we evaluate, appraise, and regulate the self: Other people. Social comparison theory (Festinger, 1954a, b) is the main theoretical approach that will guide this review, and I will consider three broad topical areas that have been the focus of much research in social comparison: Comparison motives, choice of comparison target or direction of comparison, and consequences of comparison. The literature on social comparison is enormous—a recent PsycInfo search located over two thousand papers—and I am ill-equipped for a thorough review (for this, check out Suls & Wheeler, 2000, and the 2001 special issue of *European Journal of Social Psychology* edited by Buunk & Mussweiler). In keeping with the general theme of this book, I will focus on the fact that social comparison can be conceptualized as resulting in either *assimilation* or *contrast* effects— the self is drawn toward or away from comparison to others. Perhaps the most common theme in social comparison is *contrast*—by virtue of comparing ourselves to others, we see ourselves as better or worse than they are. But assimilation occurs under specifiable conditions as well.

☐ Social Comparison—The Basics

Social comparison has been conceptualized in a variety of ways, all of which recognize the importance of other people for defining one's perceptions of the world and one's sense of self (see Wheeler, 1991; Suls & Wheeler, 2000, for reviews). Sherif's (1936) classic paper on social influence in ambiguous situations provided a compelling demonstration of how one's perceptions of reality can be socially constructed. Hyman (1942) noted that one's status on different dimensions may be determined by an understanding of oneself within the context of one's reference group. Newcomb (1943), in his famous Bennington Study, described how conservative first-year college students adopted the liberal senior class as their frame of reference and attitudinally moved toward (assimilated to) this referent group. Researchers have also conceptualized social comparison as affiliation, arguing specifically that fear-produced affiliation results from a desire to compare one's emotional reactions to those of others (Gerard & Rabbie, 1961; Schachter, 1959; see also Taylor & Lobel, 1989).

In his classic theory of social comparison, Festinger (1954a, b) argued that we are motivated to *evaluate* our abilities and opinions and will do so through the process of comparing ourselves with others. Festinger wrote, "We started out by assuming the existence of a motivation to know that one's opinions are correct and to know precisely what one is and is not capable of doing" (1954b, p. 217). In this respect, Festinger's theory is well-grounded in the social psychological tradition that paints the social perceiver as an objective information seeker who is motivated to understand, predict, and control the environment (e.g., Heider, 1944). Festinger's theory put some limits on when and with whom people compare. With regard to *when*, Festinger's (1954a) Corollary IIB suggested that we attempt to evaluate our abilities and opinions through social comparison only when we do not have access to objective, nonsocial standards of evaluation, presumably because objective standards allow for a more accurate appraisal of ourselves. With regard to *whom*, he maintained that people will compare with others who are *similar* to themselves in ability or opinion (Corollary IIIA). This occurs, presumably, because uncertainty is best reduced when comparing with similar others and because accuracy in self-assessment is more difficult to achieve through comparison with dissimilar others (Blanton, 2001; Suls & Miller, 1977).

In general, we might compare with others both to assess our abilities ("how good a tennis player am I?") and to assess our opinions ("how reasonable/correct is my opinion about George Bush?"). Festinger (1954b) assumed that abilities and opinions operate similarly within a comparative context and noted that the comparison process in both cases produces "pressures toward uniformity." For example, if one notices a discrepancy between the self and others in a reference group with respect to either abilities or opinions, one will attempt to change either one's own standing/position or the standing/position of others within the group in order to attain similarity (note the themes of assimilation). However, Festinger (1954a) postulated a "unidirectional drive upward" in the case of abilities thought to be largely absent for opinions. In the case of opinions, we gain confidence by being around others who agree with us. In the case of abilities, we would prefer to be *slightly* better than everyone else. Thus, the attempt to maintain similarity to one's group members with respect to ability always interacts with the motive to improve one's ability. "The implication is that, with respect to the evaluation of abilities, a state of social quiescence is never reached" (Festinger, 1954a, p. 125). Ultimately, then, comparison to *slightly better* others may be preferred for abilities, as this represents a compromise between the uniformity pressures and the "drive upward."

Many studies have generated support for a number of Festinger's ideas, for example, that we often choose to compare with similar others (Miller, Turnbull, & McFarland, 1988; Nosanchuk & Erickson, 1985; Taylor, Neter, & Wayment, 1995; Wheeler, 1966). But a number of researchers have taken issue with Festinger's theory on several counts. Goethals and Darley (1977), for instance, offered an attributional reformulation that emphasized a preference for comparing with others similar to us on attributes related to the performance or opinion at hand; they also argued that comparison with dissimilar others is important when seeking validity for our beliefs. Kruglanski and Mayseless (1990) disputed Festinger's distinction between opinions and abilities, arguing that comparisons involving abilities reduce to comparing opinions about abilities. Klein (1997) provided evidence that, contrary to Festinger's Corollary IIB, people will compare with others even when they have access to some objective standard for evaluation (see also Foddy & Crundall, 1993; Miller, 1977; Wood & Wilson, 2003). Also highlighting the importance of social comparison even in cases where objective standards are available, much research has documented that children's academic self-concepts are affected not only by their absolute level of achievement (as measured and communicated by objective criteria) but also by the achievement level of their peers (in a negative or contrastive direction; Marsh, 1993; Marsh & Hau, 2003).

Perhaps the most general and pervasive disagreement has been with Festinger's contention that people are objective self-evaluators who seek accurate information (e.g., Kruglanski & Mayseless, 1990; Thornton & Arrowood, 1966; Wood, 1989). Recent trends in social comparison research show quite clearly that people make comparisons for many reasons, only one of which is self-evaluation in the sense meant by Festinger (hereafter referred to as *self-assessment*; see Wood, 1989). Further, much evidence suggests that the comparison process is not unbiased—comparisons often depend on the subjective *construal* of the comparison standard rather than an "objective" appraisal. For example, one may perceive the self to be more similar to a superior other than is really the case (see Collins, 1996, for a review). These biased construals may themselves result from a variety of motives, which will be discussed in the following section.

☐ Motives of the Comparer

In contrast to Festinger's original views on the importance of self-assessment motives, evidence suggests that people compare with others for a number of other reasons (Collins, 1996; Diener & Fujita, 1997; Taylor et al., 1995; Wood, 1989). The most well-researched of these other motives are *self-enhancement* and *self-improvement*. Additionally, I will briefly consider *self-verification*, a motive much less discussed in the context of social comparison theory.

Self-Enhancement

That people wish to be held in high esteem by both themselves and others constitutes one of the most fundamental assumptions within the discipline of psychology in general as well as within social psychology in particular (Maslow, 1943; Oakes et al., 1994; Rogers, 1951; Solomon, Greenberg, & Pyszczynski, 1991; Tajfel, 1982; Taylor, 1989; Taylor & Brown, 1988; Turner, 1975). Social comparison researchers have accommodated this assumption as well with an emphasis on *self-enhancement* as a motive of comparison (Armor & Taylor, 1998; Brown et al., 1992; Buunk & Ybema, 1997; Collins, 1996; Lockwood & Kunda, 1997; Tesser, 1988; Tesser & Campbell, 1980; Tesser & Paulhus, 1983) that may involve either *attaining* or *maintaining* a positive self-concept (Taylor et al., 1995).

In Hakmiller's (1966) early demonstration of enhancement-motivated comparison, female participants were provided with information that described them as harboring strong hostility toward their parents, a personality trait that carried with it either positive or negative social implications. When presented with a rank-ordering of the likely hostility scores of other students and asked to choose a score with which to compare, participants who believed the trait to be negative as compared to positive chose a significantly more negative comparison target, on average. Hakmiller interpreted his results as reflecting the comparison function of "sustaining or reasserting the favorability of the individual's self-regard" (p. 37). Other early theorists also underscored the importance of the self-enhancement motive in social comparison (Goethals & Darley, 1977; Thornton & Arrowood, 1966; Wills, 1981).

In a more recent investigation, Sedikides (1993) found the self-enhancement motive to be the strongest of three motives of the general process of self-evaluation. Apparently, people will go to great lengths to maintain their positive self-views by making use of such strategies as being selective in the choice of dimension(s) along which to compare (Crocker & Major, 1989; Wood, 1989), attending to only certain comparison of others (Crocker & Major, 1989; Diener & Fujita, 1997; Wood, 1989), fabricating comparison targets if no self-enhancing targets are immediately available (Taylor & Lobel, 1989; Taylor, Wood, & Lichtman, 1983), denying the meaningfulness of a particular comparison (Lockwood & Kunda, 1997), elevating perceptions of those who clearly outperform the self (Alicke, LoSchiavo, Zerbst, & Zhang, 1997), and sometimes simply avoiding comparison altogether (Brickman & Bulman, 1977; Buunk, Collins, Taylor, VanYperen, & Dakof, 1990; Wood, 1989).

Among those particularly concerned with self-enhancement should be members of stigmatized groups. According to Crocker and Major (1989), the stigmatized are often faced with the difficult task of protecting their self-esteem in the face of discriminatory treatment and will utilize several creative strategies in order to do so. One of these strategies is inherently comparative in nature; specifically, Crocker and Major proposed that stigmatized individuals will make within-group comparisons in order to avoid the potential loss of self-esteem that could result from comparisons with members of relatively advantaged groups (Major, 1994; see also Tajfel, 1982).

However, when one compares *un*favorably to in-group members, self-esteem is particularly likely to be harmed—more so than when one compares unfavorably to an out-group member (Major, Sciacchitano, & Crocker, 1993; Martinot, Redersdorff, Guimond, & Dif, 2002). Thus, while in-group comparisons may be generally beneficial, they may backfire when one's performance or standing is relatively negative. But there is a caveat to this as well. Even in this situation of being outperformed, upward comparison with an *in-group* member who challenges negative ability stereotypes of one's group—as when African-American women compare with another African-American woman who outperforms them on an IQ test—can benefit self-esteem (relative to comparison with an out-group member; Blanton, Crocker, & Miller, 2000; see also Blanton et al., 2002). Those highly identified with an ingroup may be particularly attracted to high-performing ingroup members when an intergroup context is invoked (Schmitt, Silvia, & Branscombe, 2000).

But recent research suggests that it may be *non*stigmatized group members who are particularly proficient in using within-group comparisons as a self-protective strategy. In three studies, high-status group members were generally unaffected by comparisons—even upward ones—with out-group members (Martinot et al., 2002). For example, when men completed a "masculine" task (a test of verbal-spatial ability), a comparison to better-performing out-group members resulted in the same level of self-esteem as downward comparisons with either in-group or out-group members. That is, the upward out-group comparison was apparently dismissed as irrelevant. Women, however, were particularly harmed by the upward comparison with the out-group. Though stigmatized group members may *prefer* within-group comparisons, forced upward comparison to an out-group target may nonetheless be harmful to self-esteem.

Self-Improvement

Enhancement-motivated comparisons may produce a stagnant comparer who does not show the "unidirectional drive upward" discussed by Festinger. However, other research documents the existence of a *self-improvement* motive for social comparison whereby the individual looks to others in the social environment for inspiration and/or uses comparisons to motivate the self to improve (Collins, 1996, 2000; Lockwood & Kunda, 1997; Wood, 1989).

Taylor and Lobel (1989), for example, reviewed research showing that cancer patients find a source of inspiration in other patients who are coping better than themselves or who have successfully survived the disease. However, these researchers also noted that it is only affiliating with or seeking information from superior copers that patients have found inspiring; self-evaluation with respect to such "high-functioning" targets is arguably threatening and ego-deflating (see also Locke, 2003). Further, Lockwood and Kunda (1997) showed that individuals will be inspired by upward comparison targets only to the extent that (1) such targets are relevant to the comparer's self-definition, and (2) the comparer believes that he or she can also attain the target's level of success (see also Buunk & Ybema, 1997, 2003). According to Wood (1989), factors promoting self-improvement include personality variables such as the type A behavior pattern and cultural variables such as an emphasis on achievement. For example, White and Lehman (2005) documented that Asian Canadians were more likely than European Canadians to compare for the purposes of self-improvement, particularly after failure feedback and after the opportunity to improve was made salient. I will consider other moderators of this motive and its consequences later in the chapter; the key point is that *sometimes* we seek comparisons as a means of improving or inspiring the self.

Self-Verification

Self-verification theory posits a desire for coherence, to keep intact the self-views one has developed (Swann, 1987). This may be another important goal served by social comparison (Taylor et al., 1995), and it is distinct from *self-enhancement* motives in that the self-views one wants to verify may be positive *or* negative.

In one study documenting that people seek self-verification, Swann, Stein-Seroussi, and Giesler (1992) asked participants with either positive or negative self-views to choose to interact with one of two alleged partners: either a partner who saw them positively or one who saw them negatively. Results showed that 72% of participants who saw themselves positively chose the partner who confirmed their positive self-views, a finding that could be interpreted as due to either self-enhancement or self-verification strivings. However, 78% of participants with *negative* self-views chose to interact with the self-verifying partner (one who viewed them negatively). Moreover, this subgroup of participants listed a predominance of epistemic reasons (i.e., reasons emphasizing the importance of confirming self-views) for their choice, as opposed to other reasons, such as desire for self-improvement. Self-verification theory has been supported in more recent research as well (e.g., Swann, De La Ronde, & Hixon, 1994; Swann & Pelham, 2002; for a review, see Swann, Rentfrow, & Guinn, 2003).

According to Swann (1987), a person may self-verify by selecting social environments that foster self-views as well as by cognitively distorting information so that it is consistent with self-views (e.g., by preferentially attending to self-confirmatory feedback or by endorsing the validity only of self-confirmatory feedback). Social comparison is implicated in these processes. For example, by selecting social environments that confirm one's self-views (as when a teenage "computer nerd" surrounds himself or herself with other teenage computer nerds), one is likely to compare with others in that context. Given the similarity and the ease of "including" self and others in a single category (Schwarz & Bless, 1992a), assimilation may result. Cognitive distortion is also a form of assimilation—verification motives lead to the selective interpretation of self-relevant information.

Self-Assessment

Despite this evidence for a variety of comparison motives, the original *self-assessment* motive should not be ignored. Although people may not be as accuracy seeking as Festinger envisioned, evidence for the motive to self-assess does exist (Gerard, 1963; Raynor & McFarlin, 1986; Scheier & Carver, 1983; Trope, 1986). Trope (1986), for example, found that when given a choice of tasks to complete, participants selected tasks that diagnosed their abilities accurately, even if unfavorably. Research has also shown that certain individual difference variables such as depression may predispose a comparer to be more concerned with accuracy (self-assessment) than with other comparison goals (Weary, Marsh, & McCormick, 1994).

Even Sedikides (1993), who found self-enhancement to be a stronger motive than self-assessment, did not wish to suggest that people never self-assess; rather, he discussed the importance of uncovering the conditions under which each motive is likely to operate. For example, although people may be motivated to accurately assess their skills on dimensions for which *improvement* is possible, they may instead wish to see themselves more positively on aptitude-related dimensions for which ability is relatively fixed. People may also be particularly concerned with self-assessment when trying to determine whether they can actually perform a particular behavior (Wheeler, Martin, & Suls, 1997). And self-assessment may itself occur in the service of self-enhancement in the long-term (Sedikides & Strube, 1997). Further, Sedikides suggested that mood may moderate the self-evaluation process, such that a sad mood may prompt self-assessment and a happy mood may prompt self-enhancement (cf., Buunk & Ybema, 1997; Wheeler & Miyake, 1992). Such a perspective is consistent with the idea that a depressed outlook is often associated with a more realistic view of the self (Taylor, 1989; but cf. Dunning & Story, 1991).

Nonetheless, as research on self-improvement and self-enhancement makes clear, social perceivers often selectively make use of comparison information in order to satisfy goals other than discovering the "truth." Comparison choices may have less to do with an unbiased sampling of externally provided comparison information and more to do with a subjective construal of information that allows it to be used to enhance or improve the self. Thus, even though self-assessment is an important motive, it comprises only part of the social comparison picture.

☐ Choice of Comparison Target/Direction of Comparison

An issue closely tied to comparison motives concerns the particular targets that perceivers choose for comparison purposes. Much has been written on this point (Allen & Wilder, 1977; Miller & Prentice, 1996; Suls, 1986; Taylor et al., 1995). At a very general level, Kruglanski and Mayseless

(1990) suggest that one's choice of comparison target depends on three variables: (1) whether a comparison with the target will satisfy one's comparison motive, (2) whether the target is relevant to the judgment being made, and (3) the kinds of heuristics currently accessible (e.g., for teenagers, the rule "peers know best" may prompt comparison to similar others; the rule "grown-ups know best" may prompt comparison to dissimilar others). Making similar points, Levine and Moreland (1986) suggest that a perceiver will choose a given comparison target to the extent that the target is *salient* and *attractive*, where attractiveness is defined as the degree to which the target is able to satisfy the perceiver's comparison motives. The question of comparison choice ultimately boils down to whether people compare with similar others (lateral comparisons) or dissimilar others (upward or downward comparisons).

Lateral Comparison

As noted earlier, there is research evidence to suggest that individuals choose similar others with whom to compare (e.g., Kahneman & Miller, 1986; Mettee & Smith, 1977; Miller et al., 1988; Nosanchuk & Erickson, 1985; Taylor et al., 1995; Wheeler, 1966). For example, Wheeler (1966) gave participants both their own alleged scores and a rank-ordering of other participants' alleged scores on a personality test designed to select students for a course. Participants were asked to select the rank order of the participant whose score they most wanted to see. Consistent with predictions, participants chose to compare to others who had scores similar to their own. Related evidence regarding the *outcomes* of comparisons rather than choice of standards per se suggests that people are *unresponsive* to comparison information when similarity is lacking. For example, Cash, Cash, and Butters (1983) found that women rated their own attractiveness lower when exposed to attractive as compared to unattractive targets, except when they believed the attractive targets to be professional models (i.e., dissimilar in an important way; see also Brown et al., 1992).

Although I am using "similarity" to refer specifically to a perceiver's position relative to others on the comparison dimension itself, theorists have also offered broader definitions of "similarity." Goethals and Darley (1977), for instance, argued that similar others could include those who are similar to the comparer on attributes that are *related* to, not just specific to, the comparison dimension (cf., Major et al., 1991). For example, a man may choose to compare his performance at the piano with the performance of others who have studied piano for approximately the same amount of time as himself, believing years of study, a related attribute, to be a good predictor of performance, the central comparison dimension. For Goethals and Darley (1977), attributional principles come into play in the choice of someone with "related attributes" as a comparison standard: Comparing favorably with a worse-off other can lead to *discounting* of ability as the cause of our doing better; comparing favorably to a better-off other can lead to *augmentation* (Kelley, 1972). Conversely, comparing *un*favorably to a worse-off other can augment lack of ability as a cause, and comparing *un*favorably to a better-off other can discount lack of ability as a cause. The bottom line is this: "We can always learn something by comparing performances with someone who is similar on related attributes. If we compare with someone who is dissimilar, that is, more advantaged or disadvantaged, there is some chance of learning a great deal, but typically the outcome—doing better than someone who is less advantaged and worse than someone who is advantaged—is ambiguous" (Goethals & Klein, 2000, p. 26).

The "proxy model" of social comparison suggests that the role of related attributes is lessened when the effort level of a "proxy"—someone experienced on the task—is known (Martin, Suls, & Wheeler, 2002; Wheeler, Martin, & Suls, 1997). That is, when one wants to predict one's likely success at an unfamiliar task, related attributes of a proxy matter only when her or his effort is unknown. Presumably effort "disambiguates" the situation described by Goethals and Klein such that one no longer needs to be concerned with similarity on related attributes to predict one's own performance. Note that inherent in the attributional descriptions of both the related attributes hypothesis and the proxy model is the presumed *motive* for comparison—the desire to (accurately) self-assess.

Wood (1989) reviewed research that extended the definition of similarity even further than Goethals and Darley's (1977) related attributes hypothesis. She noted that people may also compare to others who are similar in terms of features *not* related to the comparison dimension. That is, similarity may be defined by features as diffuse as shared group membership (e.g., gender category) and broad personality traits (Crocker & Major, 1989; Miller et al., 1988; Tesser, 1988). Among possible explanations advanced for such comparisons are that people may (1) perceive themselves to be closer to others who are somehow similar even if on an unrelated dimension (Miller et al., 1988; Tesser, 1988), (2) make in-group comparisons to protect self-esteem (Crocker & Major, 1989), (3) believe that targets similar with respect to unrelated attributes are potential competitors and thereby relevant to one's outcomes, (4) believe attributes such as gender to be related to performance across a wide variety of domains, and (5) view some attributes (such as gender) as self-defining, even if unrelated to a given comparison dimension (see Miller et al., 1988; Wood, 1989).

But other evidence points to factors that moderate whether people prefer to compare to others with whom they share fewer, not more, attributes (Major et al., 1991; Miller, 1982, 1984; Miller et al., 1988; Oldham et al., 1982; Samuel, 1973; Suls, Gaes, & Gastorf, 1979). According to Wood (1989), similar others will be chosen when an individual is relatively certain about how to interpret his or her standing on a dimension, but *dis*similar others are especially likely candidates for comparison if the comparer is relatively unfamiliar with the comparison dimension. In such a situation, the inability to interpret one's performance in isolation may lead to interest in the entire range of performance along the dimension. Evidence also suggests that the type of judgment called for may influence the choice of comparison target. Gorenflo and Crano (1989), for example, found that when making objective judgments (those based on empirically verifiable facts about the target of judgment), people sought dissimilar others with whom to compare. When called upon to make subjective judgments (those based on one's own attitudes or values), however, people preferred to compare with similar others. For example, when students playing the role of college admission officers were told that they had "sufficient information to form an objective judgment of the candidate" under consideration, they preferred to compare their judgments with those of *out-group* members (in-group–out-group membership was created by virtue of a minimal groups manipulation). When told that their information about the candidate was "insufficient" and that they should "base their judgments on their own beliefs and preferences," they preferred to compare with *in-group* members.

Downward Comparison

Instead of a lateral comparison, one may choose to compare with another who is dissimilar in that he or she is worse-off than the self.[2] The classic paper reviewed earlier by Hakmiller (1966) supports the idea that people often compare with worse-off others, and according to Wills (1981), downward comparison serves a self-enhancing function, particularly under conditions of threat: "People do not necessarily regard misfortune to others as a desirable occurrence or view comparison with less fortunate others as a wholly admirable process; yet the psychological benefit of doing so is substantial, thus the temptation is strong, and all of the evidence suggests that people yield frequently to this temptation" (p. 265).

More recent research supports Wills' (1981) depiction of downward comparisons as highly tempting (see Affleck & Tennen, 1991; Gibbons & Gerrard, 1991; Wills, 1991). Buunk et al. (1990) examined comparisons relevant to health status and marital satisfaction. In each of two studies, self-enhancing downward comparisons that generated positive affect were made more frequently than any other type of comparison. Furthermore, consistent with Wills' theory, downward comparisons have been shown to improve an initially low level of self-esteem (Hakmiller, 1966) and to enhance positive affect more generally (for recent examples, see Locke, 2003).

But positive affect is not only a likely *result* of downward comparison. There is also evidence to suggest that positive affect may *lead to* downward comparisons (Suls & Wheeler, 2000; Wheeler & Miyake, 1992; Wood, Michela, & Giordano, 2000) and may make one more responsive to downward comparisons than to upward comparisons (Lyubomirsky & Ross, 1997). For example, individuals with high self-esteem tend to engage in downward comparisons more often than individuals with low self-esteem (Buunk & Ybema, 1997; Wheeler & Miyake, 1992; but cf., Wills, 1991) and tend to emphasize the positive qualities that they have but that others do not (Schütz & Tice, 1997).

These findings appear contradictory to Wills' (1981) conceptualization of downward comparison as a response to *threat*, and indeed a number of articles have questioned the validity of this aspect of downward comparison theory (see Gibbons, Lane, Gerrard, Reis-Bergan, Lautrup, Pexa, & Blanton, 2002; Suls & Wheeler, 2000, for reviews). However, Wills (1981) argued that downward comparison is an acute reaction to threat that dissipates over time (see also Gibbons & Gerrard, 1991). It is quite possible that many studies have failed to capture this immediate, fleeting response to threat or have looked for downward comparisons in situations where *upward* comparisons are more useful—as in a classroom, where improvement or "instrumental action" (Wills, 1981) is possible (Gibbons et al., 2002).

In a study that removed the possibility of upward comparisons as useful (because the administered test was a one-time experience), Gibbons et al. (2002) did find that poor performers (conceptualized as experiencing threat) desired comparisons with others who had also done poorly—even worse than themselves (Study 1); mood was also negatively correlated with preference for upward comparisons in a second study. More generally, Gibbons et al. (2002) noted that poor performance (threat) predicts a lower *absolute* preferred comparison level: the worse one's performance, the lower the performance level of the preferred comparison other. But this preferred comparison other need not be a *true* downward comparison, in the sense of someone who performed worse than the self. One reason for this may be that "people know that downward comparison can help them feel better about their situation, but also realize it will do little to improve that situation" (Gibbons et al., 2002, p. 877). Interestingly, across five studies, poor performers preferred *avoiding* upward comparisons except in situations where they did not need to disclose their own performance level or have face-to-face contact with the upward target.

An additional variable that may influence whether one chooses to compare downward or otherwise is the manner in which social comparison is defined in a given situation—for example, as self-evaluation or as affiliation. If the comparer's goal is an evaluative one, he or she may reap the self-enhancing benefits associated with downward comparison. If, on the other hand, an individual is seeking out someone with whom to associate, a downward target may represent a threat (Buunk et al., 1990; Buunk & Ybema, 1997; Taylor & Lobel, 1989), especially if the comparer believes the target's situation to be due to uncontrollable factors (Major et al., 1991).

Upward Comparison

Given the apparent esteem benefits of comparing downward, one might wonder why anyone would ever choose to compare upward—to a target better-off than the self. As discussed earlier, self-improvement is a viable goal of the comparison process, and upward targets are especially likely to be useful in satisfying this motive (Gibbons et al., 2002; Lockwood & Kunda, 1997; Nosanchuk & Erickson, 1985; Taylor et al., 1995). Even the goal of self-assessment embodied in the unidirectional drive upward, may be met by comparison with superior others (Festinger, 1954a). According to Wheeler and Miyake (1992), although superior others may initially evoke negative affect, they may be chosen as comparison targets to the degree that they motivate the comparer to improve. Other research is consistent with this perspective as well (Major et al., 1991; Taylor & Lobel, 1989). Surprisingly, upward targets may also be used to self-enhance; I will return to this issue in the section below on comparison consequences.

The Active Comparer?

Research on choice of comparison others makes clear that people must be adept at controlling the comparison situations they are in such that they will be sure to have at their disposal comparison targets that satisfy relevant motives. If no satisfactory targets are available, people may employ creative strategies such as comparing themselves to social stereotypes (Brickman & Bulman, 1977; Gibbons, Gerrard, Lando, & McGovern, 1991; O'Gorman, 1988; Perloff & Fetzer, 1986; Weinstein, 1980), inventing comparison targets (e.g., "I can probably do this better than most people"; see Orive, 1988; Suls, 1986; Taylor, Buunk, & Aspinwall, 1990; Taylor et al.,

1983; Wood, 1989), or avoiding comparison completely (Goethals, 1986). Thus, a picture emerges in which an *active* perceiver sorts through a variety of possible targets for comparison, perhaps constructs that comparison (Goethals et al., 1991), and makes a choice based on his or her internal state (e.g., self-esteem) or motive (e.g., self-enhancement; Buunk et al., 1990; Buunk & Ybema, 1997; Diener & Fujita, 1997; Kruglanski & Mayseless, 1990; Levine & Moreland, 1986; Taylor et al., 1995; Wheeler, 1966; Wheeler & Miyake, 1992; Wills, 1981).

Consistent with this "active" view, when considering whether environmentally imposed comparisons affected well-being, Diener and Fujita (1997) answered a resounding "no." Instead, "people may use social comparisons in a flexible and strategic way to cope with situations and enhance their subjective well-being" (p. 352). For instance, people's degree of satisfaction with outcomes such as income level and health often depends more heavily on variables such as personal goals, culturally prescribed ideals, construction of counterfactual situations, and past achievement than on environmentally imposed comparisons. Others have noted, too, the strategic nature of social comparison choices. In reviewing the "related attributes" approach to defining similarity of comparison to other, Goethals and Klein (2000) note that individuals have a lot of leeway in identifying related attributes and can then "fudge that information to make the most of the comparison outcome" (p. 28).

However, one can also consider a more active environment that forces comparisons on an unprepared perceiver. Social comparisons may often be spontaneous, effortless, and unintentional; Wood et al. (2000) reported that participants indicated some 32% of their social comparisons were unintended. Thus, comparison information present in the environment may affect one's self-evaluation even without deliberate awareness and even though one may later "correct" for such comparisons (Collins, 2000; Gilbert, Giesler, & Morris, 1995; Wood, 1996). It is also the case that proximal others are especially likely to serve as comparison targets, given their greater availability (Levine & Moreland, 1987; Major, 1994), and that efforts to distance oneself from threatening comparisons can be difficult because threatening others are typically highly salient in the environment (Miller & Prentice, 1996). Salient groups (e.g., vocal minorities) may be particularly likely to influence self-evaluations (Korte, 1972; Schanck, 1932). Furthermore, others may affect how one evaluates the self even if they are present only in a psychological sense (e.g., I think about the group "social psychologists" when evaluating how successful I am as a scholar; McFarland & Buehler, 1995; Smith & Tyler, 1997) or only at nonconscious levels (Baldwin & Holmes, 1987). And, rather than engage in an elaborate process of seeking out the appropriate comparison standard in any given situation, individuals may rely on "routine standards"—"standards that have been frequently used for self-evaluation" (Mussweiler & Rüter, 2003, p. 467). Furthermore, recent research suggests that even *subliminally presented* standards affect self-evaluation in predictable ways—self-ratings assimilate to moderate standards and are contrasted from extreme standards (Mussweiler, Rüter, & Epstude, 2004; Stapel & Blanton, 2004). In all of these examples, the environment exerts power over the perceiver merely by providing salient, available, or routinized comparison targets (sex-segregated job settings are an example of this influence; Major, 1994).

Finally, research on the "frog-pond" or "big fish in little pond" effect also points to an active environment that affects the judgments people make of themselves (Davis, 1966; Marsh & Hau, 2003). According to this line of research, people often evaluate themselves more positively if they perform well relative to others in their environment (i.e., if they are "big fish in little ponds") than if their performance suffers relative to others, assuming identical performance in both environments (i.e., if they are "small fish in big ponds"; Marsh & Hau, 2003). Boersma, Chapman, and Battle (1979) demonstrated this effect by showing that children who are below average in academic ability have higher self-concepts when placed in a classroom environment with similar peers as opposed to a regular classroom environment with average-performing peers (see also Marsh & Parker, 1984). In a recent analysis of school children from 26 countries, Marsh and Hau (2003) also documented that *across all levels of achievement—* that is, regardless of whether one performed objectively well or poorly in school—the higher the performance of peers, the less positive one's self-concept. Such findings illustrate that the environment may force comparisons on the perceiver and that these comparisons have real cognitive and emotional consequences (see also Miller & Prentice, 1996). Discussing his findings that people made upward and downward comparisons equally often yet felt better after downward comparisons, Locke (2003) writes, "Perhaps one reason why many comparison choices seem to make no sense is that in fact many comparisons are not choices" (p. 629).

Nonetheless, it seems reasonable to conclude that *within* a given environment, people may still exercise considerable choice over the target with whom they compare. To quote Gilbert et al. (1995), "a lack of complete control is not a complete lack of control" (p. 233). Gilbert and colleagues allow for the possibility that, even though comparisons may be to some extent automatic and beyond the perceiver's control, the perceiver may still be able to control with whom he or she comes into contact and which comparisons to correct or revise (for related themes on the strategic selection of social environments, see Frank, 1985; Parducci, 1995). Further, within a comparison context, people will often engage in creative strategies to satisfy various motives. Comparers have shown themselves capable of ignoring aspects of the environment in the event that they do not suit their goals. In short, there is much evidence to suggest that people will go to great lengths to "get what they want" from the comparative process (Collins, 1996; Wood, 1989).

☐ Consequences of Social Comparison

The consequences of social comparison have been hinted at throughout this chapter, but I will turn to a direct consideration of them here. It is in the outcomes or consequences of social comparison that the phenomena of assimilation and contrast can be seen.

Perhaps the most common outcomes examined in social comparison research are affective (as in measures of mood or self-esteem) or cognitive/ evaluative (as in evaluative trait ratings, particularly on the dimension of the comparison) in nature. A classic study on responses to social comparison focused on self-esteem outcomes. In Morse and Gergen's (1970) "Mr. Clean/Mr. Dirty" study, prospective job candidates' self-esteem was harmed by upward comparison to the well-dressed competitor, Mr. Clean, but improved by downward comparison to the sloppy competitor, Mr. Dirty. This basic pattern—downward comparisons feel good, upward comparisons feel bad—has been noted in many studies (for reviews, see Lockwood, 2002; Major et al., 1991; Smith, 2000; Buunk et al., 1990), and particularly in situations where comparison targets are forced upon the perceiver (Buunk & Ybema, 1997).[3] These are *contrast* effects, and they reflect the basic notion of social comparison standards as *distinct* points of reference against which the self is evaluated. However, *assimilation* to comparison standards also occurs and is facilitated by the perception of similarity between self and standard, as will be discussed below (Mussweiler, 2003).

I will note here too that how people react to comparisons often has more to do with their subjective construal of the comparison information than with its objective nature (DeVellis et al., 1991; Diener & Fujita, 1997). In one study, women with rheumatoid arthritis were asked to compare their coping ability with that of women who were portrayed as coping either better or worse than themselves (DeVellis et al., 1991). Participants exposed to the superior coper rated her coping ability higher than they rated their own on an indirect measure (in which they provided separate ratings of self and other). However, they overwhelmingly denied the superior coping of the other when asked to make a direct comparison. The authors concluded that participants may have reconstructed their perceptions of either themselves or the stimulus woman so as to avoid a comparison that would reflect badly on themselves. This kind of cognitive reconstruction is captured in some definitions of comparative consequences: Levine and Moreland (1986) defined cognitive responses to comparisons as the "source's *distortions* of his or her own outcomes or related attributes or those of the target" (p. 293, emphasis added). Thus, construal of the comparison standard—which may include an assessment of the similarity between self and other—will be key to determining the direction of the comparison outcome (assimilation or contrast).

The Similarity Principle

The role of construal in reactions to social comparison is illustrated quite nicely by considering a comparer's attempts to self-enhance through assimilation to a superior other—a topic to which I alluded earlier in this chapter. Although this phenomenon had not received a great deal of attention until fairly recently (Collins, 1996), assimilation to an upward target to self-enhance was demonstrated very early in the history of social comparison research (Wheeler, 1966). In reflecting on the paradox that people are often motivated to compare upward even though such comparisons may lead to negative affect and unfavorable evaluation, Wheeler (1966) suggested that the comparer, in such situations, assumes similarity with the superior other and will experience negative comparison consequences only to the extent that he or she is not as similar to the target as expected. Wheeler's results were consistent with this prediction: In his research, a majority (75%) of the participants who compared upward perceived themselves as similar to the comparison target, but only a minority (36%) of those who compared downward assumed they were similar to the upward targets.

More recently, Collins (1996, 2000) directly invoked the processes of assimilation and contrast to explain the consequences of comparing upward. On the one hand, if one expects to be different from an upward target, one pays particular attention to these differences and will contrast oneself from the target. This could arguably lead to the comparer seeing him- or herself as even more different from (worse than) the target than is actually the case. On the other hand, an expectation that one is similar to an upward target results in the perceptual "blurring" of actual differences between self and target, leading the comparer to assimilate the self to the target. It is through this assimilative process that an upward comparison target may actually be used to self-enhance.

These ideas are very similar to those articulated by Mussweiler (2003a, b) in his Selective Accessibility Model (SAM) and by Markman and McMullen (2003) in their Reflection-Evaluation Model, both reviewed in Chapter 3. Both models suggest that the outcome of a comparison process depends on the information that is accessible at the time of that comparison. For Mussweiler (2003), what is accessible depends on whether one engages in similarity or dissimilarity testing—is the target similar to the standard, or is the target dissimilar to the standard? Because of biased hypothesis testing, a test of similarity will make similarity information accessible, resulting in assimilation to the target, but a test of dissimilarity will make dissimilarity information accessible, resulting in contrast. For Markman and McMullen (2003), the context might prompt a reflection process that involves "as if" thinking, in which one simulates being like that target, or an evaluation process, against which one compares. Thus, in the case of an upward comparison target (say, Leon Festinger, when it comes to assessing my skill as a social psychologist), I may be prompted toward similarity testing and reflection ("Festinger and I both spent time at the Research Center for Group Dynamics at the University of Michigan; I'm like him!") or toward dissimilarity testing and evaluation ("he worked with Lewin, won every top award in psychology, and authored multiple classics in the field; I'm not in his league!"). Assimilation results in the former case, but contrast in the latter.

If upward targets are used to self-enhance, we should expect positive affect and self-evaluations to result from such comparisons. Wood (1989) reviewed evidence supporting this prediction, and highlighted "feelings of inspiration" as another component of this general positive affect (Wood and van der Zee, 1997; see also Lockwood & Kunda, 1999). In one study of interest, women's self-assessments of attractiveness were generally *contrasted* from highly attractive standards (a photograph of a very attractive woman). However, when the attractive other was similar to the self—because she shared one's attitudes or one's birthday, *assimilation* occurred—women judged themselves more attractive after exposure to very attractive, similar others (Brown et al., 1992).

But the default condition in Brown et al.'s (1992) study was dissimilarity between self and the attractive other, and this produced contrast. Wood (1989) has also argued that upward comparisons can have negative consequences if the comparison target is perceived as a competitor—again, someone *dissimilar* from the self and from whom the self is contrasted. Lockwood and Kunda's (1997) research on "superstars," discussed earlier, also found that dissimilar upward comparison targets—those whose accomplishments could not possibly be attained by the self—produced a contrast effect (negative self-evaluations on traits related to career success). And Collins (1996) noted that individuals with chronic low self-esteem are unlikely to benefit from upward comparison because of their expectations of dissimilarity with superior others. A field study of nurses also documented that upward comparisons were damaging for those with low levels of personal accomplishment or who were experiencing burnout

(Buunk, Ybema, van der Zee, Schaufeli, & Gibbons, 2001). Again, for Mussweiler (2003), these contrastive outcomes can be explained in terms of dissimilarity testing; for Markman and McMullen (2003), the "too different from me" upward others lead to "evaluation" or use of the other as a standard against which the self is (negatively) judged.

Interestingly, the inspirational effects of attainable upward comparison targets can also be undermined (and result in affective contrast) if one's *most positive self-views* are made salient (Lockwood and Kunda, 1999). For example, reminding participants of past academic success produced affective contrast from a superior–performing other compared to conditions in which the more neutral present was primed. This occurs, presumably, because remembering one's best past self "constrains the positivity of the future selves one may imagine and prevents one from generating the more spectacular future selves that the role model normally inspires" (Lockwood & Kunda, 1999, p. 214). That is, salient images of past accomplishments render *that* information accessible and reduce the odds that the present self can be assimilated to the upward target.

Other Moderators of Comparison Consequences

Also relevant to the issue of consequences of *upward* comparison is Tesser's self-evaluation maintenance (SEM) theory (Tesser, 1988; Tesser & Campbell, 1983; Tesser & Campbell, 1980; Tesser & Paulhus, 1983). The SEM assumes that people are motivated to self-enhance and offers an explanation for the finding that upward comparisons can result in either very positive or very negative consequences. Essentially, Tesser's model proposes that the *self-relevance* of the dimension on which one is outperformed determines whether reflection (assimilation) or comparison (contrast) occurs. If a close other performs well on a dimension that is *not* central to one's self-definition, one benefits by being able to *reflect* in the success of the other, or to bask in reflected glory (Cialdini et al., 1976). It is through this mechanism that one is able to boast proudly of the high school friend who went on to play professional football or the relative who climbed Mt. Everest—a kind of assimilation. One's self-esteem may suffer, on the other hand, if a close other performs well on a dimension that is important to the self. Thus, when my husband publishes a *Psychological Bulletin* article and I am rejected, jealousy, negative affect, and self-evaluation may result—a form of contrast from the upward target.

Interestingly, closeness as conceptualized in the SEM should enhance *similarity* testing—the factor in Mussweiler's (2003) SAM model that moves one toward *assimilation*. But in the case of clear outperformance by a close other, the *difference* in self- and other attainment may be highly accessible.

Specifically, such a comparison may activate the *distinctive* aspects of the self (i.e., as a worse performer), producing contrast (see Broemer & Diehl, 2004). However, closeness may also incline one toward assimilation to the extent that one construes the upward target as part of the self. Specifically, the general pattern of contrast predicted by SEM when one is outperformed by a close other can be reversed following manipulations designed to "expand" the notion of self (Gardner, Gabriel, & Hochschild, 2002).

Others have identified additional factors that moderate comparison outcomes (Brewer & Weber, 1994; Brown et al., 1992; Cash et al., 1983; McFarland & Buehler, 1995; Pelham & Wachsmuth, 1995). Mussweiler and Bodenhausen (2002) focused on in-group–out-group status as one such factor. They found that comparison to in-group members prompts similarity testing, the selective accessibility of standard-consistent information, and judgmental assimilation. For example, when men compared themselves with a "highly caring" male standard, self-assessments of caringness were high—an assimilation effect. But a comparison with a highly caring *female* standard—an out-group target—prompted dissimilarity testing and contrast. McFarland, Buehler, and MacKay (2001) also found that assimilation (to both upward and downward targets) was enhanced when participants shared an identity relationship with the standard (see also Blanton et al., 2000, 2002).

In a related study, however, in-group and out-group status did not fully explain the pattern of effects. Brewer and Weber (1994) did find that members of *minority groups* produced the pattern articulated above— they assimilated themselves to in-group members but contrasted themselves from out-group members, with respect to self-evaluations. But majority group members *contrasted* themselves from fellow in-group members and were unaffected by comparison with out-group members. Brewer and Weber (1994) suggest that this difference has to do with the level of self-categorization activated for minority versus majority group members. Members of minority groups are likely to self-categorize at the social level given the relative salience of their group membership, but members of majority groups tend to think of themselves at the individual or personal level. Thus, sharing a group membership with a comparison target may produce similarity testing and assimilation only if the group level identity is salient.

Back to the Similarity Principle

To summarize, research suggests that assimilation of the self to an upward comparison target will generally occur when an individual (1) shares group membership with the other (Mussweiler & Bodenhausen, 2002),

(2) perceives the self as similar to the other (Collins, 1996), (3) is certain about her or his standing on the comparison dimension (Pelham & Wachsmuth, 1995), (4) believes that the other's success on a self-defining dimension is attainable (Buunk & Ybema, 1997; Lockwood & Kunda, 1997), (5) views the self as mutable (Stapel & Koomen, 2000; Stapel & Suls, 2004), and (6) believes the self-standard discrepancy can be overcome and controlled (Major et al., 1991). Additionally, (7) simply simulating the idea that one is like the standard may prompt assimilation (Markman & McMullen, 2003), as may (8) making a social comparison explicit ("are you more or less intelligent than Marie Curie?") rather than implicit (simply thinking about Marie Curie; Stapel & Suls, 2004). All of these moderating factors may boil down to the basic notion of *inclusion* in Schwarz and Bless's (1992a) inclusion-exclusion model (see Chapter 3) and the *accessibility* of information that the self is similar to the target (Mussweiler, 2003). That is, if one can claim or envision or has available evidence of oneself as *included* in the category of the upward comparison target, assimilation rather than contrast will occur.

This is also the case with *downward* comparisons. To the extent that one views a downward outcome as possible for the self—particularly if one actively simulates this outcome—*assimilation* results (Lockwood, 2002). Specifically, in three studies, Lockwood (2002) found that *vulnerability* moderated the self-evaluative response to a downward target. If participants felt as though they could be like the downward target— as when college undergraduates compared to a recent graduate who was having trouble on the job market—negative self-evaluation resulted (assimilation to the downward target). But when this vulnerability was reduced— when the comparison was to a fellow undergraduate doing much worse than the self in the immediate college context—positive self-evaluation was the result (contrast). However, these effects only occurred after an active simulation of being like the downward other (e.g., "what do you think could cause you to have a similar academic experience?") (Lockwood, 2002, pp. 346–347).

More generally, comparing with a worse-off other may be threatening only if the target's outcome is perceived to be uncontrollable, in that uncontrollability implies "it could happen to me" (Major et al., 1991). In Taylor and Lobel's (1989) review of their work with cancer patients, they suggest that comparing downwardly—for instance, to a patient who is coping more poorly—may remind one of what the future may hold. Here, uncontrollability implies (potential) similarity.

Recently, Locke (2003) touched on this central notion of inclusion when he described "connections" or "solidarity" with the target of comparison. Features such as shared group membership (Mussweiler & Bodenhausen, 2002) or shared birthdays (Brown et al., 1992), vulnerability to another's negative outcomes (Lockwood, 2002), or a primed sense of the self as socially integrated or "expanded" (Gardner et al., 2002; Stapel & Koomen, 2001a) increase inclusion and assimilation.

Behavioral Consequences

Relative to affect and cognition, behavioral reactions to social comparison have been studied rarely. Nevertheless, some research on upward comparisons does point to an important positive behavioral outcome: Making upward comparisons may generate negative affect but also feelings of inspiration that can sometimes lead to behavioral improvement (Blanton, Buunk, Gibbons, & Kuyper, 1999; Gibbons et al., 2000; Major et al., 1991; Seta, 1982; Seta, Seta, & Donaldson, 1991; cf., Markman & McMullen, 2003). In one study, smokers who preferred upward comparisons—comparisons to those doing better than they in terms of quitting—were more likely to have succeeded in their cessation attempts six months later (Gerrard, Gibbons, Lane, & Reis-Bergan, 2002; cited in Gibbons et al., 2002).

As noted in Chapter 3 of this volume, Markman and McMullen's (2003) Reflection–Evaluation Model was designed to predict motivational-behavioral outcomes of comparative thinking. In this model, all behavioral consequences are mediated by affect, but positive and negative affect are posited to produce different levels of behavioral *persistence*, depending on the type of task. Specifically, through "mood as information" processes, positive affect should produce less persistence on *achievement tasks* but more persistence on *enjoyment tasks*. That is, because positive affect produces a "yes" response to the question "Have I achieved my goal?" persistence in pursuit of goals is likely to decrease. But positive affect also produces a "yes" response to the question "Am I enjoying myself?" and thus persistence should be heightened on enjoyment tasks (see Markman & McMullen, 2003; Martin, Ward, Achee, & Wyer, 1993; Schwarz, 1990).

This leads to the interesting prediction that in social comparison situations that prompt positive affect—say, in upward comparison to an attainable other (Lockwood & Kunda, 1997)—behavioral perseverance may *not* result. Instead, those inspired by the other may find themselves lacking the motivation to persist on tasks relevant to achieving the high standard. Although I am not aware of research directly testing this prediction, Markman and McMullen (2003) cite research by Oettingen and colleagues on the role of fantasy and expectations in motivation (Oettingen & Mayer, 2002; Oettingen, 1996). As discussed in Chapter 7 of this book, this research suggests that positive fantasy—"mentally enjoying future outcomes" (Oettingen & Mayer, 2002, p. 1199)—may undermine motivation and success because it takes energy away from activity that would otherwise be directed toward achieving the goal. Thus, upward comparison targets may create high expectations for one's own future success which are inspiring and motivating. But at the same time, those who compare upward may find themselves fantasizing rather than exerting effort toward meeting the high standard. Apparently, this can be overcome, however, if perceivers are led to explicitly contrast their positive fantasies with *reality*. This makes both present and future accessible and seems to produce enhanced motivation and success (Oettingen, Pak, & Schnetter, 2001).

Researchers have also linked comparison outcomes to basic self-regulatory strategies (Pennington & Roese, 2003). Specifically, Markman and McMullen (2003) have relied on Higgins' (1998) distinction between *promotion* and *prevention* strategies in predicting likely outcomes of social and other comparisons. As discussed in Chapter 7, promotion orientation involves a focus on growth, advancement, or approaching of desirable outcomes. Prevention focus, on the other hand, is regulation geared toward avoiding undesirable outcomes. "An upward comparison represents a desirable outcome and thus may activate promotion goals to obtain that outcome, whereas a downward comparison represents an undesirable outcome and thus may activate prevention goals so that the outcome does not occur" (Markman & McMullen, 2003, p. 252). Lockwood (2002) found that simulation of the self as like an attainable downward comparison target indeed enhanced *prevention* goals (measured through items like "I am more concerned with avoiding failure than with achieving success") and reduced *promotion* goals ("I see myself as someone who is striving to achieve my 'ideal self' ...").

However, direction of comparison alone cannot be directly mapped onto these regulatory strategies. Instead, the use of reflection (assimilation) versus evaluation (contrast) tells the actor where she or he stands in relation to the goal. That is, the upward comparison to Leon Festinger may generally activate promotion goals, but if the reflection process (simulating that I am like Leon Festinger) tells me I am meeting the goal (positive fantasies kick in), my promotion orientation may be weakened. And while downward comparisons may generally trigger prevention goals, the evaluation process produces a contrast effect that tells me I am successfully avoiding the undesired outcome. Again, the prevention focus may be weakened. This leads Markman and McMullen (2003) to predict that promotion goals will be most strongly activated when one engages in evaluation relative to an upward target (contrast effect) and that prevention goals will be most strongly activated when one engages in reflection with a downward target (assimilation effect). In these cases, one has feedback that a desired end state is not being attained (something like Oettingen et al.'s [2001] simultaneous activation of fantasy and reality), and motivation is heightened. These links between comparison direction, affect, and self-regulation are intriguing and await further empirical test.

The Importance of Construal, Revisited

All of the data I have reviewed on the consequences of social comparison highlight the fact that construal processes play a significant role in the process. Downward comparison, traditionally thought to be self-enhancing, can have adverse consequences just as upward comparison, traditionally considered detrimental, can have positive consequences. And much of this depends on what one does with the comparison information—one can perceive similarity or not with the comparison other; one can reconstrue information such that the self is protected even in light of negative information (DeVellis et al., 1991). The genius effect—the tendency to perceive those who outperform us as particularly brilliant—provides a very telling example of the importance of construal (Alicke LoSchiavo, Zerbst, & Zhang, 1997). By "aggrandizing the outperformer" (relative to uninvolved observers' perceptions of that person), we can stave off the self-esteem threat posed by underperforming. Interestingly, this "genius" attribution may make the other so discrepant from the self that comparison is not even viable.

Some studies have also documented *differing* effects of the *same* social comparison. For example, married women experienced more *positive* moods (assimilation) but more *negative* evaluations of their own marriages (contrast) when they compared with an upward versus downward comparison standard (another married woman; Buunk & Ybema, 2003). These authors suggest that "the mood evoked by social comparison is primarily a primitive, direct, and automatic response" whereas evaluation of one's marriage is "a separate, cognitive, process" (p. 614). Thus, one can feel inspired but concerned about one's own marriage when a comparison to better-off others occurs.

Taken as a whole, the literature relevant to comparison consequences leads to the conclusion, in the words of Buunk et al. (1990), that either direction of comparison—upward or downward—"has its ups and downs." Furthermore, although I have focused on affective responses in simplistic positive–negative terms, it is also the case that a diverse set of emotions may be experienced in response to social comparison. Depression, shame, resentment, or envy may all emerge as *contrastive* responses to *upward* comparisons; optimism, admiration, and inspiration as *assimilative* responses to upward comparisons; pride, contempt, and *schadenfreude* as *contrastive* responses to *downward* comparisons; worry, pity, and sympathy as *assimilative* responses to downward comparisons (Smith, 2000). The impact of a comparison will ultimately be determined not by its direction but by the way in which it is perceived and interpreted by the comparer.

☐ How Common Is Social Comparison?

This chapter has highlighted social comparison and its importance as "a pervasive and fundamental feature of group life" (Hogg, 2000, p. 401). But it is important to acknowledge that the social standard could also be the *self* at an earlier (or perhaps future) time. Specifically, Albert (1977) proposed a model of "temporal comparison" that paralleled Festinger's theory, though he suggested that such temporal information would be used only when objective or social information was unavailable. In a series of papers, Suls and Mullen (1982, 1984) suggested that social comparison is more common than temporal comparison *except* during developmental periods characterized by rapid change (e.g., in children aged 3 to 5 and in those over age 65; see also Suls, 1986). However, others have found a preference for temporal over social comparisons (e.g., Sedikides & Skowronski, 1995; see Wood & Wilson, 2003, for a review). In their study of undergraduates' judgments about academic and social life, Wayment and Taylor (1995) found temporal comparisons to be more frequently used than social comparisons (or objective information). Similarly, in studies of individuals coping with medical problems (rheumatoid arthritis, infertility, ill infants), *spontaneous* mentions of comparisons were more likely to be temporal than social in nature (Affleck & Tennen, 1991).

More recently, Wilson and Ross (2000, Studies 1 and 3) found temporal-past comparisons to be more frequent than social comparisons or temporal-future comparisons. Furthermore, these temporal-past comparisons tended to be *downward* in nature—that is, individuals compared themselves to a past self that was worse off. Not surprisingly, when temporal-future comparisons were made, they tended to be upward in nature. It seems likely that the choice of comparison target—temporal or social, upward or downward—is highly dependent on the goals of the perceiver in the situation. In one study, Wilson and Ross (2000, Study 4) directly manipulated goals. Some participants were instructed to give accurate self-assessments and others to describe themselves in a way that "makes you feel particularly good about yourself" (p. 936). Descriptions of social skills and self-confidence documented that those in the self-enhancement condition made more temporal-past than social comparisons, and these tended to be *downward* in direction. But those in the accuracy/self-assessment condition made more social than temporal comparisons, and these tended to be *upward* in direction. These findings make the case for the importance of both temporal and social comparisons and for the *strategic* nature of their use. Comparisons are chosen to meet the needs of the individual in a given context.

The ubiquity or inevitability of social comparisons has also been challenged on another level, in an interesting recent line of research that suggests that "explicitly comparative judgments are often focused solo judgments" (Moore & Kim, 2003, p. 1133). That is, even when individuals are asked explicitly to compare themselves to others (as in predicting the likelihood of beating a competitor), they instead base their judgments almost solely on consideration of the self. Thus, I assume I have better odds of winning an easy quiz than a difficult quiz, even though my odds of winning do not shift since my opponent faces the same constraints imposed by task difficulty (see additional discussion of this finding in Chapter 4). This has been dubbed the *myopic* or *solo comparison effect* (Moore & Kim 2003; Windschitl et al., 2003). Similarly, research suggests that relative judgments (such as "how content are you with your life, compared to the average person?") correlate more strongly with nonrelative self-judgments ("how content are you?") than with nonrelative judgments of others ("how content is the average person?"; Klar & Giladi, 1999). This suggests too that comparative judgments are more driven by consideration of the self than by consideration of others in the context (see also Eiser et al., 2001; Epley & Dunning, 2000). Moore and Kim (2003) suggest that this discrepancy between the seeming ubiquity of social comparison and findings indicating "myopia" can be reconciled by considering the "readiness of the data at one's disposal" (p. 1133). If information about others' standing is available, it will be used and produce the kinds of social comparison effects that have been highlighted in this chapter. But when people only have information about themselves—as when they are predicting likely performance on a trivia quiz or estimating contentment with life—this information is likely to be highlighted relative to information about others.

Still, social comparisons appear to occur *frequently, easily,* and *nonconsciously,* if not ubiquitously. Particularly persuasive in this regard are recent findings suggesting that subliminally presented comparison information affects self-evaluation and spontaneous *behavioral* outcomes (such as the size of one's signature as an indicator of self-regard; Stapel & Blanton, 2004, Study 4; see also Mussweiler et al., 2004).

☐ Summary

This consideration of social comparison has focused on three general topics: motives for comparing, choice of a comparison target and direction of comparison, and the consequences of comparison. It is tempting to suggest that each motive has a unique link to a comparison choice, which then produces a unique outcome. For example, the motive to self-enhance may prompt downward comparisons, which then produce affective contrast; the motive to self-improve may prompt upward comparisons and behavioral assimilation. However, decades of research, only some of which was considered here, suggests that things are much more complex than this. It may be the case that downward comparisons frequently do allow for self-enhancement, but as I hope this review makes clear, motives may lead to preferences for different kinds of comparisons under different conditions, and the outcomes of these comparisons may be assimilative *or* contrastive.

It may be more productive to think of motives, comparison choice, and comparison outcomes not in terms of their unique links to each other but rather as a series of steps through which self-judgments are gradually constructed. A person's precomparison state may determine the comparison-related motive that will operate in a given situation; that motive may affect the choice of comparison target or the construal of the target, and the information made accessible at the point of the target–self comparison will determine the ultimate consequence for the self (assimilation or contrast). For instance, an individual making slow progress toward an important goal may be motivated to improve the self and may therefore choose an upward target—a role model—with whom to compare. The goal of improving may lead this person to "similarity testing"—assuming attainability or similarity to the upward target—which renders accessible standard-consistent information about the self (Mussweiler, 2003) or simulations of the self as like the standard (Markman & McMullen, 2003). This might prompt positive affect and a promotion focus that enhances motivation to achieve the high standard. At the same time, it may activate fantasy thinking that undermines motivation in the here and now (Oettingen & Mayer, 2002).

Of course, other consequences are possible if one begins with dissimilarity testing or evaluation, or if one begins with a different motive entirely, say, self-assessment. Because goals, available comparison targets, and cues prompting assimilation versus contrast vary from person to person and context to context, perceivers are remarkably flexible (and often self-serving or self-protective) in their responsiveness to the judgment standards imposed by other people.

☐ Notes

1. This chapter is partly based on material that appeared in Biernat and Billings (2001).
2. Here I feel compelled to quote one of my daughter's current favorite books, Dr. Seuss's (1973) *Did I Ever Tell You How Lucky You Are.* This contains the downward-comparison advice: "When you think things are bad, when you feel sour and blue, when you start

to get mad, you should do what I do. Just tell yourself, Duckie, you're really quite lucky! Some people are much more … oh ever so much more … oh muchly much-much more unlucky than you."

3. It is worth noting that in the literature on counterfactual thinking, which is not reviewed in this book, similar patterns have been noted. That is, upward comparisons (to better-off outcomes) produce negative mood and self-evaluations, whereas downward comparisons (to worse-off outcomes) produce positive mood and self-evaluations (Markman, Gavanski, Sherman, & McMullen, 1993; Roese, 1994; Sanna, Turley-Ames, & Meier, 1999).

10

Assimilation and Contrast Revisited

> If we say that a thing is great or small by its own standard of great or small, then there is nothing in all creation which is not great, nothing which is not small (Chuang Tzu, *Works*, [4th–3rd century B.C.], tr. Lin Yu-tang).

This book represents my attempt to consider a wide variety of literatures on self- and other-judgment and to extract from it some general themes about how standards and expectations operate. The above quote from the Chinese philosopher Chuang Tzu appeals to me because it reflects the idea that the assessment of any object (be it self or other) requires reference to some interpretive frame or standard, that that standard can vary from object to object (and presumably also from time to time or context to context), and that depending on the standard at hand, judgment can vary dramatically—you and I can be great *and* small!

The themes of assimilation and contrast have dominated this book, and in every chapter, I have tried to highlight that both outcomes can occur depending on specifiable conditions. Chapter 2 laid out these conditions in detail, focusing on the role of contextual cues as expectations or standards. As indicated in Table 2.1, features of the judgment task, the standard/context, and the target all contribute to when assimilation and when contrast occurs. Specifically, task features such as obviousness of the prime/context or reminders of the prime and explicit instructions to form impressions contribute to *contrast* effects, whereas more subtle primes and instructions to memorize are more likely to produce *assimilation* (Moskowitz & Roman; 1992; Strack et al., 1993). With regard to features of the context itself, *extreme* and *distinct* or *non-entitative* primes or contexts are more likely to prompt contrast, whereas moderate and broad or entitative contexts prompt assimilation (Herr, 1986; Hilton & von Hippel, 1990; Stapel et al., 1996; Wedell et al., 1987). *Ambiguous* targets are more likely to be assimilated to contexts, whereas extreme or unambiguous targets are more likely to be contrasted (Stapel et al., 1997), and judgments made in subjective units are more likely to prompt contrast than those made on common-rule rating scales (Biernat et al., 1991). Furthermore, for *any* kind of context effect to occur—assimilation or contrast—there must be some relevance or *applicability* of the context to evaluating the target (Banaji et al., 1993; Brown, 1953), *and* the judgment dimension must be relevant to the target as well (Higgins et al., 1977). That is, exposure to apples should not affect judgments of oranges, unless "fruitiness" of apples—a dimension common to apples and oranges—was previously judged (Schwarz et al., 1990).

In Chapter 3, I reviewed a number of models of assimilation and contrast in social judgment. All of these represent attempts to incorporate at least some of the features and findings identified in Chapter 2; all make claims about when assimilation versus contrast is more likely. The models differ in terms of whether they claim a "default" process or not and, relatedly, whether one outcome is presumed to be more automatic than the other; they differ in whether they explicitly consider *corrective* contrast as distinct from *comparative* contrast; they differ in whether they posit a sequential or simultaneous operation of assimilative and contrastive processes; they differ in whether they deal primarily with self- or other-judgments; and they differ in the extent to which they highlight mechanisms through which context effects emerge (e.g., selective accessibility [Mussweiler, 2003]; mental simulation [Markman & McMullen, 2003]).

As a general framework, I think Schwarz and Bless's (1992a) inclusion–exclusion model is extremely useful. It highlights the bottom line of assimilation and contrast, namely, that assimilation is more likely when the target is included in the context and that contrast is more likely when the target is excluded. For related reasons, Stapel and colleagues' interpretation–comparison model is important in describing the two basic roles that context can play—a framework that affects the interpretation of a stimulus in an assimilative fashion, or a standard of comparison against which targets are compared and contrasted (Stapel & Koomen, 1998, 2001b). This model also explicitly describes features of context and target—such as distinctiveness, breadth, and extremity—that determine which role context will play in any given situation. The expectation–contrast model of Manis and Paskewitz (1984a) also incorporates these basic roles of context but makes the unique prediction that both roles can be played simultaneously. In any given situation, the interpretive and comparative roles may be triggered, but the outcome depends on the relative weight of those roles. Though not specified in the model, this weighting likely depends on the same features central to the interpretation–comparison model, namely, distinctiveness and extremity, and perhaps also target ambiguity. Like the basic principles of inclusion and exclusion, the idea that contexts play a dual role—in which one typically dominates—provides a useful lens through which to view the judgment literature. Interestingly, this model, perhaps more so than the others, also provides some basis for predicting *null effects* of context. Though null effects are problematic for theory testing, their occurrence is at least predictable from the basis of the expectation–contrast model.

Several of the models are also useful in describing the active nature of a contrastive process—that judges may desire to "partial out" the effects of a context on their judgment. That is, rather than contrast resulting from a basic comparative process, one might want to "correct" one's judgment away from the context (see also Wilson & Brekke, 1994). This theme is central to Martin's (1986) set/reset model and relevant as well to the inclusion–exclusion model (Schwarz & Bless, 1992a). It seems quite clear that *this* kind of contrast requires intent and cognitive resources, unlike comparative contrast which can function relatively automatically (e.g., see DeCoster & Claypool, 2004). However, Wegener and Petty's (1995) flexible-correction model challenges the assumption that only contrast is corrective. Instead, assimilative correction can occur as well. Central to this model is the notion of "naïve theories" about context effects. If judges believe, for example, that a context is likely to produce an assimilative effect, they may indeed "correct" in a contrastive direction. But if context is believed to produce contrast—as when perceivers assume that considering Paris will make them think less of Indianapolis as a vacation site—correction will occur in an assimilative direction. The recent general model of informational biases proposed by DeCoster and Claypool (2004) is noteworthy for its incorporation of both this active flexible correction mechanism *and* a more automatic "associative" process that can produce either assimilation or contrast, depending on the distinctiveness of the context (and the target's inclusion in it).

Also described in Chapter 3 were two process models—the selective accessibility model (SAM) (Mussweiler, 2003) and the reflection and evaluation model (REM) (Markman & McMullen, 2003). These are both noteworthy for their focus on knowledge accessibility as a key determinant of the outcome of comparative processes, a point Mussweiler and his colleagues had advanced in earlier papers as well (see Mussweiler, 2001a, b;

Mussweiler & Strack, 2000). Specifically, the SAM suggests that contexts give rise to either similarity or dissimilarity testing (which of these occurs can depend on the framing of the judgment task, among other things) and that these processes make accessible hypothesis-consistent information. That is, engaging in similarity testing will call to mind information consistent with the standard, and engaging in dissimilarity testing will call to mind information inconsistent with the standard. Accessibility directly determines the judgment outcome—assimilation or contrast, respectively. In the REM, accessibility also matters, though a process of mental simulation—in which information can be imagined rather than retrieved from memory—makes standard-consistent or-inconsistent information accessible. The REM also posits a form of parallel processing similar to that proposed by Manis and Paskewitz (1984a).

In my opinion, the contributions of the SAM and REM are extremely important to the development of the field of social judgment. By articulating process mechanisms and making links to other process literatures (biased hypothesis testing in the case of the SAM; imagination–explanation in the case of the REM), and by incorporating findings from the literatures on social comparison (in both models) and counterfactual thinking (in the REM), they provide broad and inclusive research-generative perspectives. The REM is primarily focused on self- rather than other-judgment and is noteworthy in its attempts to address affective, motivational, and behavioral consequences of the comparative process—outcomes rarely specifically addressed in the other models.

In Chapter 4, I considered self and other exemplars as standards for judging others. Here again, themes of assimilation and contrast (based on identifiable features of the judgment situation) abound. For example, findings regarding asymmetry in similarity judgments—my sense that you are more similar to me than I am to you—may be based in the fact that I can more readily "include" you in me (assimilation) than myself in you (contrast; Codol, 1990). Other findings hint at a kind of assimilative projection—my own attributes affect my characterization and judgment of others, as demonstrated through positive correlations between self- and other-ratings on relevant traits (e.g., Lambert & Wedell, 1991; Markus et al., 1982). However, even in this literature, contrast effects emerge when the target is unambiguous (a contrastive feature identified in Table 2.1; see Markus & Smith, 1981), and a pattern of "egocentric contrast" has been documented as well (e.g., Dunning & Cohen, 1992). This contrastive pattern tends to emerge in studies that determine participants' *objective* standing on some dimension (e.g., math SAT scores) and correlate these with *subjective* judgments (e.g., mathematical ability) of a target other. It seems possible that these specific self-standards function as *distinct* constructs (see Table 2.1) against which others are compared; more abstract self-conceptions are likely to produce assimilation (e.g., Beauregard & Dunning, 2001).

In these "projection" findings, a *particular* other is judged. But evidence of self-as-standard can also be seen in the literatures on false consensus and false uniqueness, which assess perceivers' views of *generalized* others (e.g., what percent of other people are X?). False consensus can be thought of in assimilation terms (we assume others are like us) and false uniqueness in contrastive terms (we assume others are different [typically, less good] than us). Moderators of these effects include the valence of the attribute, such that contrast of others from the self is more likely on positive than negative traits (Allison et al., 1989; Mullen & Goethals, 1990). This suggests that we want to be distinct when it reflects well on us. Assimilation effects (false consensus) are also more likely when the attribute being judged is broad and open to subjective construals (Gilovich, 1990) and when the "other" on whom we are projecting is the in-group rather than the out-group—presumably because of "inclusion" principles (e.g., Mullen et al., 1992). Others have noted that these phenomena may be triggered simultaneously: Judgments of self correlate positively with judgments of others, but others are judged less extremely than the self. We may expect that "others will behave like me, only less so" (Moore & Kim, 2003, p. 1132).

While the self may be special in some ways as a standard for judging others, it is also the case that other exemplars besides the self operate in the same manner. Some of the literature on asymmetry in similarity judgments, for example, highlights that any well-known standard may prompt the same kind of asymmetry; research on "myopic social prediction" has also documented that any *focal* person—not just the self—may be used as a standard in predicting the behavior of others (Moore & Kim, 2003). And some research has directly examined how exposure to one individual (the standard or context) can affect judgments of other individuals who *share some attribute* of the original standard. For example, Lewicki's (1985) classic "hairstyle" study documented that exposure to a nice experimenter led to positive judgments of another target who was similar in appearance. This is an assimilation effect that can be characterized in terms of the basic principle of "inclusion." The phenomenon of transference, in which beliefs and feelings about *significant others* are "transferred" to other people, provides another example of assimilation effects (e.g., Andersen & Baum, 1994; Andersen & Cole, 1990). Interestingly, none of the research on transference has documented contrast effects, despite the fact that exemplars were described in Chapter 2 as distinct entities that prompt comparison and contrast. What seems important to the transference and related literatures is that these "projections" occur without awareness or conscious attention; Chapter 2 described this as a feature that promotes assimilation. The similarity between known exemplar and new target may be a basic perceptual phenomenon that leads to inclusion and assimilation.

Chapter 5 turned to a consideration of stereotypes as expectancies or standards used in the judgment of others. The stereotyping literature can generally be characterized in terms of assimilation. That is, stereotyping occurs when individual targets are judged consistently with group stereotypes. This chapter reviewed several dominant models of stereotyping that are all assimilative in nature, at least when the target being judged can be construed as fitting the stereotyped category (i.e., displays behaviors that are stereotype-confirming, ambiguous, or neutral rather than clearly discrepant with the category). For example, in Brewer's (1988) and Fiske and Neuberg's (1990) dual-process models of impression formation, judgments of others will be category-based (consistent with stereotypes) unless fit is poor or unless the perceiver is highly motivated to engage in piecemeal or bottom-up processing. In Kunda and Thagard's (1996) parallel constraint satisfaction model, stereotypes play a less central role, but they nonetheless constrain the meaning of other information such that assimilation is the likely result (except when other information, such as clearly diagnostic individuating information, drowns out the impact of stereotypes). In Bodenhausen and Macrae's (1998) activation–inhibition model, there are some inhibitory factors that counteract assimilative tendencies, but these generally create rebound that results in assimilation. All of these models, then, predict either assimilative effects of stereotypes or *null effects*, but none explicitly predicts contrast.

My own work on the "shifting standards" model does conceptualize stereotypes as standards against which individuals are compared (and contrasted) in addition to "interpretive frames" that promote assimilation (Biernat et al., 1991). This model is discussed briefly in Chapter 5 and more extensively in Chapter 6, where I outlined how different types of responses to members of stereotyped groups could be categorized as assimilative or contrastive in nature. The model builds on the idea that when called upon to evaluate a member of a stereotyped group on a stereotyped dimension, we make reference to within-category expectations. Thus, women are evaluated relative to expectations for women and men to expectations for men. It is this within-category comparison that can give rise to *contrast* effects—as when a woman is judged to be highly aggressive because expectations for women's aggression are so low overall. But a signature finding in the shifting standards literature is that such contrast effects are likely only on *subjective* response scales, which specifically allow for within-category adjustment of meaning. Judgments made in common-rule units are more likely to reveal *assimilation* to stereotypes because they invite a cross-category perspective. Thus, in terms of *judgment* of others, assimilation to stereotypes is likely on common-rule response scales; contrast is likely on subjective scales.

Additionally, Chapter 6 considered how the setting of standards based on stereotypes could also reveal assimilative or contrastive influences, depending on the *type of standard* at hand. Minimal standards reveal basic expectations and as such are lower for groups stereotyped as deficient on a particular dimension (e.g., minimum competence standards are lower for women than for men; Biernat & Kobrynowicz, 1997). I characterized this as a contributor to contrast effects, because low standards can more readily be surpassed, resulting in *counterstereotypical* judgment. Confirmatory standards, however, tend to be assimilative in nature, in that they are more lenient for groups stereotyped as having a given attribute. Thus, men may achieve a lower test score and still be considered competent (relative to women). Because this serves to maintain stereotypes, confirmatory standards function as assimilative mechanisms. Finally, Chapter 6 considered how stereotypes affect *behavior* toward members of stereotyped groups, and I suggested that *zero-sum* behaviors (choices, allocation of valuable resources) will generally assimilate to stereotypes whereas *non-zero-sum* behaviors can reveal contrast—as when a female softball player, judged relative to low minimum standards, receives more congratulatory praise for a hit than a comparable man (Biernat & Vescio, 2002). That stereotypes can produce these very different outcomes depending on specifiable contextual features is consistent with the book's general theme of *relativity* and *variability* in judgment outcomes.

Chapters 7 through 9 of the book turned to judgments of *self* rather than others, though I attempted to highlight similar themes in both major sections of the book. Chapter 7 is the only "self" chapter that did not have a parallel in the other-judgment section. Here, I considered how internalized guides influence affect, judgment, and behavior. This literature, unlike much of the other considered in the book, is dominated by the theme of *contrast* rather than assimilation. Specifically, because internalized standards are typically defined as "mental representations of correct behavior, attitudes and traits" (Duval & Wicklund, 1972, p. 3), actual behavior is compared to these standards and typically found lacking. As a result, negative affect results—a contrast effect relative to the standard. This theme of contrast in emotional responses is especially dominant in self-discrepancy theory (Higgins, 1987) and the related literature on "should–would" discrepancies in prejudice expression (Monteith, 1993; Plant & Devine, 1998). Interestingly, research on possible selves (which also focuses on a kind of positive standard or goal state) has typically produced positive emotional consequences—an assimilation effect—perhaps because these future selves create optimism and belief in the mutability of the current self (Markus & Nurius, 1986). Furthermore, of course, any comparisons between reality and standards can produce positive affect—a kind of assimilation—if the comparison reveals that the standard *is* being met or at least that adequate progress is being made toward meeting the standard (Gibbons, 1990).

But assuming that most comparisons to internalized standards leave us wanting, negative affect is likely to be a common occurrence (contrast). In the theory of objective self-awareness, this negative affect also produces motivation to restore consistency—either by *changing* the attribute that does not meet the standard or by changing the standard itself (Batson et al., 1999; Duval & Lalwani, 1999). Interestingly, both of these might be considered *assimilative* effects—one behaviorally moves toward the standard or moves the standard toward reality. Many models of self-regulation incorporate this theme of assimilation as well, as individuals make changes "to diminish the gap between present location and goal" (Carver & Scheier, 2002, p. 305). In Higgins' (1998) distinction between the self-regulatory foci of *promotion* and *prevention*, however, one can see assimilation in the sense of moving toward a desired outcome, or contrast in the sense of keeping distant from an undesired outcome.

Chapter 8 considered the phenomenon of *self-stereotyping*, or the role of stereotypes in self-evaluation and behavior. As is true of other-stereotyping, most self-stereotyping research is about assimilation: Self-stereotyping occurs when one judges or perceives the self in terms consistent with group stereotypes. This chapter reviewed the self-categorization perspective on self-stereotyping (Turner et al., 1987) and highlighted the role of category salience and priming or readiness in promoting self-stereotyping. I noted, too, that stereotype threat effects might be considered a form of self-stereotyping, as the individual *behaviorally confirms* a stereotype when under threat (Steele & Aronson, 1995). Stereotype threat effects are interesting for a number of other reasons, however. One is that they represent a case in which the individual does not want to confirm the stereotype, so the desire or intent may be in a stereotype-contrastive direction. Another is that conditions of stereotype threat seem to produce contrast in the behavior of members of the *nonstereotyped* group, a phenomenon that has come to be called stereotype "lift" (Walton & Cohen, 2003). This chapter also considered related findings that behavior may be affected by stereotypes even when one is not a member of the stereotyped group, either in an assimilative (Bargh et al., 1996) or in a contrastive direction (Schubert & Häfner, 2003; Spears et al., 2004). In this latter work, contrast from stereotypes is likely when the stereotype is instantiated in terms of an exemplar (a distinct construct; Dijksterhuis et al., 1998) or when the intergroup context is made salient, such that one desires distance from this outgroup (Spears et al., 2004).

Finally, Chapter 9 tackled the rich literature on social comparison—the use of other people as standards to judge the self (Festinger, 1954a, b). This chapter reviewed commonly noted motives for engaging in social comparison, including self-assessment, self-enhancement, and self-improvement, along with self-verification. Additionally, I considered how choice of comparison to other may be determined by these motives, as when the desire to self-improve leads individuals to choose an upward comparison target (Collins, 1996), and the desire to feel good about the self promotes downward comparison (Wills, 1981).

Comparison typically implies contrast, as noted in the famous "Mr. Clean/Mr. Dirty" study, in which self-esteem was harmed by an upward comparison (to a job applicant much better than the self) and enhanced by a downward comparison (to a shabby-looking applicant). But the review in Chapter 9 highlighted instead that *both* upward and downward comparisons may produce either assimilation or contrast, again depending on a number of specifiable conditions. *Similarity* and *inclusion* are extremely important in this regard. Upward comparisons can be beneficial to the self (resulting in assimilation effects) if one perceives that the other's status is attainable (Lockwood & Kunda, 1997), if the upward other is an in-group member (Mussweiler & Bodenhausen, 2002) or shares some attributes with the self (Brown et al., 1992), or if one generally "blurs" the distinction between self and other (Collins, 1996). Contrast is likely when dissimilarity reigns, as when the upward other is a competitor (Wood, 1989) or an individual whose accomplishments are out of reach (Buunk et al., 2001; Lockwood & Kunda, 1997). Similarly, downward comparisons, though generally proposed to have beneficial self-esteem consequences (a contrast effect), can lead to assimilation if *similarity* with the downward other is heightened. For example, if one feels vulnerable to the same outcome as the downward other (Lockwood, 2002) or if that individual's outcome is perceived as uncontrollable—"it could happen to me!"—negative affect is likely to result (Major et al., 1991; Taylor & Lobel, 1989).

Furthermore, recent research has documented that the same comparison situation may prompt *both* assimilation and contrast, depending on the outcome of interest. For example, the positive affective benefits of comparing to an attainable upward other may not produce positive behavioral effects if the individual engages in "fantasy" that preempts effective motivation and action (see Markman & McMullen, 2003; Oettingen & Mayer, 2002). Or an upward comparison may make one feel happy but at the same time *cognitively* concerned about one's own situation (Buunk & Ybema, 2003).

In all of this research on the consequences of social comparison, construal matters. After engaging in an upward comparison, for example, one might come to see the self as similar to that person (Wheeler, 1966), or one might manipulate images of the self or other in such a way that the self is still perceived as *superior* to the upward other (DeVellis et al., 1991). The "genius effect" is a construal mechanism that allows one to deflect the potentially negative consequences of comparing with an outperforming other by paradoxically seeing that person as so brilliant, the comparison to self is inappropriate (Alicke et al., 1997). In short, perceivers may be active in their choice of comparison target and active (even creative) in what they do with comparison information once it is received. Even if not so active—as when comparisons are made without intent or awareness—it is clear that either upward or downward comparisons can have positive or negative consequences depending on features of the comparison situation, the construal of those features, and the type of comparsion outcome.

☐ Concluding Comments

Daily life compels us to make judgments such as whether we have what it takes to succeed in a chosen profession, whether the salesperson can be trusted, or whether a new acquaintance has an aggressive streak. In making these types of judgments, we are likely to refer to the types of standards discussed throughout this book. Stereotypes, for example, may affect consideration of my own and others' suitability for a job, recent exposure to one helpful salesperson may lead me to judge a newly encountered salesperson as trustworthy, and my own aggressiveness may affect how aggressive I judge the new acquaintance to be. In these situations, one may seek accuracy, but one may also be inclined to support a preexisting belief such as a social stereotype or a positive view of the self (see Kruglanski & Webster, 1996). In self-judgment in particular, one may also be striving to enhance or inspire the self, such that downward or upward social comparisons, respectively, become appealing standards to instantiate.

The dual role of expectations (interpretive frameworks) and standards (points of comparison) in social judgment have been emphasized throughout this book. Whether any given contextual cue (a prime, a stereotype, the self, another person) plays these roles simultaneously or does not may be a matter of debate, but it is clear that virtually any cue may have an assimilative or a contrastive influence depending on the variety of circumstantial factors described in this volume. In general, I assume that much of our life experience—what we observe about others and ourselves—is ambiguous, leaving room for perception, interpretation, and construal consistent with expectations. Thus, for example, the influence of stereotypes may be primarily assimilative, because we are likely to see in ambiguous others what we expect to see (von Hippel et al., 1995). At the same time, unambiguous or unexpected targets are less prone to these interpretive biases, and comparative processes may dominate in these cases. However, more research on how aspects of the to-be-judged target and features of the context interact to produce different patterns of judgment would be beneficial.

I would also like to see further work geared toward addressing the fact that different judgmental patterns (assimilation, contrast, or null effects) often appear on different measures or outcomes. In research on social comparison, for example, direct comparative measures may indicate that one perceives similarity to a superior other at the same time that separate ratings of self and other recognize the other's superiority (DeVellis et al., 1991; Miyake & Zuckerman, 1993). There is a parallel to this finding in the racism literature, in which White perceivers recognized a competent Black target as intelligent but still thought of themselves as *relatively* more so (Dovidio & Gaertner, 1981). Relative deprivation effects (a literature not reviewed here) tend to appear on affective and direct comparative measures rather than on nonaffective or indirect measures (Pettigrew, 2002). In stereotyping, whether judgments are assessed on common-rule scales or on subjective scales, whether a minimum or confirmatory standard has been evoked, or whether behavioral outcomes are zero-sum or non-zero-sum in nature, all may determine the pattern of effects that emerge (Biernat, 2003; Biernat et al., 1991). And particularly with respect to self-judgment, affect, cognition, and behavior, each may be differentially affected by comparison standards. Thus, comparison to some internalized standard may prompt negative affect but positive behavioral consequences (Silvia & Duval, 2001); comparison to a worse-off other may prompt positive affect or self-evaluation but poor behavioral motivation (Markman & McMullen, 2003).

These findings hint at the importance of research that includes a variety of measures, such that classes of outcomes and potential explanations for them can be identified. More research on the role of affect as a potential mediator of judgment and behavior outcomes is also warranted (see Markman & McMullen, 2003, for a good example of such an approach). Considerations of *time course* are also lacking in this literature. We know almost nothing about how long-lasting the consequences of priming or of a social comparison are likely to be. Some of the diversity of outcomes alluded to above may play out, in part, over time, as some effects decay and some emerge with distance from the comparative process.

Finally, in a number of places in this book I have differentiated between cognitive and motivational accounts of a variety of judgment effects. I do not advocate "between-theory confrontation" to settle the hot versus cold debate for any given phenomenon or to discover the "true" account of a particular effect (Tetlock & Levi, 1982). Instead, I recommend continued attention to the interplay of cognitive and motivational factors in the study of expectancy- and standard-based judgment. The influence of motives is least clearly articulated in the literature on contextual priming effects and perhaps most clearly articulated in the literature on social comparison. In the former, it is typically assumed that the perceiver is passively influenced by context and that knowledge accessibility (along with "cold" phenomena such as attention or anchoring) is responsible for judgment effects. In the latter, the perceiver is viewed as an active processor of information, motivated to fill certain needs or extract what is desired out of available information. Perhaps the role of motives (e.g., for self-enhancement, status, belonging) could be further explored in the priming literature. In social comparison, we see a more cognitive emphasis offered by Mussweiler's (2003) selective-accessibility model and Markman and McMullen's (2003) reflection–evaluation model, which highlight knowledge accessibility as a key construct.

Expectations and standards play an important and seemingly ubiquitous role in our encounters with, perceptions of, judgments about, and behavior within the social environment. This book has attempted to highlight basic features of the judgment context that determine the manner in which these expectations and standards guide social life. The themes of assimilation versus contrast, inclusion versus exclusion, and interpretation versus comparison have pervaded this book, and I hope that noting their relevance to domains as different as priming, stereotyping, social comparison, and goal striving has been a (comparatively) useful exercise.

References

Abele, A. E., & Petzold, P. (1998). Pragmatic use of categorical information in impression formation. *Journal of Personality and Social Psychology, 75*, 347–358.

Abeles, R. P. (1976). Relative deprivation, rising expectations, and black militancy. *Journal of Social Issues, 32*, 119–137.

Abelson, R. P. (1976). Script processing in attitude formation and decision making. In J. S. Carroll & J. W. Payne (Eds.), *Cognition and social behavior*. Oxford, England: Lawrence Erlbaum.

Abelson, R. P., & Levi, A. (1985). Decision making and decision theory. In G. Lindzey & E. Aronson (Eds.), *Handbook of social psychology* (3rd ed., Vol. 1, pp. 231–309). New York: Random House.

Abramson, P. R., Goldberg, P. A., Greenberg, J. H., & Abramson, L. M. (1977). The talking platypus phenomenon: Competency ratings as a function of sex and professional status. *Psychology of Women Quarterly, 2*, 114–124.

Affleck, G., & Tennen, H. (1991). Social comparison and coping with major medical problems. In J. Suls & T. A. Wills (Eds.), *Social comparison: Contemporary theory and research* (pp. 369–394). Hillsdale, NJ: Erlbaum.

Agostinelli, G., Sherman, S. J., Presson, C. C., & Chassin, L. (1992). Self-protection and self-enhancement biases in estimates of population prevalence. *Personality and Social Psychology Bulletin, 18*, 631–642.

Ajzen, I., & Fishbein, M. (1980). *Understanding attitudes and predicting social behavior*. Englewood Cliffs, NJ: Prentice-Hall.

Albert, S. (1977). Temporal comparison theory. *Psychological Review, 84*, 485–503.

Alicke, M. D., & Largo, E. (1995). The role of the self in the false consensus effect. *Journal of Experimental Social Psychology, 31*, 28–47.

Alicke, M. D., LoSchiavo, F. M., Zerbst, J., & Zhang, S. (1997). The person who outperforms me is a genius: Maintaining perceived competence in upward social comparison. *Journal of Personality and Social Psychology, 73*, 781–789.

Allen, V. L., & Wilder, D. A. (1977). Veridical social support, extreme social support and conformity. *Representative Research in Social Psychology, 8*, 33–41.

Allison, S. T., Messick, D. M., & Goethals, G. R. (1989). On being better but not smarter than others: The Muhammad Ali effect. *Social Cognition, 7*, 275–295.

Allport, F. H. (1924). *Social psychology.* Boston: Houghton-Mifflin.

Amodio D. M., Shah, J. Y., Sigelman, J., Brazy, P. C., & Harmon-Jones, E. (2004). Implicit regulatory focus associated with asymmetrical frontal cortical activity. *Journal of Experimental and Social Psychology, 40,* 255–232.

Andersen, S. M., & Baum, A. (1994). Transference in interpersonal relations: Inferences and affect based on significant-other representations. *Journal of Personality, 62,* 459–498.

Andersen, S. M., & Cole, S. W. (1990). "Do I know you?": The role of significant others in general social perception. *Journal of Personality and Social Psychology, 59,* 384–399.

Andersen, S. M., Glassman, N. S., Chen, S., & Cole, S. W. (1995). Transference in social perception: The role of chronic accessibility in significant-other representations. *Journal of Personality and Social Psychology, 69,* 41–57.

Andersen, S. M., Reznik, I., & Manzella, L. M. (1996). Eliciting facial affect, motivation, and expectancies in transference: Significant-other representations in social relations. *Journal of Personality and Social Psychology, 71,* 1108–1129.

Anderson, N. H. (1981). *Foundations of information integration theory.* New York: Academic Press.

Anderson, R. C. (1974). Substance recall of sentences. *Quarterly Journal of Experimental Psychology, 26,* 530–541.

Armor, D. A., & Taylor, S. E. (1998). Situated optimism: Specific outcome expectancies and self-regulation. In M. P. Zanna (Ed.), *Advances in experimental social psychology* (Vol. 30, pp. 309–379). Orlando, FL: Academic Press.

Aronson, J., Lustina, M. J., Good, C., Keough, K., Steele, C. M., & Brown, J. (1999). When White men can't do math: Necessary and sufficient factors in stereotype threat. *Journal of Experimental Social Psychology, 35,* 29–46.

Ashmore, R. D., & Del Boca, F. K. (1981). Conceptual approaches to stereotypes and stereotyping. In D. L. Hamilton (Ed.), *Cognitive processes in stereotyping and intergroup behavior* (pp. 1–35). Hillsdale, NJ: Erlbaum.

Atkinson, J. W. (1957). Motivational determinants of risk-taking behavior. *Psychological Review, 64,* 359–372.

Atkinson, J. W., & Feather, N. T. (Eds.). (1966). *A theory of achievement motivation.* New York: Wiley.

Augoustinos, M., Ahrens, C., & Innes, J. M. (1994). Stereotypes and prejudice: The Australian experience. *British Journal of Social Psychology, 33,* 125–141.

Baldwin, M. W., & Holmes, J. G. (1987). Salient private audiences and awareness of the self. *Journal of Personality and Social Psychology, 52,* 1087–1098.

Banaji, M. R., Hardin, C., & Rothman, A. J. (1993). Implicit stereotyping in person judgment. *Journal of Personality and Social Psychology, 65,* 272–281.

Bandura, A. (1977). Self-efficacy: Toward a unifying theory of behavioral change. *Psychological Review, 84,* 191–215.

Bandura, A. (1991). Social cognitive theory of self-regulation. *Organizational Behavior and Human Decision Processes, 50,* 248–287.

Bandura, A. (1997). *Self-efficacy: The exercise of control.* New York: W. H. Freeman.

Bargh, J. A. (1992). Does subliminality matter to social psychology? Awareness of the stimulus versus awareness of its influence. In R. F. Bornstein & T. S. Pittman (Eds.), *Perception without awareness: Cognitive, clinical, and social perspectives* (pp. 236–255). New York: Guilford Press.

Bargh, J. A., Chen, M., & Burrows, L. (1996). Automaticity of social behavior: Direct effects of trait construct and stereotype activation on action. *Journal of Personality and Social Psychology, 71,* 230–244.

Bargh, J. A., & Pietramonaco, P. (1982). Automatic information processing and social perception: The influence of trait information presented outside of conscious awareness on impression formation. *Journal of Personality and Social Psychology, 43,* 437–449.

Batson, C. S., Thompson, E. R., Seuferling, G., Whitney, H., & Strongman, J. A. (1999). Moral hypocrisy: Appearing moral to oneself without being so. *Journal of Personality and Social Psychology, 77,* 525–537.

Baumeister, R. F. (1990). Suicide as escape from self. *Psychological Review, 97,* 90–113.

Beauregard, K. S., & Dunning, D. (1998). Turning up the contrast: Self-enhancement motives prompt egocentric contrast effects in social judgment. *Journal of Personality and Social Psychology, 74,* 606–621.

Beauregard, K. S., & Dunning, D. (2001). Defining self-worth: Trait self-esteem moderates the use of self-serving trait definitions in social judgment. *Motivation and Emotion, 25,* 135–161.

Bem, S. L. (1981). Gender schema theory: A cognitive account of sex typing. *Psychological Review, 88,* 354–364.

Bem, S. L., & Lewis, S. A. (1975). Sex role adaptability: One consequence of psychological androgyny. *Journal of Personality and Social Psychology, 31,* 634–643.

Bem, S. L., Martyna, W., & Watson, C. (1976). Sex typing and androgyny: Further explorations of the expressive domain. *Journal of Personality and Social Psychology, 34,* 1016–1023.

Berk, M. S., & Andersen, S. M. (2000). The impact of past relationships on interpersonal behavior: Behavioral confirmation in the social-cognitive process of transference. *Journal of Personality and Social Psychology, 79,* 546–562.

Berkowitz, L. (1960). The judgmental process in personality functioning. *Psychological Review, 67,* 130–142.

Berry, D. S., & Zebrowitz-McArthur, L. (1988). What's in a face?: Facial maturity and the attribution of legal responsibility. *Personality and Social Psychology Bulletin, 14,* 23–33.

Bettencourt, B. A., Dill, K. E., Greathouse, S. A., Charlton, K., & Mulholland, A. (1997). Evaluations of ingroup and outgroup members: The role of category-based expectancy violation. *Journal of Experimental Social Psychology, 33,* 244–275.

Biernat, M. (2003). Toward a broader view of social stereotyping. *American Psychologist, 58,* 1019–1027.

Biernat, M., & Billings, L. S. (2001). Standards, expectancies, and social comparison. In A. Tesser & N. Schwarz (Eds.), *Blackwell handbook of social psychology: Intraindividual processes* (pp. 257–283). London: Blackwell.

Biernat, M., Crandall, C. S., Young, L. V., Kobrynowicz, D., & Halpin, S. M. (1998). All that you can be: Stereotyping of self and others in a military context. *Journal of Personality and Social Psychology, 75,* 301–317.

Biernat, M., Eidelman, S., & Fuegen, K. (2002). Judgment standards and the social self: A shifting standards perspective. In J. P. Forgas and K. D. Williams (Eds.), *The social self: Cognitive, interpersonal, and intergroup perspectives* (pp. 51–72). New York: Psychology Press.

Biernat, M., & Fuegen, K. (2001). Shifting standards and the evaluation of competence: Complexity in gender-based judgment and decision making. *Journal of Social Issues, 57,* 707–724.

Biernat, M & Kobrynowicz, D. (1997). Gender- and race-based standards of competence: Lower minimum standards but higher ability standards for devalued groups. *Journal of Personality and Social Psychology, 72,* 544–557.

Biernat, M., Kobrynowicz, D., & Weber, D. (2003). Stereotyping and shifting standards: Some paradoxical effects of cognitive load. *Journal of Applied Social Psychology, 33,* 2060–2079.

Biernat, M., & Ma, J. E. (2005). Stereotypes and the confirmability of trait concepts. *Personality and Social Psychology Bulletin, 31,* 443–495.

Biernat, M., Ma, J. E., & Nario-Redmond, M. R. (2005). The role of stereotypes and judgment standards in trait diagnosis. Manuscript under review.

Biernat, M., & Manis, M. (1994). Shifting standards and stereotype-based judgments. *Journal of Personality and Social Psychology, 66,* 5–20.

Biernat, M., Manis, M., & Kobrynowicz, D. (1997). Simultaneous assimilation and contrast effects in judgments of self and other. *Journal of Personality and Social Psychology, 73,* 254–269.

Biernat, M., Manis, M., & Nelson, T. F. (1991). Comparison and expectancy processes in human judgment. *Journal of Personality and Social Psychology, 61,* 203–211.

Biernat, M., & Thompson, E. R. (2002). Shifting standards and contextual variation in stereotyping. In W. Stroebe and M. Hewstone (Eds.), *European review of social psychology,* (Vol. 12, pp. 103–137). London: John Wiley & Sons.

Biernat, M., & Vescio, T. K. (2002). She swings, she hits, she's great, she's benched: Implications of gender-based shifting standards for judgment and behavior. *Personality and Social Psychology Bulletin, 28,* 66–77.

Biernat, M., Vescio, T. K., & Billings, L. S. (1999). Black sheep and expectancy violation: Integrating two models of social judgment. *European Journal of Social Psychology, 29,* 523–542.

Biernat, M., Vescio, T. K., & Green, M. L. (1996). Selective self-stereotyping. *Journal of Personality Social psychology, 71,* 1194–1209.

Biernat, M., Vescio, T. K., & Manis, M. (1998). Judging and behaving toward members of stereotyped groups: A shifting standards perspective. In C. Sedikides, J. Schopler, & C. A. Insko (Eds.), *Intergroup cognition and intergroup behavior* (pp. 151–175). Mahwah, NJ: Lawrence Erlbaum Associates.

Blair, I. V., & Banaji, M. R. (1996). Automatic and controlled processes in stereotype priming. *Journal of Personality and Social Psychology, 70,* 1142–1163.

Blanchard, F. A., Lilly, T., & Vaughn, L. A. (1991). Reducing the expression of racial prejudice. *Psychological Science, 2,* 101–105.

Blanton, H. (2001). Evaluating the self in the context of another: The three-selves model of social comparison assimilation and contrast. In G. B. Moskowitz (Ed.), *Cognitive social psychology: The Princeton Symposium on the legacy and future of social cognition* (pp. 75–87). Mahwah, NJ: Lawrence Erlbaum Associates.

Blanton, H., Buunk, B. P., Gibbons, F. X., & Kuyper, H. (1999). When better-than-others compare upward: Choice of comparison and comparative evaluation as independent predictors of academic performance. *Journal of Personality and Social Psychology, 7,* 420–430.

Blanton, H., Christie, C., & Dye, M. (2002). Social identity versus reference frame comparisons: The moderating role of stereotype endorsement. *Journal of Experimental Social Psychology, 38,* 253–267.

Blanton, H., Crocker, J., & Miller, D. T. (2000). The effects of in-group versus out-group social comparison on self-esteem in the context of a negative stereotype. *Journal of Experimental Social Psychology, 36,* 519–530.

Bobes, M. A., Valdes-Sosa, M., & Olivares, E. (1994). An ERP study of expectancy violation in face perception. *Brain and Cognition, 26,* 1–22.

Bodenhausen, G. V. (1988). Stereotypic biases in social decision making and memory: Testing process models for stereotype use. *Journal of Personality and Social Psychology, 55,* 726–737.

Bodenhausen G. V., & Macrae, C. N. (1998). Stereotype activation and inhibition. In R. S. Wyer, Jr. (Ed.), *Stereotype activation and inhibition. Advances in social cognition* (pp. 1–52). Mahway, NJ: Lawrence Erlbaum Associates.

Bodenhausen, G. V., Schwarz, N., Bless, H., & Wänke, M. *(1995).* Effects of atypical exemplars on racial beliefs: Enlightened racism or generalized appraisals? *Journal of Experimental Social Psychology, 31,* 48–63.

Boersma, F. J., Chapman, J. W., & Battle, J. (1979). Academic self-concept change in special education students: Some suggestions for interpreting self-concept scores. *Journal of Special Education, 13,* 433–442.

Boldero, J., & Francis, J. (2000). The relation between self-discrepancies and emotion: The moderating roles of self-guide importance, location relevance, and social self-domain centrality. *Journal of Personality and Social Psychology, 78,* 38–52.

Bosveld, W., Koomen, W., & van der Pligt, J. (1994). Selective exposure and the false consensus effect: The availability of similar and dissimilar others. *British Journal of Social Psychology, 33,* 457–466.

Bosveld, W., Koomen, W., & van der Pligt, J. (1996). Estimating group size: Effects of category membership, differential construal and selective exposure. *European Journal of Social Psychology, 26,* 523–535.

Bosveld, W., Koomen, W., van der Pligt, J., & Plaisier, J. W. (1995). Differential construal as an explanation for false consensus and false uniqueness effects. *Journal of Experimental Social Psychology, 31,* 518–532.

Bosveld, W., Koomen, W., & Vogelaar, R. (1997). Construing a social issue: Effects on attitudes and the false consensus effects. *British Journal of Social Psychology, 36,* 263–272.

Bramel, D. (1963). Selection of a target for defensive projection. *Journal of Abnormal and Social Psychology, 66,* 318–324.

Branscombe, N. R., Schmitt, M. T., & Harvey, R. D. (1999). Perceiving pervasive discrimination among African Americans: Implications for group identification and well-being. *Journal of Personality and Social Psychology, 77,* 135–149.

Branscombe, N. R., & Smith, E. R. (1990). Gender and racial stereotypes in impression formation and social decision-making processes. *Sex Roles, 22,* 627–647.

Brehm, J. W. (1966). *A theory of psychological reactance.* Oxford, England: Academic Press.

Brewer, M. B. (1988). A dual process model of impression formation. In T. K. Srull & R. S. Wyer, Jr. (Eds.), *Advances in social cognition* (Vol. 1, pp. 1–36). Hillsdale, NJ: Lawrence Erlbaum Associates.

Brewer, M. B. (1991). The social self: On being the same and different at the same time. *Personality and Social Psychology Bulletin, 17,* 475–482.

Brewer, M. B. (1996). When stereotypes lead to stereotyping: The use of stereotypes in person perception. In C. N. Macrae, C. Stangor, & M. Hewstone (Eds.) *Stereotypes and Stereotyping* (pp. 254–275). New York: Guilford Press.

Brewer, M. B., & Pickett, C. L. (1999). Distinctiveness motives as a source of the social self. In T. R. Tyler & R. M. Kramer (Eds.), *The psychology of the social self. Applied social research* (pp. 71–87). Mahwah, NJ: Lawrence Erlbaum Associates.

Brewer, M. B., & Weber, J. G. (1994). Self-evaluation effects of interpersonal versus intergroup social comparison. *Journal of Personality and Social Psychology, 66,* 268–275.

Brickman, P., & Bulman, R. J. (1977). Pleasure and pain in social comparison. In J. M. Suls & R. L. Miller (Eds.), *Social comparison processes: Theoretical and empirical perspectives* (pp. 149–186). Washington, DC: Hemisphere.

Brickman, P., Coates, D., & Janoff-Bulman, R. (1978). Lottery winners and accident victims: Is happiness relative? *Journal of Personality and Social Psychology, 36,* 917–927.

Broemer, P., & Diehl, M. (2004). Evaluative contrast in social comparison: The role of distinct and shared features of the self and comparison others. *European Journal of Social Psychology, 34,* 25–38.

Brown, D. R. (1953). Stimulus similarity and the anchoring of subjective scales. *American Journal of Psychology, 66,* 199–214.

Brown, J. D., Novick, N. J., Lord, K. A., & Richards, J. M. (1992). When Gulliver travels: Social context, psychological closeness, and self-appraisals. *Journal of Personality and Social Psychology, 62,* 717–727.

Bruner, J. S. (1957). Going beyond the information given. In H. E. Gruber, K. R. Hammond, & R. Jessor (Eds.), *Contemporary approaches to cognition* (pp. 41–69). Cambridge, MA: Harvard University Press.

Burgoon, J. (1993). Interpersonal expectations, expectancy violations, and emotional communication. *Journal of Language and Social Psychology, 12,* 30–48.

Buunk, B. P., Collins, R. L., Taylor, S. E., Van Yperen, N. W., & Dakof, G. A. (1990). The affective consequences of social comparison: Either direction has its ups and downs. *Journal of Personality and Social Psychology, 59,* 1238–1249.

Buunk, B. P., & Mussweiler, T. (2001). New directions in social comparison research. *European Journal of Social Psychology, 31,* 467–475.

Buunk, B. P., & Ybema, J. F. (1997). Social comparisons and occupational stress: The identification-contrast model. In B. P. Buunk & F. X. Gibbons (Eds.), *Health, coping, and well-being: Perspectives from social comparison theory* (pp. 359–387). Mahwah, NJ: Lawrence Erlbaum.

Buunk, B. P., & Ybema, J. F. (2003). Feeling bad, but satisfied: The effects of upward and downward comparison upon mood and marital satisfaction. *British Journal of Social Psychology, 42,* 613–628.

Buunk, B. P., Ybema, J. F., van der Zee, K., Schaufeli, W. B., & Gibbons, F. X. (2001). Affect generated by social comparisons among nurses high and low in burnout. *Journal of Applied Social Psychology, 31,* 1500–1520.

Campbell, D. T. (1958). Common fate, similarity, and other indices of the status of aggregates of persons as social entities. *Behavioral Science, 3,* 14–25.

Campbell, J. (1986). Similarity and uniqueness: The effects of attribute type, relevance, and individual differences in self-esteem and depression. *Journal of Personality and Social Psychology, 50,* 281–294.

Carpenter, S. (1988). Self-relevance and goal-directed processing in the recall and weighting of information about others. *Journal of Experimental Social Psychology, 24,* 310–332.

Carter, S. L. (1993). *Reflections of an affirmative action baby.* New York: Basic Books.

Carver, C. S. (2001). Affect and the functional bases of behavior: On the dimensional structure of affective experience. *Personality and Social Psychology Review, 5,* 345–356.

Carver, C. S., Blaney, P. H., & Scheier, M. F. (1979). Reassertion and giving up: The interactive role of self-directed attention and outcome expectancy. *Journal of Personality and Social Psychology, 37,* 1859–1870.

Carver, C. S., Lawrence, J. W., & Scheier, M. F. (1999). Self-discrepancies and affect: Incorporating the role of feared selves. *Personality and Social Psychology Bulletin, 25,* 783–792.

Carver, C. S., & Scheier, M. F. (1981). *Attention and self-regulation: A control-theory approach to human behaviors.* New York: Springer-Verlag.

Carver, C. S., & Scheier, M. F. (1990). Origins and functions of positive and negative affect: A control-process view. *Psychological Review, 97,* 19–35.

Carver, C. S., & Scheier, M. F. (1998). *On the self-regulation of behavior.* New York: Cambridge University Press.

Carver, C. S., & Scheier, M. F. (2002). The hopeful optimist. *Psychological Inquiry, 13,* 288–290.

Cash, T. F., Cash, D. W., & Butters, J. W. (1983). "Mirror, mirror, on the wall ...?": Contrast effects and self-evaluations of physical attractiveness. *Personality and Social Psychology Bulletin, 9,* 351–358.

Catrambone, R., Beike, D., & Niedenthal, P. (1996). Is the self-concept a habitual referent in judgments of similarity? *Psychological Science, 7,* 158–163.

Catrambone, R., & Markus, H. (1987). The role of self-schemas in going beyond the information given. *Social Cognition, 5,* 349–368.

Chiu, C., Hong, Y., Lam, I. C., Fu, J. H. Y., Tong, J. Y., & Lee, V. S. (1998). Stereotyping and self-presentation: Effects of gender stereotype activation. *Group Processes and Intergroup Relations, 1,* 81–96.

Cialdini, R. B., Borden, R. J., Thorne, A., Walker, M. R., Freeman, S., & Sloan, L. R. (1976). Basking in reflected glory: Three (football) field studies. *Journal of Personality and Social Psychology, 34,* 366–375.

Cialdini, R. B., Kallgren, C. A., & Reno, R. R. (1991). A focus theory of normative conduct: A theoretical refinement and reevaluation of the role of norms in human behavior. In M. P. Zanna (Ed.), *Advances in experimental social psychology* (Vol. 24, pp. 201–234). Orlando, FL: Academic Press.

Clark, H. H. (1985). Language use and language users. In G. Lindzey & E. Aronson (Eds.), *Handbook of social psychology* (3rd ed., pp. 179–231). New York: Random House.

Clark, H. H., & Haviland, S. E. (1977). *Psychology and language: An introduction to psycholinguistics.* New York: Harcourt, Brace, Jovanovich.

Clary, E. G., & Tesser, A. (1983). Reaction to unexpected events: The naive scientist and interpretive activity. *Personality and Social Psychology Bulletin, 9,* 609–620.

Clement R. W., & Krueger, J. (2000). The primacy of self-referent information in perceptions of social consensus. *British Journal of Social Psychology, 39,* 279–299.

Clore, G. L., Schwarz, N., & Conway, M. (1994). Affective causes and consequences of social information processing. In R. S. Wyer & T. K. Srull (Eds.), *Handbook of social cognition: Vol. 1. Basic Processes* (2nd ed.). Hillsdale, NJ: Lawrence Erlbaum.

Coan, J. A., & Allen, J. J. B. (2003). Frontal EEG asymmetry and the behavioral activation and inhibition systems. *Psychophysiology, 40,* 106–114.

Codol, J.-P. (1987). Comparability and incompatability between oneself and others: Means of differentiation and comparison reference points. *Current Psychology of Cognition, 7,* 87–105.

Codol, J.-P. (1990). Studies on self-centered assimilation processes. In J.-P. Caverni, J.-M. Fabre, & M. Gonzalez (Eds.), *Cognitive biases* (pp. 387–400). North-Holland, Amsterdam, Netherlands: Elsevier Science.

Codol, J.-P., Jarymowicz, M., Kaminska-Feldman, M., & Szuster-Zbrojewicz, A. (1989). Asymmetry in the estimation of interpersonal distance and identity affirmation. *European Journal of Social Psychology, 19,* 11–22.

Collins, R. L. (1996). For better or worse: The impact of upward social comparison on self-evaluation. *Psychological Bulletin, 119,* 51–69.

Collins, R. L. (2000). Among the better ones: Upward assimilation in social comparison. In J. Suls & L. Wheeler (Eds.), *Handbook of social comparison: Theory and research* (pp. 159–171). New York: Kluwer Academic Publishers.

Cooley, C. H. (1902/1964). *Human nature and the social order.* New York: Charles Scribner's Sons.

Costrich, N., Feinstein, J., Kidder, L., Marecek, J., & Pascale, L. (1975). When stereotypes hurt: Three studies of penalties for sex-role reversals. *Journal of Experimental Social Psychology, 11,* 520–530.

Cozzarelli, C., & Karafa, J. A. (1998). Cultural estrangement and terror management theory. *Personality and Social Psychological Bulletin, 24,* 253–267.

Crandall, C. S. (1988). Social contagion of binge eating. *Journal of Personality and Social Psychology, 55,* 588–598.

Crandall, C. S., & Eshleman, A. (2003). A justification-suppression model of the expression and experience of prejudice. *Psychological Bulletin, 129,* 414–446.

Crandall, C. S., Eshleman, A., & O'Brien, L. (2002). Social norms and the expression and suppression of prejudice: The struggle for internalization. *Journal of Personality and Social Psychology, 82,* 359–378.

Crano, W. D. (1983). Assumed consensus of attitudes: The effect of vested interest. *Personality and Social Psychology Bulletin, 9,* 597–608.

Crocker, J., & Major, B. (1989). Social stigma and self-esteem: The self-protective properties of stigma. *Psychological Review, 96,* 608–630.

Cronbach, L. J. (1955). Processes affecting scores on "understanding of others" and "assumed similarity." *Psychological Bulletin, 52,* 177–193.

Crosby, F. (1976). A model of egoistical relative deprivation. *Psychological Review, 83,* 85–113.

Crosby, F. J., Pufall, A., Snyder, R. C., O'Connell, M., & Whalen, P. (1989). The denial of personal disadvantage among you, me, and all the other ostriches. In M. Crawford & M. Gentry (Eds.), *Gender and thought* (pp. 79–99). New York: Springer-Verlag.

Cross, S. E., & Madson, L. (1997). Models of the self: Self-construal and gender. *Psychological Bulletin, 122,* 5–37.

Davis, J. A. (1966). The campus as a frog pond: An application of the theory of relative deprivation to career decisions of college men. *American Journal of Sociology, 72,* 17–31.

Dawes, R. M. (1989). Statistical criteria for establishing a truly false consensus effect. *Journal of Experimental Social Psychology, 25,* 1–17.

Deaux, K., & Lewis, L. L. (1984). Structure of gender stereotypes: Interrelationships among components and gender label. *Journal of Personality and Social Psychology, 46,* 991–1004.

Deaux, K., & Taynor, J. (1973). Evaluation of male and female ability: Bias works two ways. *Psychological Reports, 32,* 261–262.

DeCoster, J., & Claypool, H. M. (2004). A meta-analysis of priming effects on impression formation supporting a general model of informational biases. *Personality and Social Psychology Review, 8,* 2–27.

DeVellis, R. F., Blalock, S. J., Holt, K., Renner, B. R., Blanchard, L. W., & Klotz, M. L. (1991). Arthritis patients' reactions to unavoidable social comparisons. *Personality and Social Psychology Bulletin, 17,* 392–399.

Devine, P. G. (1989). Stereotypes and prejudice: Their automatic and controlled components. *Journal of Personality and Social Psychology, 56,* 5–18.

Devine, P. G., Monteith, M. J., Zuwerink, J. R., & Elliot, A. J. (1991). Prejudice with and without compunction. *Journal of Personality and Social Psychology, 60,* 817–830.

Diener, E., & Fujita, F. (1997). Social comparisons and subjective well-being. In B. P. Buunk & F. X. Gibbons (Eds.), *Health, coping, and well-being: Perspectives from social comparison theory* (pp. 329–357). Mahwah, NJ: Lawrence-Erlbaum.

Dijksterhuis, A., & Bargh, J. A. (2001). The perception-behavior expressway: Automatic effects of social perception on social behavior. In M. P. Zanna (Ed.), *Advances in experimental social psychology* (pp. 1–40). San Diego, CA: Academic Press.

Dijksterhuis, A., Spears, R., & Lépinasse, V. (2001). Reflecting and deflecting stereotypes: Assimilation and contrast in impression formation and automatic behavior. *Journal of Experimental Social Psychology, 37,* 286–299.

Dijksterhuis, A., Spears, R., Postmes, T., Stapel, D., Koomen, W., van Knippenberg, A., & Scheepers, D. (1998). Seeing one thing and doing another: Contrast effects in automatic behavior. *Journal of Personality and Social Psychology, 75,* 862–871.

Dijksterhuis, A., & van Knippenberg, A. (2000). Behavioral indecision: Effects of self-focus on automatic behavior. *Social Cognition, 18*, 55–74.

Dijksterhuis, A., & van Knippenberg, A. (1998). Inhibition, Aberdeen, and other cloudy subjects. In R. S. Wyer Jr. (Ed.), *Stereotype activation and inhibition. Advances in social cognition* (pp. 83–96). Mahwah, NJ: Lawrence-Erlbaum.

Dion, K. L. (1975). Women's reactions to discrimination from members of the opposite sex. *Journal of Research in Personality, 9*, 294–306.

Dion, K. L., & Earn, B. M. (1975). The phenomenology of being a target of prejudice. *Journal of Personality and Social Psychology, 32*, 944–950.

Dipboye, R. L., & Wiley, J. W. (1977). Reactions of college recruiters to interviewee sex and self-presentation style. *Journal of Vocational Behavior, 10*, 1–12.

Doosje, B., & Ellemers, N. (1997). Stereotyping under threat: The role of group identification. In R. Spears, P. J. Oakes, N. Ellemers, & S. A. Haslam (Eds.), *The social psychology of stereotyping and group life* (pp. 257–272). Cambridge, MA: Blackwell.

Dornbush, S. M., Hastorf, A. H., Richardson, S. A., Muzzy, R. E., & Vreeland, R. S. (1965). The perceiver and the perceived: Their relative influence on the categories of interpersonal cognition. *Journal of Personality and Social Psychology, 3*, 434–440.

Dovidio, J. F., Brigham, J. C., Johnson, B. T., & Gaertner, S. L. (1996). Stereotyping, prejudice, and discrimination: Another look. In C. N. Macrae, C. Stangor, & M. Hewstone (Eds.), *Stereotypes and stereotyping* (pp. 276–319). New York: Guilford.

Dovidio, J. F., & Fazio, R. H. (1992). New technologies for the direct and indirect assessment of attitudes. In J. M. Tanur (Ed.), *Questions about questions: Inquiries into the cognitive bases of surveys* (pp. 204–237). New York: Russell Sage Foundation.

Dovidio, J. F. & Gaertner, S. L. (1981). The effects of race, status, and ability on helping behavior. *Social Psychology Quarterly, 44*, 192–203.

Dovidio, J. F., Kawakami, K., Johnson, C., Johnson, B., & Howard, A. (1997). On the nature of prejudice: Automatic and controlled processes. *Journal of Experimental and Social Psychology, 33*, 510–540.

Dunning, D. (1993). Words to live by: The self and definitions of social concepts and categories. In J. M. Suls (Ed.), *The self in social perspective: Vol. 4. Psychological perspectives on the self* (pp. 99–126). Hillsdale, NJ: Lawrence Erlbaum and Associates.

Dunning, D., & Beauregard, K. S. (2000). Regulating impressions of others to affirm images of the self. *Social-Cognition, 18*, 198–222.

Dunning D., & Cohen, G. L. (1992). Egocentric definitions of traits and abilities in social judgment. *Journal of Personality and Social Psychology, 63*, 341–355.

Dunning, D., & Hayes, A. F. (1996). Evidence for egocentric comparison in social judgment. *Journal of Personality and Social Psychology, 71*, 213–229.

Dunning, D., & McElwee, R. O. (1995). Idiosyncratic trait definitions: Implications for self-description and social judgment. *Journal of Personality and Social Psychology, 68*, 936–946.

Dunning, D., Meyerowitz, J. A., & Holzberg, A. D. (1989). Ambiguity and self-evaluation: The role of idiosyncratic trait definitions in self-serving assessments of ability. *Journal of Personality and Social Psychology, 57*, 1082–1090.

Dunning, D., Perie, M., & Story, A. L. (1991). Self-serving prototypes of social categories. *Journal of Personality and Social Psychology, 61*, 957–968.

Dunning, D., & Sherman, D. A. (1997). Stereotypes and tacit inference. *Journal of Personality and Social Psychology, 73*, 459–471.

Dunning, D., & Story, A. L. (1991). Depression, realism, and the overconfidence effect: Are the sadder wiser when predicting future actions and events? *Journal of Personality and Social Psychology, 61*, 521–532.

Duval, T. S., Duval, V. H., & Mulilis, J. P. (1992). Effects of self-focus, discrepancy between self and standard, and outcome expectancy favorability on the tendency to match self to standard or to withdraw. *Journal of Personality and Social Psychology, 62*, 340–348.

Duval, T. S., & Lalwani, N. (1999). Objective self-awareness and causal attributions for self-standard discrepancies: Changing self or changing standards of correctness. *Personality and Social Psychology Bulletin, 25*, 1220–1229.

Duval, T. S., & Silvia, P. J. (2002). Self-awareness, probability of improvement, and the self-serving bias. *Journal of Personality and Social Psychology, 82,* 49–61.

Duval, T. S., & Wicklund, R. A. (1972). *A theory of objective self-awareness.* San Diego, CA: Academic Press.

Eagly, A. H., & Steffen, V. J. (1984). Gender stereotypes stem from the distribution of women and men into social roles. *Journal of Personality and Social Psychology, 46,* 735–754.

Eidelman, S. (2004). Self-categorization and self-stereotyping. Unpublished manuscript, University of Kansas.

Eiser, J. R. (1990). *Social judgment.* Pacific Grove, CA: Brooks/Cole Publishing Co.

Eiser, J. R., & Mower White, C. J. (1974). Evaluative consistency and social judgment. *Journal of Personality and Social Psychology, 30,* 349–359.

Eiser, J. R., Pahl, S., & Prins, Y. R. A. (2001). Optimism, pessimism, and the direction of self-other comparisons. *Journal of Experimental Social Psychology, 37,* 77–84.

Eiser, J. R., & Stroebe, W. (1972). *Categorization and social judgment.* New York: Academic Press.

Eiser, J. R., & van der Pligt, J. (1982). Accentuation and perspective in attitudinal judgment. *Journal of Personality and Social Psychology, 42,* 224–238.

Epley, N., & Dunning, D. (2000). Feeling "holier than thou": Are self-serving assessments produced by errors in self- or social prediction? *Journal of Personality and Social Psychology, 79,* 861–875.

Erber, R., & Fiske, S. T. (1984). Outcome dependency and attention to inconsistent information. *Journal of Personality and Social Psychology, 47,* 709–726.

Erdley, C. A., & D'Agostino, P. R. (1988). Cognitive and affective components of automatic priming effects. *Journal of Personality and Social Psychology, 54,* 741–747.

Fabrigar, L. R., & Krosnick, J. A. (1995). Attitude importance and the false consensus effect. *Personality and Social Psychology Bulletin, 21,* 408–479.

Fagen, J. W., & Ohr, P. S. (1985). Temperament and crying in response to the violation of a learned expectancy in early infancy. *Infant Behavior and Development, 8,* 157–166.

Fazio, R. H., Jackson, J. R., Dunton, B. C., & Williams, C. J. (1995). Variability in automatic activation as an unobtrusive measure of racial attitudes: A bona fide pipeline? *Journal of Personality and Social Psychology, 69,* 1013–1027.

Fazio, R. H., Powell, M. C., & Herr, P. M. (1983). Toward a process model of the attitude-behavior relation: Accessing one's attitude upon mere observation of the attitude object. *Journal of Personality and Social Psychology, 44,* 723–735.

Feather, N. T. (1967). An expectancy-value model of information-seeking behavior. *Psychological Review, 74,* 342–360.

Feather, N. T. (1990). Bridging the gap between values and actions: Recent applications of the expectancy-value model. In E. T. Higgins & R. M. Sorrentino (Eds.), *Handbook of motivation and cognition* (Vol. 2, pp. 151–192). New York: Guilford Press.

Fechner, G. T. (1860). *Elemente der Psychophysik.* Leipzig: Breitkopf & Hartel (translated in English in Fechner, G. T. (1966). *Elements of psychophysis.* New York: Holt, Rhinehart, & Winston).

Federoff, N. A., & Harvey, J. A. (1976). Focus of attention, self-esteem and attribution of causality. *Journal of Research, 10,* 336–345.

Felson, R. B. (1990). Comparison processes in parents' and children's appraisals of academic performance. *Social Psychology Quarterly, 53,* 264–273.

Felson, R. B. (1993). The (somewhat) social self: How others affect self-appraisals. In J. Suls (Ed.), *Psychological perspectives on the self,* (Vol. 4, pp. 1–26). Hillsdale, NJ: Erlbaum.

Festinger, L. (1942). A theoretical interpretation of shifts in level of aspiration. *Psychological Review, 49,* 235–250.

Festinger, L. (1954a). A theory of social comparison processes. *Human Relations, 7,* 117–140.

Festinger, L. (1954b). Motivation leading to social behavior. In M. R. Jones (Ed.), *Nebraska symposium on motivation* (Vol. 2, pp. 191–218). Lincoln, NE: University of Nebraska Press.

Fishbein, M., & Ajzen, I. (1975). *Belief, attitude, intention, and behavior: An introduction to theory and research.* Reading, MA: Addison-Wesley.

Fiske, S. T. (1993). Controlling other people: The impact of power on stereotyping. *American Psychologist, 48,* 621–628.

Fiske, S. T. (1998). Stereotyping, prejudice, and discrimination. In D. T. Gilbert, S. T. Fiske, & G. Lindzey (Ed.), *The handbook of social psychology* (4th ed., Vol. 2, pp. 357–411). New York: McGraw-Hill.

Fiske, S. T., Lin, M., & Neuberg, S. L. (1999). The continuum model: Ten years later. In S. Chaiken & Y. Trope (Eds.), *Dual-process theories in social psychology* (pp. 231–254). New York: Guilford Press.

Fiske, S. T., & Neuberg, S. L. (1990). A continuum of impression formation, from category-based to individuating processes: Influences of information and motivation on attention and interpretation. In M. Zanna (Ed.), *Advances in experimental social psychology* (Vol. 23, pp. 1–74). New York: Academic Press.

Fiske, S. T., Neuberg, S. L., Beattie, A. E., & Milberg, S. J. (1987). Category-based and attribute-based reactions to others: Some informational conditions of stereotyping and individuating processes. *Journal of Experimental Social Psychology, 23,* 399–427.

Foddy, M., & Crundall, I. (1993). A field study of social comparison processes in ability evaluation. *British Journal of Social Psychology, 32,* 287–305.

Foddy, M., & Smithson, M. (1989). Fuzzy sets and double standards: Modeling the process of ability inference. In J. Berger, M. Zelditch, & B. Anderson (Eds.), *Sociological theories in progress: New formulations* (pp. 73–99). Newbury Park, CA: Sage.

Förster, J., Higgins, E. T., & Idson, L. C. (1998). Approach and avoidance strength during goal attainment: Regulatory focus and the "goal looms larger" effect. *Journal of Personality and Social Psychology, 75,* 1115–1131.

Foschi, M. (1992). Gender and double standards for competence. In C. L. Ridgeway (Ed.), *Gender, interaction, and inequality* (pp. 181–207). New York: Springer-Verlag.

Foschi, M. (1998). Double standards: Types, conditions, and consequences. *Advances in group processes, 15,* 59–80.

Foschi, M. (2000). Double standards for competence: Theory and research. *Annual Review of Sociology, 26,* 21–42.

Foschi, M., & Foddy, M. (1988). Standards, performances, and the formation of self-other expectations. In M. Webster, Jr., & M. Foschi (Eds.), *Status generalization: Theory and research* (pp. 248–260, 501–503). Stanford, CA: Stanford University Press.

Frable, D. E. S. (1993). Being and feeling unique: Statistical deviance and psychological marginality. *Journal of Personality, 61,* 85–110.

Frank, R. H. (1985). *Choosing the right pond.* New York: Oxford University Press.

Fransella, F. (1968). Self concepts and the stutterer. *British Journal of Psychiatry, 114,* 1531–1535.

Gaertner, S. L., & Dovidio, J. F. (1986). The aversive form of racism. In J. F. Dovidio & S. L. Gaertner (Eds.), *Prejudice, discrimination, and racism* (pp. 61–89). Orlando, FL: Academic Press.

Gardner, W. L., Gabriel, S., & Hochschild, L. (2002). When you and I are "we," you are not threatening: The role of self-expansion in social comparison. *Journal of Personality and Social Psychology, 82,* 239–251.

Gerard, H. B. (1963). Emotional uncertainty and social comparison. *Journal of Abnormal and Social Psychology, 66,* 568–573.

Gerard, H. B., & Rabbie, J. M. (1961). Fear and social comparison. *Journal of Abnormal and Social Psychology, 62,* 586–592.

Gibbons, F. X. (1985). Stigma perception: Social comparison among mentally retarded persons. *American Journal of Mental Deficiency, 90,* 98–106.

Gibbons, F. X. (1990). Self-attention and behavior: A review and theoretical update. *Advances in Experimental Social Psychology, 23,* 249–303.

Gibbons, F. X., & Gerrard, M. (1991). Downward comparison and coping with threat. In J. Suls & T. A. Wills (Eds.), *Social comparison: Contemporary theory and research* (pp. 317–346). Hillsdale, NJ: Erlbaum.

Gibbons, F. X., & Gerrard, M. (1995). Predicting young adults' health-risk behavior. *Journal of Personality and Social Psychology, 69,* 505–517.

Gibbons, F. X., & Gerrard, M. (1997). Health images and their effects on health behavior. In B. P. Buunk & F. X. Gibbons (Eds.), *Health, coping, and well-being: Perspectives from social comparison theory* (pp. 63–94). Mahway, NJ: Erlbaum.

Gibbons, F. X., Gerrard, M., Lando, H. A., & McGovern, P. G. (1991). Social comparison and smoking cessation: The role of the "typical smoker." *Journal of Experimental Social Psychology, 27,* 239–258.

Gibbons, F. X., Lane, D. J., Gerrard, M., Reis-Bergan, M., Lautrup, C. L., Pexa, N. A., & Blanton, H. (2002). Comparison-level preferences after performance: Is downward comparison theory still useful? *Journal of Personality and Social Psychology, 83,* 865–880.

Gilbert, D. T., Giesler, R. B., & Morris, K. A. (1995). When comparisons arise. *Journal of Personality and Social Psychology, 69,* 227–236.

Gilbert, D. T., & Hixon, J. G. (1991). The trouble of thinking: Activation and application of stereotypic beliefs. *Journal of Personality and Social Psychology, 60,* 509–517.

Gilbert, D. T., Pelham, B. W., & Krull, D. S. (1988). On cognitive busyness: When person perceivers meet persons perceived. *Journal of Personality and Social Psychology, 54,* 733–740.

Gilovich, T. (1981). Seeing the past in the present: The effect of associations to familiar events on judgments and decisions. *Journal of Personality and Social Psychology, 40,* 797–808.

Gilovich, T. (1990). Differential construal and the false consensus effect. *Journal of Personality and Social Psychology, 59,* 623–634.

Glassman, N. S., & Andersen, S. M. (1999). Activating transference without consciousness: Using significant others to go beyond what is subliminally given. *Journal of Personality and Social Psychology, 77,* 1146–1162.

Goethals, G. R. (1986). Fabricating and ignoring social reality: Self-serving estimates of consensus. In J. Olson, C. P. Herman, & M. P. Zanna (Eds.), *Relative deprivation and social comparison: The Ontario Symposium on Social Cognition* (Vol. 4, pp. 135–157). Hillsdale, NJ: Erlbaum.

Goethals, G. R., Allison, S. J., & Frost, M. (1979). Perceptions of the magnitude and diversity of social support. *Journal of Experimental Social Psychology, 15,* 570–581.

Goethals, G. R., & Darley, J. M. (1977). Social comparison theory: An attributional approach. In J. M. Suls & R. L. Miller (Eds.), *Social comparison processes: Theoretical and empirical perspectives* (pp. 259–278). Washington, DC: Hemisphere.

Goethals, G. R., & Klein, W. M. (2000). Interpreting and inventing social reality: Attributional and constructive elements in social comparison. In J. Suls & L. Wheeler (Eds.), *Handbook of social comparison: Theory and research* (pp. 23–44). New York: Kluwer Academic Publishers.

Goethals, G. R., Messick, D., & Allison, S. (1991). The uniqueness bias: Studies of constructive social comparison. In J. Suls & T. A. Wills (Eds.), *Social comparison: Contemporary theory and research* (pp. 149–176). Hillsdale, NJ: Erlbaum.

Gollwitzer, P. M. (1990). Action phases and mind-sets. In E. T. Higgins & R. M. Sorrentino (Eds.), *Handbook of motivation and cognition: Foundations of social behavior, Vol. 2* (pp. 53–92). New York: Guilford Press.

Gollwitzer, P. M. (1996). The volitional benefits of planning. In P. M. Gollwitzer & J. A. Bargh (Eds.), *The psychology of action: Linking cognition and motivation to behavior* (pp. 287–312). New York: Guilford Press.

Gonzales, M. H., Burgess, D. J., & Mobilio, L. J. (2001). The allure of bad plans: Implications of plan quality for progress toward possible selves and postplanning energization. *Basic and Applied Social Psychology, 23,* 87–108.

Goodwin, S. A., Gubin, A., Fiske, S. T., & Yzerbyt, V. Y. (2000). Power can bias impression processes: Stereotyping subordinates by default and by design. *Group Processes and Intergroup Relations, 3,* 227–256.

Gordijn, E. H., Hindriks, I., Koomen, W., Dijksterhuis, A., & van Knippenberg, A. (2004). Consequences of stereotype suppression and internal suppression motivation: A self-regulation approach. *Personality and Social Psychology Bulletin, 30,* 212–224.

Gorenflo, D. W., & Crano, W. D. (1989). Judgmental subjectivity/objectivity and locus of choice in social comparison. *Journal of Personality and Social Psychology, 57,* 605–614.

Greenberg, J., & Musham, C. (1981). Avoiding and seeking self-focused attention. *Journal of Research in Personality, 15,* 191–200.

Greenwald, A. G., & Banaji, M. R. (1989). The self as a memory system: Powerful, but ordinary. *Journal of Personality and Social Psychology, 57,* 41–54.

Grice, H. P. (1975). Logic and conversation. In P. Cole & J. L. Morgan (Eds.), *Syntax and semantics 3: Speech acts* (pp. 41–58). New York: Academic Press.

Gross, S. R., Holtz, R., & Miller, N. (1995). Attitude certainty. In R. E. Petty & J. A. Krosnick (Eds.), *Attitude strength: Antecedents and consequences* (pp. 215–245). Mahwah, NJ: Erlbaum.

Gross, S. R., & Miller, N. (1997). The "golden section" and bias in perceptions of social consensus. *Personality and Social Psychology Review, 1,* 241–271.

Guimond, S., Chatard, A., Martinot, D., Crisp, R. J., & Redersdorff, S. (in press). Social comparsion, self-stereotyping, and gender differences in self-construal. *Journal of Personality and Social Psychology.*

Gupta, N., Jenkins, G. D., Jr., & Beehr, T. A. (1983). Employee gender, gender similarity, and supervisor-subordinate cross-evaluations. *Psychology of Women Quarterly, 8,* 174–184.

Haddock, G., Macrae, C. N., & Fleck, S. (2002). Syrian science and smart supermodels: On the when and how of perception-behavior effects. *Social Cognition, 20,* 461–479.

Häfner, M. (2004). How dissimilar other may still resemble the self: Assimilation and contrast after social comparison. *Journal of Consumer Psychology, 14,* 187–196.

Hakmiller, K. L. (1966). Threat as a determinant of downward comparison. *Journal of Experimental Social Psychology, 2* (Suppl. 1), 32–39.

Hamilton D. L., & Sherman, S. J. (1994). Stereotypes. In R. S. Wyer, Jr., & T. K. Srull (Eds.), *Handbook of social cognition* (pp. 1–68). Hillsdale, NJ: Erlbaum.

Harber, K. D. (1998). Feedback to minorities: Evidence of a positive bias. *Journal of Personality and Social Psychology, 74,* 622–628.

Hausdorff, J. M., Levy, B. R., & Wei, J. Y. (1999). The power of ageism on physical function of older persons: Reversibility of age-related gait changes. *Journal of the American Geriatrics Society, 47,* 1346–1349.

Heckhausen, H. (1967). *The anatomy of achievement motivation.* New York: Academic Press.

Heckhausen, H. (1991). *Motivation and action.* Heidelberg: Springer-Verlag.

Heider, F. (1944). Social perception and phenomenal causality. *Psychological Review, 51,* 358–374.

Heilman, M. E. (2001). Description and prescription: How gender stereotypes prevent women's ascent up the organizational ladder. *Journal of Social Issues, 57,* 657–674.

Helson, H. (1947). Adaptation-level as frame of reference for prediction of psychophysical data. *American Journal of Psychology, 60,* 1–29.

Helson, H. (1964). *Adaptation-level theory: An experimental and systematic approach to behavior.* New York: Harper & Row.

Henderson-King, E. I., & Nisbett, R. E. (1996). Anti-black prejudice as a function of exposure to the negative behavior of a single black person. *Journal of Personality and Social Psychology, 71,* 654–664.

Herr, P. M. (1986). Consequences of priming: Judgment and behavior. *Journal of Personality and Social Psychology, 51,* 1106–1115.

Herr, P. M., Sherman, S. J., & Fazio, R. H. (1983). On the consequences of priming: Assimilation and contrast effects. *Journal of Experimental Social Psychology, 19,* 323–340.

Higgins, E. T. (1987). Self-discrepancy: A theory relating self and affect. *Psychological Review, 94,* 319–340.

Higgins, E. T. (1989). Knowledge accessibility and activation: Subjectivity and suffering from unconscious sources. In J. S. Uleman & J. A. Bargh (Eds.), *Unintended thought: The limits of awareness, intention and control* (pp. 75–123). New York: Guilford.

Higgins, E. T. (1990). Personality, social psychology, and person-situated relations: Standards and knowledge activation as a common language. In L. A. Pervin (Ed.), *Handbook of personality* (pp. 301–338). New York: Guilford.

Higgins, E. T. (1996). Knowledge activation: Accessibility, applicability, and salience. In E. T. Higgins & A. W. Kruglanski (Eds.), *Social psychology: Handbook of basic principles* (pp. 133–168). New York: The Guilford Press.

Higgins, E. T. (1997). Beyond pleasure and pain. *American Psychologist, 52,* 1280–1300.

Higgins, E. T. (1998). The aboutness principle: A pervasive influence on human inference. *Social Cognition, 16,* 173–198.

Higgins, E. T. (1999). When do self-discrepancies have specific relations to emotions? The second generation question of Tangney, Niedenthal, Covert, & Barlow (1998). *Journal of Personality and Social Psychology, 77,* 1313–1317.

Higgins, E. T., & Chaires, W. M. (1980). Accessibility of interrelational constructs: Implications for stimulus encoding and creativity. *Journal of Experimental Social Psychology, 16,* 348–361.

Higgins, E. T., & King, G. (1981). Accessibility of social constructs: Information processing consequences of individual and contextual variability. In N. Cantor & J. Kihlstrom (Eds.), *Personality, cognition, and social interaction* (pp. 69–121). Hillsdale, NJ: Erlbaum.

Higgins, E. T., Klein, R., & Strauman, T. (1985). Self-concept discrepancy theory: A psychological model for distinguishing among different aspects of depression and anxiety. *Social Cognition, 3,* 51–76.

Higgins, E. T., & Liberman, A. (1994). Memory errors from a change of standard: A lack of awareness or understanding? *Cognitive Psychology, 27,* 227–258.

Higgins, E. T., & Lurie, L. (1983). Context, categorization, and memory: The "change of standard" effect. *Cognitive Psychology, 15,* 525–547.

Higgins, E. T., Rholes, W. S., & Jones, C. R. (1977). Category accessibility and impression formation. *Journal of Experimental Social Psychology, 13,* 141–154.

Higgins, E. T., Roney, C., Crowe, E., & Hymes, C. (1994). Ideal versus ought predilections for approach and avoidance: Distinct self-regulatory systems. *Journal of Personality and Social Psychology, 66,* 276–286.

Higgins, E. T., Shah, J., & Friedman, R. (1997). Emotional responses to goal attainment: Strength of regulatory focus as moderator. *Journal of Personality and Social Psychology, 72,* 515–525.

Higgins, E. T., & Stangor, C. (1988). A "change of standard" perspective on the relations among context, judgment, and memory. *Journal of Personality and Social Psychology, 54,* 181–192.

Higgins, E. T., Strauman, T., & Klein, R. (1986). Standards and the process of self-evaluation. In R. M. Sorrentino & E. T. Higgins (Eds.), *Handbook of motivation and cognition* (Vol. 1, pp. 23–63). New York: Guilford.

Hilton, J. L., & von Hippel, W. (1990). The role of consistency in the judgment of stereotype-relevant behaviors. *Personality and Social Psychology Bulletin, 16,* 430–448.

Hilton, J. L., & von Hippel, W. (1996). Stereotypes. *Annual Review of Psychology, 47,* 237–271.

Hinkley, K., & Andersen, S. M. (1996). The working self-concept in transference: Significant-other activation and self-change. *Journal of Personality and Social Psychology, 71,* 211–225.

Hogg, M. A. (2000). Social identity and social comparison. In J. Suls & L. Wheeler (Eds.), *Handbook of social comparison: Theory and research* (pp. 401–421). New York: Kluwer Academic Publishers.

Hogg, M. A., & Abrams, D. (1988). *Social identifications: A social psychology of intergroup relations and group processes.* London: Routledge.

Hogg, M. A., & Turner, J. C. (1987). Intergroup behaviour, self-stereotyping, and the salience of social categories. *British Journal of Social Psychology, 26,* 325–340.

Holmes, D. S. (1968). Dimensions of projection. *Psychological Bulletin, 69,* 248–268.

Holmes, D. S. (1978). Projection as a defense mechanism. *Psychological Bulletin, 85,* 677–688.

Holyoak, K. J., & Gordon, P. C. (1983). Social reference points. *Journal of Personality and Social Psychology, 44,* 881–887.

Holyoak, K. J., & Mah, W. A. (1982). Cognitive reference points in judgments of symbolic magnitude. *Cognitive Psychology, 14,* 328–352.

Hoorens, V., & Buunk, B. P. (1993). Social comparison of health risks: Locus of control, the person-positivity bias, and unrealistic optimism. *Journal of Applied Social Psychology, 23,* 291–302.

House, W. C., & Perney, V. (1974). Valence of expected and unexpected outcomes as a function of locus of goal and type of expectancy. *Journal of Personality and Social Psychology, 29,* 454–463.

Houston, D. A. (1990). Empathy and the self: Cognitive and emotional influences on the evaluation of negative affect in others. *Journal of Personality and Social Psychology, 59,* 859–868.

Houston, D. A., & Sherman, S. J. (1995). Cancellation and focus: The role of shared and unique features in the choice process. *Journal of Experimental Social Psychology, 31,* 357–378.

Hovland, C. I., Harvey, O. J., & Sherif, M. (1957). Assimilation and contrast effects in reactions to communication and attitude change. *Journal of Abnormal and Social Psychology, 55*, 244–252.

Hovland, C. I., & Sherif, M. (1952). Judgmental phenomena and scales of attitude measurement: Item displacement in Thurstone scales. *Journal of Abnormal and Social Psychology, 47*, 822–832.

Hoy, R. M. (1977). Some findings concerning beliefs and alcoholism. *British Journal of Medical Psychology, 50*, 227–235.

Hugenberg, K., & Bodenhausen, G. V. (2004). Category membership moderates the inhibition of social identities. *Journal of Experimental Social Psychology, 40*, 233–238.

Huttenlocher, J., & Higgins, E. T. (1971). Adjectives, comparatives, and syllogisms. *Psychological Review, 78*, 487–504.

Hyman, H. (1942). The psychology of subjective status. *Psychological Bulletin, 39*, 473–474.

Ickes, W. J., Wicklund, R. A., & Ferris, C. B. (1973). Objective self awareness and self esteem. *Journal of Experimental Social Psychology, 9*, 202–219.

Idson, L. C., Liberman, N., & Higgins, E. T. (2000). Distinguishing gains from losses and losses from nongains: A regulatory focus perspective on hedonic intensity. *Journal of Experimental Social Psychology, 36*, 252–274.

Insko, C. A., Murashima, F., & Saiyadain, M. (1966). Communicator discrepancy, stimulus ambiguity, and influence. *Journal of Personality, 34*, 262–274.

Jackman, M. R. (1994). *The velvet glove: Paternalism and conflict in gender, class, and race relations*. Berkeley, CA: University of California Press.

Jackson, L. A., Sullivan, L. A., & Hodge, C. N. (1993). Stereotype effects of attributions, predictions, and evaluations: No two social judgments are quite alike. *Journal of Personality and Social Psychology, 65*, 69–84.

James, W. (1890/1948). *Principles of psychology*. New York: Holt.

Jones, E. E. (1986). Interpreting interpersonal behavior: The effects of expectancies. *Science, 234*, 41–46.

Judd, C. M., & Harackiewicz, J. M. (1980). Contrast effects in attitude judgment: An examination of the accentuation hypothesis. *Journal of Personality and Social Psychology, 38*, 390–398.

Jussim, L. (1986). Self-fulfilling prophesies: A theoretical and integrative review. *Psychological Review, 93*, 429–445.

Jussim, L., Coleman, L. M., & Lerch, L. (1987). The nature of stereotypes: A comparison and integration of three theories. *Journal of Personality and Social Psychology, 52*, 536–546.

Jussim, L., Eccles, J., & Madon, S. (1996). Social perception, social stereotypes, and teacher expectations: Accuracy and the quest for the powerful self-fulfilling prophecy. In M. P. Zanna (Ed.), *Advances in experimental social psychology* (Vol. 28, pp. 281–388).

Jussim, L., Nelson, T. E., Manis, M., & Soffin, S. (1995). Prejudice, stereotypes, and labeling effects: Sources of bias in person perception. *Journal of Personality and Social Psychology, 68*, 228–246.

Kahneman, D., & Miller, D. T. (1986). Norm theory: Comparing reality to its alternatives. *Psychological Review, 93*, 136–153.

Karniol, R. (2003). Egocentrism versus protocentrism: The status of self in social prediction. *Psychological Review, 110*, 564–580.

Karylowski, J. J. (1990). Social reference points and accessibility of trait-related information in self-other similarity judgments. *Journal of Personality and Social Psychology, 58*, 975–983.

Karylowski, J. J., & Skarzynska, K. (1992). Asymmetric self-other similarity judgments depend on priming self-knowledge. *Social Cognition, 10*, 235–254.

Katz, D., & Allport, F. H. (1928). *Student attitudes: A report of the Syracuse University research study*. Syracuse, NY: Craftsman Press.

Kawada, C. L. K., Oettingen, G., Gollwitzer, P. M., & Bargh, J. A. (2004). The Projection of implicit and explicit goals. *Journal of Personality and Social Psychology, 86*, 545–559.

Kawakami, K., Dovidio, J. F., & Dijksterhuis, A. (2003). Effect of social category priming on personal attitudes. *Psychological Science, 14*, 315–319.

Kelley, H. H. (1950). The warm-cold variable in first impressions of persons. *Journal of Personality, 18*, 431–439.

Kelley, H. H. (1952). Two functions of reference groups. In G. E. Swanson, T. M. Newcomb, & E. L. Hartley (Eds.), *Readings in social psychology* (2nd ed., pp. 410–430). New York: Holt, Rinehart & Winston.

Kelley, H. H. (1972). Attribution in social interaction. In E. E. Jones, D. E. Kanouse, H. H. Kelley, R. E. Nisbett, S. Valins, & B. Weiner (Eds.), *Attribution: Perceiving the causes of behavior* (pp. 1–26). Morristown, NJ: General Learning Press.

Kelley, H. H., & Stahelski, A. J. (1970). Social interaction basis of cooperators' and competitors' beliefs about others. *Journal of Personality and Social Psychology, 16,* 66–91.

Kenny, D. A. (1994). *Interpersonal perception: A social relations analysis.* New York: Guilford.

Kihlstrom, J. F., & Klein, S. B. (1994). The self as a knowledge structure. In R. S. Wyer & T. K. Srull (Eds.), *Handbook of social cognition* (Vol. 1, pp. 153–208). Hillsdale, NJ: Erlbaum.

Klar, Y., & Giladi, E. E. (1999). Are most people happier than their peers, or are they just happy? *Personality and Social Psychology Bulletin, 25,* 585–594.

Klein, W. M. (1997). Objective standards are not enough: Affective, self-evaluative, and behavioral responses to social comparison information. *Journal of Personality and Social Psychology, 72,* 763–774.

Klein, W. M. & Weinstein, N. D. (1997). Social comparison and unrealistic optimism about personal risk. In F. X. Gibbons & B. P. Buunk, (Eds.), *Health, coping, and well-being: Perspectives from social comparison theory* (pp. 25–61). Mahwah, NJ: Lawrence Erlbaum Associates.

Kobrynowicz, D., & Biernat, M. (1997). Decoding subjective evaluations: How stereotypes provide shifting standards. *Journal of Experimental Social Psychology, 33,* 579–601.

Koehler, D. J. (1991). Explanation, imagination, and confidence in judgment. *Psychological Bulletin, 110,* 499–519.

Koomen, W., Stapel, D. A., Jansen, S. S., & In 't Veld, K. H. R. (1998). Priming and timing: A test of two perspectives. *European Journal of Social Psychology, 28,* 681–686.

Korte, C. (1972). Pluralistic ignorance about student radicalism. *Sociometry, 35,* 576–587.

Krantz, D. L., & Campbell, D. T. (1961). Separating perceptual and linguistic effects of context shifts upon absolute judgments. *Journal of Experimental Psychology, 62,* 35–42.

Krueger, J. (1998). Enhancement bias in descriptions of self and others. *Personality and Social Psychology Bulletin, 24,* 505–516.

Krueger, J. (2000). The projective perception of the social world: A building block of social comparison processes. In J. Suls & L. Wheeler (Eds.), *Handbook of social comparison: Theory and research* (pp. 323–351). New York: Kluwer Academic Publishers.

Krueger, J., & Clement, R. W. (1994). The truly false consensus effect: An ineradicable and egocentric bias in social perception. *Journal of Personality and Social Psychology, 67,* 596–610.

Krueger, J., & Clement, R. W. (1997). Estimates of social consensus by majorities and minorities: The case for social projection. *Personality and Social Psychology Review, 1,* 299–313.

Krueger, J., & Rothbart, M. (1988). The use of categorical and individuating information in making inferences about personality. *Journal of Personality and Social Psychology, 55,* 187–195.

Krueger, J. & Stanke, D. (2001). The role of self-referent and other-referent knowledge in perceptions of group characterictics. *Personality and Social Psychology Bulletin, 27,* 878–888.

Krueger, J., & Zeiger, J. S. (1993). Social categorization and the truly false consensus effect. *Journal of Personality and Social Psychology, 65,* 670–680.

Kruglanski, A. W., & Freund, T. (1983). The freezing and unfreezing of lay-inferences: effects on impressional primacy, ethnic stereotyping, and numerical anchoring. *Journal of Experimental Social Psychology, 19,* 448–468.

Kruglanski, A. W., & Mayseless, O. (1990). Classic and current social comparison research: Expanding the perspective. *Psychological Bulletin, 108,* 195–208.

Kruglanski, A. W., & Webster, D. M. (1996). Motivated closing of the mind: "Seizing" and "freezing." *Psychological Review, 103,* 263–283.

Kuhl, J. (1994). Motivation and volition. In G. d'Y dewalle, P. Eelen, & P. Bertelson (Eds.), *International perspectives on psychological science, Vol. 2: The state of the art* (pp. 311–340). Hillsdale, NJ: Lawrence Erlbaum Associates.

Kunda, Z. (1990). The case for motivated reasoning. *Psychological Bulletin, 108,* 480–498.

Kunda, Z., & Sherman-Williams, B. (1993). Stereotypes and the construal of individuating information. *Personality and Social Psychological Bulletin, 19*, 90–99.

Kunda, Z., Sinclair, L., & Griffin, D. (1997). Equal ratings but separate meanings: Stereotypes and the construal of traits. *Journal of Personality and Social Psychology, 72*, 720–734.

Kunda, Z., & Thagard, P. (1996). Forming impressions from stereotypes, traits, and behaviors: A parallel-constraint satisfaction theory. *Psychological Review, 103*, 284–308.

Lambert, A. J., & Wedell, D. H. (1991). The self and social judgment: Effects of affective reaction and "own position" on judgments of unambiguous and ambiguous information about others. *Journal of Personality and Social Psychology, 61*, 884–897.

Langer, E. J., & Abelson, R. P. (1974). A patient by any other name …: Clinician group difference in labeling bias. *Journal of Consulting and Clinical Psychology, 42*, 4–9.

Latané, B., & Darley, J. (1970). *The unresponsive bystander: Why doesn't he help?* New York: Appleton-Century-Crofts.

LeBoeuf, R. A., & Estes, Z. (2004). "Fortunately, I'm no Einstein": Comparison relevance as a determinant of behavioral assimilation and contrast. *Social Cognition, 22*, 607–636.

Lemon, N., & Warren, N. (1976). Salience, centrality, and self-relevance of traits in construing others. *British Journal of Social and Clinical Psychology, 13*, 119–124.

Lepore, L., & Brown, R. (1997). Category and stereotype activation: Is prejudice inevitable? *Journal of Personality and Social Psychology, 72*, 275–287.

Levine, J. M., & Moreland, R. L. (1986). Outcome comparisons in group contexts: Consequences for the self and others. In R. Schwarzer (Ed.), *Self-related cognitions in anxiety and motivation* (pp. 285–303). Hillsdale, NJ: Lawrence Erlbaum Associates.

Levine, J. M., & Moreland, R. L. (1987). Social comparison and outcome evaluation in group concepts. In J. C. Masters & W. P. Smith (Eds.), *Social comparison, social justice, and relative deprivation: Theoretical, empirical, and policy perspectives* (pp. 105–127). Hillsdale, NJ: Lawrence Erlbaum Associates.

Levy, B. (1996). Improving memory in old age through implicit self-stereotyping. *Journal of Personality and Social Psychology, 71*, 1092–1107.

Lewicki, P. (1983). Self-image bias in person perception. *Journal of Personality and Social Psychology, 45*, 384–393.

Lewicki, P. (1985). Nonconscious biasing effects of single instances on subsequent judgments. *Journal of Personality and Social Psychology, 48*, 563–574.

Lewicki, P. (1986). *Nonconscious social information processing.* San Diego, CA: Academic Press.

Lewin, K. (1935). *A dynamic theory of personality.* New York: McGraw-Hill.

Lewin, K. (1951). *Field theory in social science: Selected theoretical papers.* Oxford, England: Harpers.

Lewin, K., Dembo, T., Festinger, L., & Sears, P. S. (1944). Level of aspiration. In J. M. Hunt (Ed.), *Personality and the behavior disorders* (pp. 333–378). New York: Roland Press.

Leyens, J. P., Yzerbyt, V., & Schadron, G. (1994). *Stereotypes and social cognition.* London: Sage.

Liberman, N., & Förster, J. (2000). Expression after suppression: A motivational explanation of postsuppressional rebound. *Journal of Personality and Social Psychology, 79*, 51–56.

Linville, P. W., & Jones, E. E. (1980). Polarized appraisals of outgroup members. *Journal of Personality and Social Psychology, 38*, 689–703.

Locke, K. D. (2003). Status and solidarity in social comparison: Agentic and communal values and vertical and horizontal directions. *Journal of Personality and Social Psychology, 84*, 619–631.

Locke, V., MacLeod, C., & Walker, I. (1994). Automatic and controlled activation of stereotypes: Individual differences associated with prejudice. *British Journal of Social Psychology, 33*, 29–46.

Locksley, A., Borgida, E., Brekke, N., & Hepburn, C. (1980). Sex stereotypes and judgments of individuals: An instance of the base-rate fallacy. *Journal of Experimental Social Psychology, 18*, 23–42.

Lockwood, P. (2002). Could it happen to you? Predicting the impact of downward comparisons on the self. *Journal of Personality and Social Psychology, 82*, 343–358.

Lockwood, P., & Kunda, Z. (1997). Superstars and me: Predicting the impact of role models on the self. *Journal of Personality and Social Psychology, 73*, 91–103.

Lockwood, P., & Kunda, Z. (1999). Increasing the salience of one's best selves can undermine inspiration by outstanding role models. *Journal of Personality and Social Psychology, 76*, 214–228.

Lombardi, W. J., Higgins, E. T., & Bargh, J. A. (1987). The role of consciousness in priming effects on categorization. *Personality and Social Psychology Bulletin, 13*, 411–429.

Lord, C. G., Ross, L., & Lepper, M. R. (1979). Biased assimilation and attitude polarization: The effects of prior theories on subsequently considered evidence. *Journal of Personality and Social Psychology, 37*, 2098–2109.

Lorenzi-Cioldi, F. (1991). Self-stereotyping and self-enhancement in gender groups. *European Journal of Social Psychology 21*, 403–417.

Lyubomirsky, S., & Ross, L. (1997). Changes in attractiveness of elected, rejected, and precluded alternatives: A comparison of happy and unhappy individuals. *Journal of Personality and Social Psychology, 76*, 988–1007.

Maass, A., Montalcini, F., & Biciotti, E. (1998). On the (dis-)confirmability of stereotypic attributes. *European Journal of Social Psychology, 28*, 383–402.

Macrae, C. N., Bodenhausen, G. V., & Milne, A. B. (1995). The dissection of selection in person perception: Inhibitory processes in social stereotyping. *Journal of Personality and Social Psychology, 69*, 397–407.

Macrae, C. N., Bodenhausen, G. V., & Milne, A. B. (1998). Saying no to unwanted thoughts: Self-focus and the regulation of mental life. *Journal of Personality and Social Psychology, 74*, 578–589.

Macrae, C. N., Bodenhausen, G. V., Milne, A. B., & Jetten, J. (1994). Out of mind but back in sight: Stereotypes on the rebound. *Journal of Personality and Social Psychology, 67*, 808–817.

Major, B. (1994). From social inequality to personal entitlement: The role of social comparison, legitimacy appraisals, and group membership. In M. P. Zanna (Ed.), *Advances in experimental social psychology* (Vol. 26, pp. 293–355). Orlando, FL: Academic Press.

Major, B., Sciacchitano, A. M., & Crocker, J. (1993). In-group versus out-group comparisons and self-esteem. *Personality and Social Psychology Bulletin, 19*, 711–721.

Major, B., Testa, M., & Bylsma, W. H. (1991). Responses to upward and downward social comparisons: The impact of esteem-relevance and perceived control. In J. Suls & T. A. Wills (Eds.), *Social comparison: Contemporary theory and research* (pp. 237–260). Hillsdale, NJ: Lawrence-Erlbaum.

Mandler, G. (1975). *Mind and emotions.* New York: Wiley.

Manis, M., Biernat, M., & Nelson, T. (1991). Comparison and expectancy processes in human judgment. *Journal of Personality and Social Psychology, 61*, 203–211.

Manis, M., & Blake, J. B. (1963). Interpretation of persuasive messages as a function of prior immunization. *Journal of Abnormal and Social Psychology, 66*, 225–230.

Manis, M., & Moore, J. C. (1978). Summarizing controversial messages: Retroactive effects due to subsequent information. *Social Psychology, 41*, 62–68.

Manis, M., Nelson, T. E., & Shedler, J. (1988). Stereotypes and social judgment: Extremity, assimilation, and contrast. *Journal of Personality and Social Psychology, 55*, 28–36.

Manis, M., & Paskewitz, J. R. (1984a). Judging psychopathology: Expectation and contrast. *Journal of Experimental Social Psychology, 20*, 363–381.

Manis, M., & Paskewitz, J. R. (1984b). Specificity in contrast effects: Judgments of psychopathology. *Journal of Experimental Social Psychology, 20*, 217–230.

Manis, M., Paskewitz, J. R., & Cotler, S. (1986). Stereotypes and social judgment. *Journal of Personality and Social Psychology, 50*, 461–473.

Manstead, A. S. R. (1982). Perceived social support for opinions: A test of the magnitude and diversity hypothesis. *British Journal of Social Psychology, 21*, 35–41.

Markman, K. D., Gavanski, I., Sherman, S. J., & McMullen, M. N. (1993). The mental stimulation of better and worse possible worlds. *Journal of Experimental Social Psychology, 29*, 87–109.

Markman, K. D., & McMullen, M. N. (2003). A reflection and evaluation model of comparative thinking. *Personality and Social Psychology Review, 7*, 244–267.

Marks, G. (1984). Thinking one's abilities are unique and one's opinions are common. *Personality and Social Psychology Bulletin, 10*, 203–208.

Marks, G., & Duval, S. (1991). Availability of alternative positions and estimates of consensus. *British Journal of Social Psychology, 30,* 179–183.

Marks, G., & Miller, N. (1985). The effect of certainty on consensus judgments. *Personality and Social Psychology Bulletin, 11,* 165–177.

Marks, G., & Miller, N. (1987). Ten years of research on the false consensus effect: An empirical and theoretical review. *Psychological Bulletin, 102,* 72–90.

Markus, H., Crane, M., Bernstein, S., & Siladi, M. (1982). Self-schemas and gender. *Journal of Personality and Social Psychology, 42,* 38–50.

Markus, H., & Nurius, P. (1986). Possible selves. *American Psychologist, 41,* 954–969.

Markus, H., & Smith, J. (1981). The influence of self-schemata on the perception of others. In N. Cantor & J. Kihlstrom (Eds.), *Personality, cognition, and social interaction* (pp. 233–262). Hillsdale, NJ: Erlbaum.

Markus, H., Smith, J., & Moreland, R. L. (1985). Role of the self-concept in perception of others. *Journal of Personality and Social Psychology, 49,* 1494–1512.

Markus, H., & Wurf, E. (1987). The dynamic self-concept: A social psychological perspective. *Annual Review of Psychology, 38,* 299–337.

Marsh, H. W. (1993). Academic self-concept: Theory, measurement, and research. In J. Suls (Ed.), *Psychological perspectives on the self* (Vol. 4, pp. 1–26). Hillsdale, NJ: Lawrence Erlbaum and Associates.

Marsh, H. W., & Hau, K. T. (2003). Big-fish–little-pond effect on academic self-concept: A cross-cultural (26-country) test of the negative effects of academically selective schools. *American Psychologist, 58,* 364–376.

Marsh, H. W., & Parker, J. W. (1984). Determinants of student self-concept: Is it better to be a relatively large fish in a small pond even if you don't learn to swim as well? *Journal of Personality and Social Psychology, 47,* 213–231.

Martin, C. L. (1987). A ratio measure of sex stereotyping. *Journal of Personality and Social Psychology, 52,* 489–499.

Martin, L. L. (1986). Set/reset: Use and disuse of concepts in impression formation. *Journal of Personality and Social Psychology, 51,* 493–504.

Martin, L. L., & Achee, J. W. (1992). Beyond accessibility: The role of processing objectives in judgment. In L. L. Martin & A. Tesser (Eds.), *The construction of social judgments* (pp. 195–216). Hillsdale, NJ: Erlbaum.

Martin, L. L., & Seta, J. J. (1983). Perceptions of unity and distinctiveness as determinants of attraction. *Journal of Personality and Social Psychology, 44,* 755–764.

Martin, L. L., Seta, J. J., & Crelia, R. A. (1990). Assimilation and contrast as a function of people's willingness and ability to expend effort in forming an impression. *Journal of Personality and Social Psychology, 59,* 27–37.

Martin, L. L., Ward, D. W., Achee, J. W., & Wyer, R. S. (1993). Mood as input: People have to interpret the motivational implications of their moods. *Journal of Personality and Social Psychology, 64,* 317–326.

Martin, R., Suls, J., & Wheeler, L. (2002). Ability evaluation by proxy: The role of maximal performance and related attributes in social comparison. *Journal of Personality and Social Psychology, 82,* 781–791.

Martinot, D., Redersdorff, S., Guimond, S., & Dif, S. (2002). Ingroup versus outgroup comparisons and self-esteem: The role of group status and ingroup identification. *Personality and Social Psychology Bulletin, 28,* 1586–1600.

Maslow, A. H. (1943). A theory of human motivation. *Psychological Review, 50,* 370–396.

Massey G. C., Scott, M. V., & Dornbusch, S. M. (1975). Racism without racists: Institutional racism in urban schools. *Black Scholar, 7,* 10–19.

McClelland, D. C., Atkinson, J. W., Clark, R. A., & Lowell, E. L. (1953). The achievement motive. New York: Appleton-Century-Crofts.

McFarland, C., & Buehler, R. (1995). Collective self-esteem as a moderator of the frog-pond effect in reactions to performance feedback. *Journal of Personality and Social Psychology, 68,* 1055–1070.

McFarland, C., Buehler, R., & MacKay, L. (2001). Affective responses to social comparison with extremely close others. *Social Cognition, 19,* 547–586.

McFarland, C., & Miller, D. T. (1990). Judgments of self-other similarity—just like other people, only more so. *Personality and Social Psychology Bulletin, 16,* 475–484.

McGill, A. L. (1993). Selection of a causal background: Role of expectation versus feature mutability. *Journal of Personality and Social Psychology, 64,* 701–707.

McGuire, W. J., & McGuire, C. V. (1988). Content and process in the experience of the self. In L. Berkowitz (Ed.), *Advances in experimental social psychology* (Vol. 21, pp. 97–144). San Diego, CA: Academic Press.

McMullen, M. N. (1997). Affective contrast and assimilation in counterfactual thinking. *Journal of Experimental Social Psychology, 33,* 77–100.

Messé, L. A., & Sivacek, J. M. (1979). Predictions of others' responses in a mixed-motive game: Self-justification or false consensus? *Journal of Personality and Social Psychology, 37,* 602–607.

Mettee, D. R., & Smith, G. (1977). Social comparison and interpersonal attraction: The case for dissimilarity. In J. M. Suls & R. L. Miller (Eds.), *Social comparison processes: Theoretical and empirical perspectives* (pp. 69–101). Washington, DC: Hemisphere.

Miller, C. T. (1982). The role of performance-related similarity in social comparison of abilities: A test of the related attributes hypothesis. *Journal of Experimental Social Psychology, 18,* 513–523.

Miller, C. T. (1984). Self-schemas, gender, and social comparison: A clarification of the related attributes hypothesis. *Journal of Personality and Social Psychology, 46,* 1222–1229.

Miller, D. T., & McFarland, C. (1987). Pluralistic ignorance: When similarity is interpreted as dissimilarity. *Journal of Personality and Social Psychology, 53,* 298–305.

Miller, D. T., & Prentice, D. A. (1996). The construction of social norms and standards. In E. T. Higgins & A. W. Kruglanski (Eds.), *Social psychology: Handbook of basic principles* (pp. 799–829). New York, NY: Guilford Press.

Miller, D. T., Turnbull, W., & McFarland, C. (1988). Particularistic and universalistic evaluation in the social comparison process. *Journal of Personality and Social Psychology, 55,* 908–917.

Miller, D. T., Turnbull, W., & McFarland, C. (1990). Counterfactual thinking and social perception: Thinking about what might have been. In M. P. Zanna (Ed.), *Advances in experimental social psychology* (Vol. 23, pp. 305–331). Orlando, FL Academic Press.

Miller, R. L. (1977). Preferences for social vs. non-social comparison as a means of self-evaluation. *Journal of Personality, 45,* 343–355.

Mischel, W., Cantor, N., & Feldman, S. (1996). Principles of self-regulation: The nature of willpower and self-control. In E. T. Higgins & A. W. Kruglanski (Eds.), *Social psychology: Handbook of basic principles* (pp. 329–360). New York, NY: Guilford Press.

Miyake, K., & Zuckerman, M. (1993). Beyond personality impressions: Effects of physical and vocal attractiveness on false consensus, social comparison, affiliation, and assumed and perceived similarity. *Journal of Personality, 61,* 411–437.

Monin, B., & Norton, M. I. (2003). Perceptions of a fluid consensus: Uniqueness bias, false consensus, false polarization, and pluralistic ignorance in a water conservation crisis. *Personality and Social Psychology Bulletin, 29,* 559–567.

Monteith, M. J. (1993). Self-regulation of prejudiced responses: Implications for progress in prejudice-reduction efforts. *Journal of Personality and Social Psychology, 65,* 469–485.

Monteith, M. J. (1996). Contemporary forms of prejudice-related conflict: In search of a nutshell. *Personality and Social Psychology Bulletin, 22,* 461–473.

Monteith, M. J., Ashburn-Nardo, L., Voils, C. I., & Czopp, A. M. (2002). Putting the brakes on prejudice: On the development and operations of cues for control. *Journal of Personality and Social Psychology, 83*(5), 1029–1050.

Monteith, M. J., Devine, P. G., & Zuwerink, J. R. (1993). Self-directed versus other-directed affect as a consequence of prejudice-related discrepancies. *Journal of Personality and Social Psychology, 64,* 198–210.

Monteith, M. J., Sherman, J. W., & Devine, P. G. (1998). Suppression as a stereotype control strategy. *Personality and Social Psychology Review, 2,* 63–82.

Monteith, M. J., & Walters, G. L. (1998). Egalitarianism, moral obligation, and prejudice-related personal standards. *Personality and Social Psychology Bulletin, 24,* 186–199.

Moore, D. A., & Kim, T. G. (2003). Myopic social prediction and the solo comparison effect. *Journal of Personality and Social Psychology, 85,* 1121–1135.

Morse, S., & Gergen, K. J. (1970). Social comparison, self-consistency, and the concept of self. *Journal of Personality and Social Psychology, 16,* 148–156.

Moskowitz, G. B., & Roman, R. J. (1992). Spontaneous trait inferences as self-generated primes: Implications for conscious social judgment. *Journal of Personality and Social Psychology, 62,* 728–738.

Moskowitz, G. B., & Skurnik, I. W. (1999). Contrast effects as determined by the type of prime: Trait versus exemplar primes initiate processing strategies that differ in how accessible constructs are used. *Journal of Personality and Social Psychology, 76,* 911–927.

Mullen, B., Atkins, J. L., Champion, D. S., Edwards, C., Hardy, D., Story, J. E., & Vanderklok, M. (1985). The false consensus effect: A meta-analysis of 155 hypothesis tests. *Journal of Experimental Social Psychology, 21,* 262–283.

Mullen, B., Dovidio, J. F., Johnson, C., & Copper, C. (1992). In-group-out-group differences in social projection. *Journal of Experimental Social Psychology, 28,* 422–440.

Mullen, B., Driskell, J. E., & Smith, C. (1989). Availability and social projection: The effects of sequence of measurement and wording of question on estimates of consensus. *Personality and Social Psychology Bulletin, 15,* 84–90.

Mullen, B., & Goethals, G. R. (1990). Social projection, actual consensus and valence. *British Journal of Social Psychology, 29,* 279–282.

Mullen, B., & Hu, L. (1988). Social projection as a function of cognitive mechanisms: Two meta-analytic integrations. *British Journal of Social Psychology, 27,* 333–356.

Murphy, K. R., & Cleveland, J. N. (1995). *Understanding performance appraisal: Social, organizational, and goal-based perspectives.* Thousand Oaks, CA: Sage Publications.

Murray, C. B., & Jackson, J. S. (1982–83). The conditioned failure model of Black educational underachievement. *Humboldt Journal of Social Relations, 10,* 276–300.

Murstein, B. I., & Pryer, R. S. (1959). The concept of projection: A review. *Psychological Bulletin, 56,* 353–374.

Mussweiler, T. (2001a). Focus of comparison as a determinant of assimilation and contrast in social comparison. *Personality and Social Psychology Bulletin, 27,* 38–47.

Mussweiler, T. (2001b). "Seek and ye shall find": Antecedents of assimilation and contrast in social comparison. *European Journal of Social Psychology, 31,* 499–509.

Mussweiler, T. (2003a). Comparison processes in social judgment: Mechanisms and consequences. *Psychological Review, 110,* 472–489.

Mussweiler, T. (2003b). "Everything is relative": Comparison processes in social judgment: The 2002 Jaspars Lecture. *European Journal of Social Psychology, 33,* 719–733.

Mussweiler, T., & Bodenhausen, G. V. (2002). I know you are, but what am I? Self-evaluative consequences of judging in-group and out-group members. *Journal of Personality and Social Psychology, 82,* 19–32.

Mussweiler, T., & Rüter, K. (2003). What friends are for! The use of routine standards in social comparison. *Journal of Personality and Social Psychology, 85,* 467–481.

Mussweiler, T., & Rüter, K., & Epstude, K. (2004). The man who wasn't there: Subliminal social comparsion standards influence self-evaluation. *Journal of Experimental Social Psychology, 40,* 689–696.

Mussweiler, T., & Strack, F. (2000). The "relative self": Informational and judgmental consequences of comparative self-evaluation. *Journal of Personality and Social Psychology, 79,* 23–38.

Neuberg, S. L., & Fiske, S. T. (1987). Motivational influences on impression formation: Outcome dependency, accuracy-driven attention, and individuating processes. *Journal of Personality and Social Psychology, 53,* 431–444.

Newcomb, T. M. (1943). *Personality and social change.* Fort Worth, TX: Dryden Press.

Newman, L. S., & Uleman, J. S. (1990). Assimilation and contrast effects in spontaneous trait inference. *Personality and Social Psychology Bulletin, 16,* 224–240.

Newman, L. S., Higgins, E. T., & Vookles, J. (1992). Self-guide strength and emotional vulnerability: Birth order as a moderator of self-affect relations. *Personality and Social Psychology Bulletin, 18,* 402–411.

Newman, S. E., & Benassi, V. A. (1989). Putting judgments of control into context: Contrast effects. *Journal of Personality and Social Psychology, 56,* 876–889.

Nisbett, R. E., & Kunda, Z. (1985). Perception of social distributions. *Journal of Personality and Social Psychology, 48,* 297–311.

Nisbett, R. E., & Ross, L. (1980). *Human inference: Strategies and shortcomings of social judgment.* Englewood Cliffs, NJ: Prentice-Hall.

Nisbett, R. E., & Valins, S. (1972). Perceiving the causes of one's own behavior. In E. E. Jones, D. E. Kanouse, H. H. Kelley, R. E. Nisbett, S. Valins, & B. Weiner (Eds.), *Attribution: Perceiving the causes of behavior* (pp. 63–78). Hillsdale, NJ, England: Lawrence Erlbaum.

Nisbett, R. E., Zukier, H., & Lemley, R. E. (1981). The dilution effect: Nondiagnostic information weakens the implications of diagnostic information. *Cognitive Psychology, 13*, 248–277.

Nosanchuk, T. A., & Erickson, B. H. (1985). How high is up? Calibrating social comparison in the real world. *Journal of Personality and Social Psychology, 48*, 624–634.

Oakes, P. J., Haslam, S. A., & Turner, J. C. (1994). *Stereotyping and social reality*. Oxford: Blackwell.

Oakes, P. J., Turner, J. C., & Haslam, S. A. (1991). Perceiving people as group members: the role of fit in the salience of social categorizations. *British Journal of Social Psychology, 30*, 125–144.

Oettingen, G. (1996). Positive fantasy and motivation. In P. M. Gollwitzer & J. A. Bargh (Eds.), *The psychology of action: Linking cognition and motivation to behavior* (pp. 236–259). New York: Guilford Press.

Oettingen, G., & Mayer, D. (2002). The motivating function of thinking about the future: Expectations versus fantasies. *Journal of Personality and Social Psychology, 83*, 1198–1212.

Oettingen, G., Pak, H., & Schnetter, K. (2001). Self-regulation of goal-setting: Turning free fantasies about the future into binding goals. *Journal of Personality and Social Psychology, 80*, 736–753.

O'Gorman, H. J. (1988). Pluralistic ignorance and reference groups: The case of ingroup ignorance. In H. J. O'Gorman (Ed.), *Surveying social life: Papers in honor of H. H. Hyman* (pp. 145–173). Middletown, CT: Wesleyan University Press.

Oldham, G., Nottenburg, G., Kasner, M., Ferris, G., Fedor, D., & Masters, M. (1982). The selection and consequences of job comparisons. *Organizational Behavior and Human Performance, 29*, 84–111.

Olson, J. M., & Hafer, C. L. (1996). Affect, motivation, and cognition in relative deprivation research. In R. M. Sorrentino & E. T. Higgins (Eds.), *Handbook of motivation and cognition, Vol. 3: The interpersonal context* (pp. 85–117). New York, NY: Guilford Press.

Olson, J. M., Roese, N. J., & Zanna, M. P. (1996). Expectancies. In E. T. Higgins & A. W. Kruglanski (Eds.), *Social psychology: Handbook of basic principles* (pp. 211–238). New York, NY: The Guilford Press.

O'Mahony, P. D. (1982). Psychiatric patient denial of mental illness as a normal process. *British Journal of Medical Psychology, 55*, 109–118.

Orive, R. (1988). Social projection and social comparison of opinions. *Journal of Personality and Social Psychology, 54*, 953–964.

Ostrom, T. M., & Upshaw, H. S. (1968). Psychological perspective and attitude change. In A. G. Greenwald, T. C. Brock, & T. M. Ostrom (Eds.), *Psychological foundations of attitudes* (pp. 217–242). San Diego, CA: Academic Press.

Ottati, V. C., Riggle, E. J., Wyer, R. S., Schwarz, N., & Kuklinski, J. (1989). Cognitive and affective bases of opinion survey responses. *Journal of Personality and Social Psychology, 57*, 404–415.

Otten, S. (2003). "Me and us" or "us and them"?: The self as a heuristic for defining novel ingroups. In W. Stroebe & M. Hewstone (Eds.), *European Review of Social Psychology* (Vol. 13, pp. 1–34). Philadelphia, PA: Psychology Press.

Otten, W., van der Pligt, J. (1996). Context effects in the measurement of comparative optimism in probability judgments. *Journal of Social and Clinical Psychology, 15*, 80–101.

Oyserman, D. (2001). Self concept and identity. In A. Tesser & N. Schwarz (Eds.), *Blackwell handbook of social psychology* (pp. 449–517). Malden, MA: Blackwell Press.

Oyserman, D., Bybee, D., Terry, K., & Hart-Johnson, T. (2004). Possible selves as roadmaps. *Journal of Research in Personality, 38*, 130–149.

Parducci, A. (1956). Direction of shift in the judgment of single stimuli. *Journal of Experimental Psychology, 51*, 169–178.

Parducci, A. (1963). Range-frequency compromise in judgment. *Psychological Monographs, 77*, 1–29.

Parducci, A. (1965). Category judgment: A range-frequency model. *Psychological Review, 72*, 407–418.

Parducci, A. (1992). Elaborations upon psychophysical contexts for judgment: Implications of cognitive models. In H. G. Geissler & S. W. Link (Eds.), *Cognition, information processing, and psychophysics: Basic issues* (pp. 207–223). Hillsdale, NJ: Lawrence Erlbaum Associates.

Parducci, A. (1995). *Happiness, pleasure, and judgment.* Mahwah, NJ: Erlbaum.

Parducci, A., Knobel, S., & Thomas, C. (1976). Independent contexts for category ratings: A range-frequency analysis. *Perception and Psychophysics, 20,* 360–366.

Parducci, A., & Wedell, D. H. (1986). The category effect with rating scales: Number of categories, number of stimuli, and method of presentation. *Journal of Experimental Psychology: Human Perception and Performance, 12,* 496–516.

Parducci, A., & Wedell, D. H. (1990). The context for evaluative judgment: Psychophysics and beyond. In H. G. Geissler, M. H. Miller, & W. Prinz (Eds.), *Psychophysical explorations of mental structures* (pp. 94–103). Kirkland, WA: Hogrefe and Huber Publishers.

Park, B., & Hastie, R. (1987). Perception of variability in category development: Instance-versus abstraction-based stereotypes. *Journal of Personality and Social Psychology, 53,* 621–635.

Pelham, B. W., & Wachsmuth, J. O. (1995). The waxing and waning of the social self: Assimilation and contrast in social comparison. *Journal of Personality and Social Psychology, 69,* 825–838.

Pennington, G. L., & Roese, N. J. (2003). Regulatory focus and temporal distance. *Journal of Experimental Social Psychology, 39,* 563–576.

Perdue, C. W., & Gurtman, M. B. (1990). Evidence for the automaticity of ageism. *Journal of Experimental Social Psychology, 26,* 199–216.

Perloff, L. S., & Brickman, P. (1982). False consensus and false uniqueness: Biases in perceptions of similarity. *Academic Psychology Bulletin, 4,* 475–494.

Perloff, L. S., & Fetzer, B. K. (1986). Self-other judgments and perceived vulnerability to victimization. *Journal of Personality and Social Psychology, 50,* 502–510.

Pervin, L. A. (1982). The stasis and flow of behavior: Toward a theory of goals. *Nebraska Symposium on Motivation, 30,* pp. 1–53.

Pettigrew, T. F. (1967). Social evaluation theory: Convergences and applications. *Nebraska Symposium on Motivation, 15,* 241–311.

Pettigrew, T. F. (2002). Summing up: Relative deprivation as a key social psychological concept. In I. Walker (Ed.), *Relative deprivation: Specification, development, and integration* (pp. 351–373). New York, NY: Cambridge University Press.

Pettigrew, T., & Martin, J. (1987). Shaping the organizational context for Black American inclusion. *Journal of Social Issues, 43,* 41–78.

Petty, R. E., & Wegener, D. T. (1993). Flexible correction processes in social judgment: Correcting for context-induced contrast. *Journal of Experimental Social Psychology, 29,* 137–165.

Philippot, P., Schwarz, N., Carrera, P., De Vries, N., & Van Yperen, N. W. (1991). Differential effects of priming at the encoding and judgment stage. *European Journal of Social Psychology, 21,* 293–302.

Pickett, C. L., Bonner, B. L., & Coleman, J. M. (2002). Motivated self-stereotyping: Heightened assimilation and differentiation needs result in increased levels of positive and negative self-stereotyping. *Journal of Personality and Social Psychology, 82,* 543–562.

Plant, E. A., & Devine, P. G. (1998). Internal and external motivation to respond without prejudice. *Journal of Personality and Social Psychology, 75,* 811–832.

Plant, E. A., & Devine, P. G. (2001). Response to other-imposed pro-Black pressure: Acceptance or backlash? *Journal of Experimental Social Psychology, 37,* 486–501.

Postman, L., & Miller, G. A. (1945). Anchoring of temporal judgments. *American Journal of Psychology, 58,* 43–53.

Postmes, T., & Spears, R. (2002). Behavior online: Does anonymous computer communication reduce gender inequality? *Personality and Social Psychology Bulletin, 28,* 1073–1083.

Pratto, F., & Bargh, J. A. (1991). Stereotyping based on apparently individuating information: Trait and global components of sex stereotypes under attention overload. *Journal of Experimental Social Psychology, 27,* 26–47.

Prentice, D. A. (1990). Familiarity and differences in self- and other-representations. *Journal of Personality and Social Psychology, 59,* 369–383.

Prentice, D. A., & Miller, D. T. (1993). Pluralistic ignorance and alcohol use on campus: Some consequences of misperceiving the social norm. *Journal of Personality and Social Psychology, 64*, 243–256.

Prentice, D. A., & Miller, D. T. (1996). Pluralistic ignorance and the perpetuation of social norms by unwitting actors. In M. P. Zanna (Ed.), *Advances in experimental social psychology* (Vol. 26, pp. 161–209). Orlando, FL: Academic Press.

Pyszczynski, T., & Greenberg, J. (1987). Toward an integration of cognitive and motivational perspectives on social inference: A biased hypothesis-testing model. In L. Berkowitz (Ed.), *Advances in experimental social psychology* (Vol. 20, pp. 297–340). San Diego, CA: Academic Press.

Rabbie, J. M., & Horwitz, M. (1988). Categories versus groups as explanatory concepts in intergroup relations. *European Journal of Social Psychology, 18*, 117–123.

Raynor, J. O. (1969). Future orientation and motivation of immediate activity: An elaboration of the theory of achievement motivation. *Psychological Review, 76*, 606–610.

Raynor, J. O., & McFarlin, D. B. (1986). Motivation and the self-system. In R. M. Sorrentino & E. T. Higgins (Eds.), *Handbook of motivation and cognition: Foundations of social behavior* (pp. 315–349). New York: Guilford.

Read, S. J. (1983). Once is enough: Causal reasoning from a single instance. *Journal of Personality and Social Psychology, 45*, 323–334.

Read, S. J. (1984). Analogical reasoning in social judgment: The importance of causal theories. *Journal of Personality and Social Psychology, 46*, 14–25.

Read, S. J., & Cessa, I. L. (1991). This reminds me of the time when …: Expectation failures in reminding and explanation. *Journal of Experimental Social Psychology, 27*, 1–25.

Reisenzein, R. (1996). Emotional action generation. In W. Battmann & S. Dutke (Eds.). *Processes of the molar regulation of behavior* (pp. 151–165). Scottsdale, AZ: Pabst Science Publishers.

Roese, N. J. (1994). The functional biases of counterfactual thinking. *Journal of Personality and Social Psychology, 66*, 805–818.

Roese, N. J., & Olson, J. M. (1997). Counterfactual thinking: The intersection of affect and function. In M. P. Zanna (Ed.), *Advances in experimental social psychology* (Vol. 29, pp. 1–59). San Diego, CA: Academic Press.

Rogers, C. R. (1951). *Client-centered therapy: Its current practice, implications, and theory*. Boston: Houghton-Mifflin.

Rogers, T. B. (1981). A model of the self as an aspect of the human information processing system. In N. Cantor & J. Kihlstrom (Eds.), *Personality, cognition, and social interaction* (pp. 193–214). Hillsdale, NJ: Erlbaum.

Rogers, T. B., Kuiper, N. A., & Rogers, P. J. (1979). Symbolic distance and congruity effects for paired-comparisons judgments of degree of self-reference. *Journal of Research in Personality, 13*, 433–449.

Rosch, E. (1975). Cognitive reference points. *Cognitive Psychology, 7*, 532–547.

Rosen, S., Mickler, S. E., & Collins, J. E. (1987). Reactions of would-be helpers whose offer of help is spurned. *Journal of Personality and Social Psychology, 53*, 288–297.

Rosenkrantz, P., Vogel, S., Bee, H., Broverman, I., & Broverman, D. M. (1968). Sex-role stereotypes and self-concepts in college students. *Journal of Consulting and Clinical Psychology, 32*, 287–295.

Rosenthal, R., & Jacobson, L. (1968). *Pygmalion in the classroom*. New York: Holt, Rinehart & Winston.

Ross, L., Greene, D., & House, P. (1977). The false consensus effect: An egocentric bias in social perception and attribution processes. *Journal of Experimental Social Psychology, 13*, 279–301.

Ross, L. D., Lepper, M. R., Strack, F., & Steinmetz, J. (1977). Social explanation and social expectation: Effects of real and hypothetical explanations on subjective likelihood. *Journal of Personality and Social Psychology, 35*, 817–829.

Rotter, J. B. (1966). Generalized expectancies for internal versus external control of reinforcement. *Psychological Monographs, 80*, 1–28.

Ruscher, J. B., & Fiske, S. T. (1990). Interpersonal competition can cause individuating processes. *Journal of Personality and Social Psychology, 58*, 832–843.

Ruvolo, A. P., & Markus, H. R. (1992). Possible selves and performance: The power of self-relevant imagery. *Social Cognition, 10*, 95–124.

Sadalla, E. K., Burroughs, W. J., & Staplin, L. J. (1980). Reference points in spatial cognition. *Journal of Experimental Psychology: Human Learning and Memory, 6*, 516–528.

Samuel, W. (1973). On clarifying some interpretations of social comparison theory. *Journal of Experimental Social Psychology, 9*, 450–465.

Sanna, L. J., Turley-Ames, K. J., & Meier, S. (1999). Mood, self-esteem, and simulated alternatives: Thought-provoking affective influences on counterfactual direction. *Journal of Personality and Social Psychology, 76*, 543–558.

Schachter, S. (1959). *The psychology of affiliation*. Stanford, CA: Stanford University Press.

Schanck, R. L. (1932). A study of community and its group institutions conceived of as behavior of individuals. *Psychological Monographs, 43*, 1–133.

Schank, R. C., & Abelson, R. P. (1977). *Scripts, plans, goals and understanding: An inquiry into human knowledge structures*. Oxford, England: Lawrence Erlbaum.

Scheier, M., & Carver, C. (1983). Self-directed attention and the comparison of self with standards. *Journal of Experimental Social Psychology, 19*, 205–222.

Schlenker, B. R. (1985). Identity and self-identification. In B. R. Schlenker (Ed.), *The self and social life* (pp. 65–100). New York: McGraw-Hill.

Schmitt, M. T., Silvia, P. J., & Branscombe, N. R. (2000). The intersection of self-evaluation maintenance and social identity theories: Intragroup judgment in interpersonal and intergroup contexts. *Personality and Social Psychology Bulletin, 26*, 1598–1606.

Schneider, D. J. (2004). *The psychology of stereotyping*. New York: The Guilford Press.

Schubert, T. W., & Häfner, M. (2003). Contrast from social stereotypes in automatic behavior. *Journal of Experimental Social Psychology, 39*, 577–584.

Schütz, A., & Tice, D. M. (1997). Associative and competitive indirect self-enhancement in close relationships moderated by trait self-esteem. *European Journal of Social Psychology, 27*, 257–273.

Schwarz, N. (1990). Feelings as information: Informational and motivational functions of affective states. In R. M. Sorrentino & E. T. Higgins (Eds.), *Handbook of motivation and cognition: Foundations of social behavior* (Vol. 2, pp. 527–561). New York: Guilford Press.

Schwarz, N., & Bless, H. (1992a). Constructing reality and its alternatives: An inclusion/exclusion model of assimilation and contrast effects in social judgment. In L. L. Martin & A. Tesser (Eds.), *The construction of social judgments* (pp. 217–245). Hillsdale, NJ: Lawrence Erlbaum Associates.

Schwarz, N., & Bless, H. (1992b). Scandals and the public's trust in politicians: Assimilation and contrast effects. *Personality and Social Psychology Bulletin, 18*, 574–579.

Schwarz, N., Münkel, T., & Hippler, H. J. (1990). What determines a "perspective"? Contrast effects as a function of the dimension tapped by preceding questions. *European Journal of Social Psychology, 20*, 357–361.

Schwarz, N., Strack, F., & Mai, H. P. (1991). Assimilation and contrast effects in part-whole question sequences: A conversational-logic analysis. *Public Opinion Quarterly, 55*, 3–23.

Sechrist, G. B., & Stangor, C. (2001). Perceived consensus influences intergroup behavior and stereotype accessibility. *Journal of Personality and Social Psychology, 80*, 645–654.

Sedikides, C. (1990). Effects of fortuitously activated constructs versus activated communication goals on person impressions. *Journal of Personality and Social Psychology, 58*, 397–408.

Sedikides, C. (1993). Assessment, enhancement, and verification determinants of the self-evaluation process. *Journal of Personality and Social Psychology, 65*, 317–338.

Sedikides, C., & Skowronski, J. J. (1995). On the sources of self-knowledge: The perceived primacy of self-reflection. *Journal of Social and Clinical Psychology, 14*, 244–270.

Sedikides, C., & Strube, M. J. (1997). To thine own self be good, to thine own self be sure, to thine own self be true, and to thine own self be better. In M. P. Zanna (Ed.), *Advances in experimental social psychology, Vol. 29* (pp. 209–269). San Diego, CA: Academic Press.

Seibt, B., & Förster, J. (2004). Stereotype threat and performance: How self-stereotypes influence processing by inducing regulatory foci. *Journal of Personality and Social Psychology, 87*, 38–56.

Seta, J. J. (1982). The impact of comparison processes on coactors' task performance. *Journal of Personality and Social Psychology, 42*, 281–291.

Seta, J. J., Martin, L., & Capehart, G. (1979). Effects of contrast and generalization on the attitude similarity-attraction relationship. *Journal of Personality and Social Psychology, 37,* 462–467.

Seta, J. J., & Seta, C. E. (1993). Stereotypes and the generation of compensatory and noncompensatory expectancies of group members. *Personality and Social Psychology Bulletin, 19,* 722–731.

Seta, J. J., Seta, C. E., & Donaldson, S. (1991). The impact of comparison processes on coactor's frustration and willingness to expend effort. *Personality and Social Psychology Bulletin, 17,* 560–568.

Shah, J. Y., Brazy, P. B., & Higgins, E. T. (2004). Promoting us or preventing them: Regulatory focus and the nature of ingroup bias. *Personality and Social Psychology Bulletin, 30,* 433–466.

Shah, J., & Higgins, E. T. (2001). Regulatory concerns and appraisal efficiency: The general impact of promotion and prevention. *Journal of Personality and Social Psychology, 80,* 693–705.

Shah, J., Higgins, T., & Friedman, R. S. (1998). Performance incentives and means: How regulatory focus influences goal attainment. *Journal of Personality and Social Psychology, 74,* 285–293.

Sherif, M. A. (1936). *The psychology of social norms.* New York: Harper.

Sherif, M., & Hovland, C. I. (1961). *Social judgment: Assimilation and contrast effects in communication and attitude change.* New Haven, CT: Yale University Press.

Sherman, S. J., Presson, C. C., & Chassin, L. (1984). Mechanisms underlying the false consensus effect: The special role of threats to the self. *Personality and Social Psychology Bulletin, 10,* 127–138.

Sherman, S. J., Presson, C. C., Chassin, L., Corty, E., & Olshavsky, R. (1983). The false consensus effect in estimates of smoking prevalence: Underlying mechanisms. *Personality and Social Psychology Bulletin, 9,* 197–207.

Shih, M., Pittinsky, T. L., & Ambady, N. (1999). Stereotype susceptibility: Identity salience and shifts in quantitative performance. *Psychological Science, 10,* 80–83.

Shrauger, J. S., & Patterson, M. B. (1976). Self-evaluation and the selection of dimensions for evaluating others. *Journal of Personality, 42,* 569–585.

Sigelman, C. (1991). Social distance from stigmatized groups: False consensus and false uniqueness effects on responding. *Rehabilitation Psychology, 36,* 139–151.

Silvia, P. J., & Duval, T. S. (2001). Objective self-awareness theory: Recent progress and enduring problems. *Personality and Social Psychology Review, 5,* 230–241.

Silvia, P. J., & Gendolla, G. H. E. (2001). On introspection and self-perception: Does self-focused attention enable accurate self-knowledge? *Review of General Psychology, 37,* 333–340.

Simon, B., & Hamilton, D. L. (1994). Self-stereotyping and social context: The effects of relative in-group size and in-group status. *Journal of Personality and Social Psychology, 66,* 699–711.

Simon, B., Loewy, M., Sturmer, S., Weber, U., Freytag, P., Habig, C., Kampmeier, C., & Spahlinger, P. (1998). Collective identification and social movement participation. *Journal of Personality and Social Psychology, 74,* 646–658.

Skowronski, J. J., Carlston, D. E., & Isham, J. T. (1993). Implicit versus explicit impression formation: The differing effects of overt labeling and covert priming on memory and impressions. *Journal of Experimental Social Psychology, 29,* 17–41.

Smith, E. R., & DeCoster, J. (1998). Person perception and stereotyping: Simulation using distributed representations in a recurrent connectionist network. In S. J. Read & L. C. Miller (Eds.), *Connectionist models of social reasoning and social behavior* (pp. 111–140). Mahwah, NJ: Lawrence Erlbaum Associates.

Smith, E. R., & DeCoster, J. (2000). Dual-process models in social and cognitive psychology: Conceptual integration and links to underlying memory systems. *Personality and Social Psychology Review, 4,* 108–131.

Smith, E. R., & Zárate, M. A. (1992). Exemplar-based model of social judgment. *Psychological Review, 99,* 3–21.

Smith, H. J., & Tyler, T. R. (1997). Choosing the right pond: The impact of group membership on self-esteem and group-oriented behavior. *Journal of Experimental Social Psychology, 33,* 146–170.

Smith, R. H. (2000). Assimilative and contrastive emotional reactions to upward and downward social comparisons. In J. Suls & L. Wheeler (Eds.), *Handbook of social comparison: Theory and research* (pp. 173–200). New York: Kluwer Academic Publishers.

Snyder, M., & Swann, W. B., Jr. (1978). Hypothesis-testing processes in social interaction. *Journal of Personality and Social Psychology, 36,* 1202–1212.

Solomon, S., Greenberg, J., & Pyszczynski, T. (1991). Terror management theory of self-esteem. In C. R. Snyder & D. Forsyth (Eds.), *Handbook of social and clinical psychology: The health perspective* (pp. 21–40). New York: Pergamon.

Spears, R., Doosje, B., & Ellemers, N. (1997). Self-stereotyping in the face of threats to group status and distinctiveness: The role of group identification. *Personality and Social Psychology Bulletin, 23,* 538–553.

Spears, R., Gordijn, E., Dijksterhuis, A., & Stapel, D. A. (2004). Reaction in action: Intergroup contrast in automatic behavior. *Personality and Social Psychology Bulletin, 30,* 605–616.

Spears, R., & Manstead, A. S. R. (1990). Consensus estimation in social context. In W. Stroebe & M. Hewstone (Eds.), *European review of social psychology* (Vol. 1, pp. 81–109). Chichester, U.K.: Wiley.

Spellman, B. A., & Holyoak, K. J. (1992). If Saddam is Hitler then who is George Bush? Analogical mapping between systems of social roles. *Journal of Personality and Social Psychology, 62,* 913–933.

Spence, J. T., & Buckner, C. E. (2000). Instrumental and expressive traits, trait stereotype, and sexist attitudes. *Psychology of Women Quarterly, 24,* 44–62.

Spence, J. T., Helmreich, R., & Stapp, J. (1975). Ratings of self and peers on sex role attributes and their relation to self-esteem and conceptions of masculinity and femininity. *Journal of Personality and Social Psychology, 32,* 29–39.

Spencer, S. J., Steele, C. M., & Quinn, D. M. (1999). Stereotype threat and women's math performance. *Journal of Experimental and Social Psychology, 35,* 4–28.

Srull, T. K., & Gaelick, L. (1983). General principles and individual differences in the self as a habitual reference point: An examination of self-other judgments of similarity. *Social Cognition, 2,* 108–121.

Srull, T. K., & Wyer, R. S., Jr. (1979). The role of category accessibility in the interpretation of information about persons: Some determinants and implications. *Journal of Personality and Social Psychology, 37,* 1660–1672.

Srull, T. K., & Wyer, R. S., Jr. (1980). Category accessibility and social perception: Some implications for the study of person memory and interpersonal judgments. *Journal of Personality and Social Psychology, 38,* 841–856.

Srull, T. K, & Wyer, R. S., Jr. (1989). Person memory and judgment. *Psychological Review, 96,* 58–83.

Stangor, C., & Lange, J. E. (1994). Mental representations of social groups: Advances in understanding stereotypes and stereotyping. In M. P. Zanna (Ed.), *Advances in experimental social psychology* (Vol. 26, pp. 357–416). Orlando, FL: Academic Press.

Stangor, C., & McMillan, D. (1992). Memory for expectancy-congruent and expectancy-incongruent information: A review of the social and social developmental literatures. *Psychological Bulletin, 111,* 42–62.

Stapel, D. A., & Blanton, H. (2004). From seeing to being: Subliminal social comparsions affect implicit and explicit self-evaluations. *Journal of Personality and Social Psychology, 87,* 468–481.

Stapel, D. A., & Koomen, W. (1996). Differential consequences of trait inferences: A direct test of the trait-referent hypothesis. *European Journal of Social Psychology, 26,* 827–837.

Stapel, D. A., & Koomen, W. (1997). Using primed exemplars during impression formation: Interpretation or comparison? *European Journal of Social Psychology, 27,* 357–367.

Stapel, D. A., & Koomen, W. (1998). When stereotype activation results in (counter) stereotypical judgments: Priming stereotype-relevant traits and exemplars. *Journal of Experimental Social Psychology, 34,* 136–163.

Stapel, D. A., & Koomen, W. (2000). How far do we go beyond the information given? The impact of knowledge activation on interpretation and inference. *Journal of Personality and Social Psychology, 78*, 19–37.

Stapel, D. A., & Koomen, W. (2001a). I, we, and the effects of others on me: How self-construal moderates social comparison effects. *Journal of Personality and Social Psychology, 80*, 766–781.

Stapel, D. A., & Koomen, W. (2001b). The impact of interpretation versus comparison mind-sets on knowledge accessibility effects. *Journal of Experimental Social Psychology, 37*, 134–149.

Stapel, D. A., Koomen, W., & van der Pligt, J. (1996). The referents of trait inferences: The impact of trait concepts versus actor-trait links on subsequent judgments. *Journal of Personality and Social Psychology, 70*, 437–450.

Stapel, D. A., Koomen, W., & van der Pligt, J. (1997). Categories of category accessibility: The impact of trait concept versus exemplar priming on person judgments. *Journal of Experimental Social Psychology, 33*, 47–76.

Stapel, D. A., & Schwarz, N. (1998). The Republican who did not want to become president: Colin Powell's impact on evaluations of the Republican party and Bob Dole. *Personality and Social Psychology Bulletin, 24*, 690–698.

Stapel, D. A., & Spears, R. (1996). Event accessibility and context effects in causal inference: Judgments of a different order. *Personality and Social Psychology Bulletin, 22*, 979–992.

Stapel, D. A., & Suls, J. (2004). Method matters: Effects of explicit versus implicit social comparisons on activation, behavior, and self-views. *Journal of Personality and Social Psychology, 87*, 860–875.

Stapel, D. A., & Winkielman, P. (1998). Assimilation and contrast as a function of context-target similarity, distinctness, and dimensional relevance. *Personality and Social Psychology Bulletin, 24*, 634–646.

Steele, C. (1992, April). Race and the schooling of Black Americans. *The Atlantic Monthly*, 68–78.

Steele, C. M. (1997). A threat in the air: How stereotypes shape intellectual identity and performance. *American Psychologist, 52*, 613–629.

Steele, C. M., & Aronson, J. (1995). Stereotype threat and the intellectual performance of African Americans. *Journal of Personality and Social Psychology, 69*, 797–811.

Steele, C. M., Spencer, S. J., & Aronson, J. (2002). Contending with group image: The psychology of stereotype and social identity threat. In M. P. Zanna (Ed.), *Advances in experimental social psychology, Vol. 34* (pp. 379–440). San Diego, CA: Academic Press.

Stevens, S. S. (1957). On the psychophysical law. *Psychological Review, 64*, 153–181.

Strack, F. (1992). The different routes to social judgments: Experiential versus informational strategies. In L. L. Martin & A. Tesser (Eds.), *The construction of social judgments* (pp. 249–275). Hillsdale, NJ: Lawrence Erlbaum.

Strack, F., Martin, L. L., & Schwarz, N. (1988). Priming and communication: Social determinants of information use in judgments of life satisfaction. *European Journal of Social Psychology, 18*, 429–442.

Strack, F., Schwarz, N., Bless, H., Kübler, A., & Wänke, M. (1993). Awareness of influence as a determinant of assimilation versus contrast. *European Journal of Social Psychology, 23*, 53–62.

Strack, F., Schwarz, N., & Gschneidinger, E. (1985). Happiness and reminiscing: The role of time perspective, affect, and mode of thinking. *Journal of Personality and Social Psychology, 49*, 1460–1469.

Strauman, T. J. (1989). Self-discrepancies in clinical depression and social phobia: Cognitive structures that underlie emotional disorders? *Journal of Abnormal Psychology, 98*, 14–22.

Strauman, T. J. (1992). Self-guides, autobiographical memory, anxiety, and dysphoria: Toward a cognitive model of vulnerability to emotional distress. *Journal of Abnormal Psychology, 101*, 87–95.

Strauman, T. J., & Higgins, E. T. (1987). Automatic activation of self-discrepancies and emotional syndromes: When cognitive structures influence affect. *Journal of Personality and Social Psychology, 53*, 1004–1014.

Suls, J. (1986). Notes on the occasion of social comparison theory's thirtieth birthday. *Personality and Social Psychology Bulletin, 12*, 289–296.

Suls, J. M., Gaes, G. G., & Gastorf, J. W. (1979). Evaluating a sex-related ability: Comparison with same-, opposite-, and combined-sex norms. *Journal of Research in Personality, 13,* 294–304.

Suls, J. M., & Miller, R. L. (Eds.) (1977). *Social comparison processes: Theoretical and empirical perspectives.* Oxford, England: Hemisphere.

Suls, J., & Mullen, B. (1982). From the cradle to the grave: Comparison and self-evaluation across the life-span. In J. Suls (Ed.), *Psychological perspectives on the self* (pp. 173–200). Hillsdale, NJ: Erlbaum.

Suls, J., & Mullen, B. (1984). Social and temporal bases of self-evaluation in the elderly: Theory and evidence. *International Journal of Aging and Human Development, 18,* 111–120.

Suls, J. M., & Wan, C. K. (1987). Social comparison choices for evaluating a sex- and age-related ability. *Personality and Social Psychology Bulletin, 4,* 102–105.

Suls, J., Wan, C. K., Barlow, D. H., & Heimberg, R. G. (1990). The fallacy of uniqueness: Social consensus perceptions of anxiety disorder patients and community residents. *Journal of Research in Personality, 24,* 415–432.

Suls, J., Wan, C. K., & Sanders, G. S. (1988). False consensus and false uniqueness in estimating the prevalence of health-protective behaviors. *Journal of Applied Social Psychology, 18,* 66–79.

Suls, J., & Wheeler, L. (2000). A selective history of classic and neo-social comparison theory. In J. Suls & L. Wheeler (Eds.), *Handbook of social comparison: Theory and research* (pp. 3–19). New York: Kluwer Academic Publishers.

Suls, J., & Wills, T. A. (Eds.) (1991). *Social comparison: Contemporary theory and research.* Hillsdale, NJ: Erlbaum.

Swann, W. B., Jr. (1987). Identity negotiation: Where two roads meet. *Journal of Personality and Social Psychology, 53,* 1038–1051.

Swann, W. B., Jr., De La Ronde, C., & Hixon, J. G. (1994). Authenticity and positivity strivings in marriage and courtship. *Journal of Personality and Social Psychology, 66,* 857–869.

Swann, W. B., Jr., & Pelham, B. (2002). Who wants out when the going gets good? Psychological investment and preference for self-verifying college roommates. *Self and Identity, 1,* 219–233.

Swann, W. B., Jr., Rentfrow, P. J., & Guinn, J. S. (2003). Self-verification: The search for coherence. In M. R. Leary & J. P. Tangney (Eds.), *Handbook of self and identity* (pp. 367–383). New York: Guilford Press.

Swann, W. B., Jr., Stein-Seroussi, A., & Giesler, R. B. (1992). Why people self-verify. *Journal of Personality and Social Psychology, 62,* 392–401.

Tajfel, H. (1957). Value and the perceptual judgment of magnitude. *Psychological Review, 64,* 192–204.

Tajfel, H. (1982). Social psychology of intergroup relations. *Annual Review of Psychology, 33,* 1–39.

Tajfel, H., & Wilkes, A. L. (1963). Classification and quantitative judgement. *British Journal of Social and Clinical Psychology, 54,* 101–114.

Tangney, J. P., Niedenthal, P. M., Covert, M. V., & Barlow, D. H. (1998). Are shame and guilt related to distinct self-discrepancies? A test of Higgins's (1987) hypotheses. *Journal of Personality and Social Psychology, 75,* 256–268.

Taylor, S. E. (1989). *Positive illusions: Creative deception and the healthy mind.* New York: Basic Books.

Taylor, S. E., & Brown, J. D. (1988). Illusion and well-being: A social psychological perspective on mental health. *Psychological Bulletin, 103,* 193–210.

Taylor, S. E., Buunk, B. P., & Aspinwall, L. G. (1990). Social comparison, stress, and coping. *Personality and Social Psychology Bulletin, 16,* 74–89.

Taylor, S. E., & Lobel, M. (1989). Social comparison activity under threat: Downward evaluation and upward contacts. *Psychological Review, 96,* 569–575.

Taylor, S. E., Neter, E., & Wayment, H. A. (1995). Self-evaluation processes. *Personality and Social Psychology Bulletin, 21,* 1278–1287.

Taylor, S. E., Wood, J. V., & Lichtman, R. R. (1983). It could be worse: Selective evaluation as a response to victimization. *Journal of Social Issues, 39,* 19–40.

Taynor, J., & Deaux, K. (1973). When women are more deserving than men: Equity, attribution, and perceived sex differences. *Journal of Personality and Social Psychology, 28,* 360–367.

Tesser, A. (1988). Toward a self-evaluation maintenance model of social behavior. In M. P. Zanna (Ed.), *Advances in experimental social psychology* (Vol. 21, pp. 181–226). New York: Academic Press.

Tesser, A., & Campbell, J. (1980). Self-definition: The impact of the relative performance and similarity of others. *Social Psychological Quarterly, 43*, 341–347.

Tesser, A., & Campbell, J. (1983). Self-definition and self-evaluation maintenance. In J. Suls & A. Greenwald (Eds.), *Social psychological perspectives on the self* (pp. 1–31). Hillsdale, NJ: Erlbaum.

Tesser, A., & Paulhus, D. (1983). The definition of self: Private and public self-evaluation management strategies. *Journal of Personality and Social Psychology, 44*, 672–682.

Tetlock, P. E., & Levi, A. (1982). Attribution bias: On the inconclusiveness of the cognition-motivation debate. *Journal of Experimental Social Psychology, 18*, 68–88.

Thompson, E. P., Roman, R. J., Moskowitz, G. B., Chaiken, S., & Bargh, J. A. (1994). Accuracy motivation attenuates covert priming effects: The systematic reprocessing of social information. *Journal of Personality and Social Psychology, 66*, 474–489.

Thornton, D., & Arrowood, A. J. (1966). Self-evaluation, self-enhancement, and the locus of social comparison. *Journal of Experimental Social Psychology,* Suppl. 1, 40–48.

Thurstone, L. L. (1928). Attitudes can be measured. *American Journal of Sociology, 33*, 529–554.

Tourangeau, R., & Rasinski, K. A. (1988). Cognitive processes underlying context effects in attitude measurement. *Psychological Bulletin, 103*, 299–314.

Trope, Y. (1986). Identification and inferential processes in dispositional attribution. *Psychological Review, 93*, 239–257.

Trope, Y., & Liberman, A. (1996). Social hypothesis testing: Cognitive and motivational mechanisms. In E. T. Higgins & A. W. Kruglanski (Eds.), *Social psychology: Handbook of basic principles* (pp. 239–270). New York: Guilford Press.

Turner, J. C. (1975). Social comparison and social identity: Some prospects for intergroup behaviour. *European Journal of Social Psychology, 5*, 5–34.

Turner, J. C. (1984). Social identification and psychological group formation. In H. Tajfel (Ed.), *The social dimension: European developments in social psychology* (Vol. 2). Cambridge: Cambridge University Press.

Turner, J. C. (1985). Social categorization and the self-concept: A social cognitive theory of group behaviour. In E. J. Lawler (Ed.), *Advances in group processes: Theory and research* (Vol. 2). Greenwich, CT: JAI.

Turner, J. C., Hogg, M. A., Oakes, P. J., Reicher, S. D., & Wetherell, M. S. (1987). *Rediscovering the social group: A self-categorization theory*. New York: Basil Blackwell.

Turner, J. C., Oakes, P. J., Haslam, S. A., & McGarty, C. (1994). Self and collective: Cognition and social context. *Personality and Social Psychology Bulletin, 20*, 454–463.

Turner, J. C., & Onorato, R. S. (1999). Social identity, personality, and the self-concept: A self-categorizing perspective. In T. R. Tyler & R. M. Roderick (Eds.), *The psychology of the social self. Applied social research* (pp. 11–46). Mahwah, NJ: Lawrence Erlbaum.

Tversky, A. (1977). Features of similarity. *Psychological Review, 84*, 327–352,

Tversky, A., & Gati, I. (1978). Studies of similarity. In E. Rosch & B. B. Lloyd (Eds.), *Cognition and categorization* (pp. 79–98). Hillsdale, NJ: Erlbaum.

Uleman, J. S. (1989). A framework for thinking intentionally about unintended thoughts. In J. S. Uleman & J. A. Bargh (Eds.), *Unintended thought* (pp. 425–449). New York: Guilford Press.

Upshaw, H. S. (1962). Own attitudes as an anchor in equal appearing intervals. *Journal of Abnormal and Social Psychology, 64*, 85–96.

Upshaw, H. S. (1965). The effect of variable perspectives on judgments of opinion statements for Thurstone scales: Equal-appearing intervals. *Journal of Personality and Social Psychology, 2*, 60–69.

Upshaw, H. S. (1969). Stimulus range and the judgmental unit. *Journal of Experimental Social Psychology, 5*, 1–11.

Upshaw, H. S. (1978). Social influence on attitudes and on anchoring of congeneric attitude scales. *Journal of Experimental Social Psychology, 14*, 327–339.

Upshaw, H. S., & Ostrom, T. M. (1984). Psychological perspective in attitude research. In J. R. Eiser (Ed.), *Attitudinal judgment*. New York: Springer-Verlag.

van den Eijnden, R. J. J. M., Buunk, B. P.,& Bosveld, W. (2000). Feeling similar or feeling unique: How men and women perceive their own sexual behaviors. *Personality and Social Psychology Bulletin, 26,* 1540–1549.

van der Pligt, J., Ester, P., & van der Linden, J. (1983). Attitude extremity, consensus, and diagnosticity. *European Journal of Social Psychology, 13,* 437–439.

Verkuyten, M., & Nekuee, S. (1999). Ingroup bias: The effect of self-stereotyping, identification and group threat. *European Journal of Social Psychology, 29,* 411–418.

Vescio, T. K., Gervais, S. J., Snyder, M., & Hoover, A. (2005). Power and the creation of patronizing environments: The stereotype-based behaviors of the powerful and their effects on female performance in masculine domains. *Journal of Personality and Social Psychology, 88,* 658–672.

Vescio, T. K., Snyder, M., & Butz, D. A. (2003). Power in stereotypically masculine domains: A social influence strategy X stereotype match model. *Journal of Personality and Social Psychology, 85,* 1062–1078.

Volkmann, J. (1951). Scales of judgment and their implications for social psychology. In J. H. Rohrer & M. Sherif (Eds.), *Social psychology at the crossroads* (pp. 273–294). New York: Harper.

von Hippel, W., Sekaquaptewa, D., & Vargas, P. (1995). On the role of encoding processes in stereotype maintenance. In M. P. Zanna (Ed.), *Advances in experimental social psychology* (Vol. 27, pp. 177–254). New York: Academic Press.

Wallen, R. (1943). Individuals' estimates of group opinions. *Journal of Social Psychology, 17,* 269–274.

Walton, G. M., & Cohen, G. L. (2003). Stereotype lift. *Journal of Experimental Social Psychology, 39,* 456–467.

Wayment, H. A., & Taylor, S. E. (1995). Self-evaluation processes: Motives, information, and self-esteem. *Journal of Personality, 63,* 729–757.

Weary, G., Marsh, K. L., & McCormick, L. (1994). Depression and social comparison motives. *European Journal of Social Psychology, 24,* 117–129.

Wedell, D. H., Parducci, A., & Geiselman, R. E. (1987). A formal analysis of ratings of physical attractiveness: Successive contrast and simultaneous assimilation. *Journal of Experimental Social Psychology, 23,* 230–249.

Wegener, D. T., & Petty, R. E. (1995). Flexible correction processes in social judgment: The role of naive theories in corrections for perceived bias. *Journal of Personality and Social Psychology, 68,* 36–51.

Wegener, D. T., & Petty, R. E. (1997). The flexible correction model: The role of naive theories of bias in bias correction. In M. P. Zanna (Ed.), *Advances in experimental social psychology* (Vol. 29, pp. 141–208). New York: Academic Press.

Weinstein, N. D. (1980). Unrealistic optimism about future life events. *Journal of Personality and Social Psychology, 39,* 806–820.

Weitz, S. (1972). Attitude, voice, and behavior: A repressed affect model of interracial interaction. *Journal of Personality and Social Psychology, 24,* 14–21.

Wever, E. G., & Zener, K. E. (1928). The method of absolute judgment in psychophysics. *Psychological Review, 35,* 466–493.

Wheeler, L. (1966). Motivation as a determinant of upward comparison. *Journal of Experimental Social Psychology, 2* (Suppl. 1), 27–31.

Wheeler, L. (1991). A brief history of social comparison theory. In J. Suls, & T. A. Wills (Eds.), *Social comparison: Contemporary theory and research* (pp. 3–21). Hillsdale, NJ: Lawrence-Erlbaum.

Wheeler, L., Martin, R., & Suls, J. (1997). The proxy model of social comparison for self-assessment of ability. *Personality and Social Psychology Review, 1,* 54–61.

Wheeler, L., & Miyake, K. (1992). Social comparison in everyday life. *Journal of Personality and Social Psychology, 62,* 760–773.

Wheeler, S. C., Jarvis, W. B. G., & Petty, R. E. (2001). Think unto others: The self-destructive impact of negative racial stereotypes. *Journal of Experimental Social Psychology, 37,* 173–180.

Wheeler, S. C., & Petty, R. E. (2001). The effects of stereotype activation on behavior: A review of possible mechanisms. *Psychological Bulletin, 127,* 797–826.

White, G. L., & Shapiro, D. (1987). Don't I know you? Antecedents and social consequences of perceived familiarity. *Journal of Experimental Social Psychology, 23,* 75–92.

White, K., & Lehman, D. R. (2005). Culture and social comparison seeking: The role of self-motives. *Personality and Social Psychology Bulletin, 31,* 232–242.

Wilder, D. A., & Shapiro, P. (1991). Facilitation of outgroup stereotypes by enhanced ingroup identity. *Journal of Experimental Social Psychology, 27,* 431–452.

Wills, T. A. (1981). Downward comparison principles in social psychology. *Psychological Bulletin, 90,* 245–271.

Wills, T. A. (1991). Similarity and self-esteem in downward comparison. In J. M. Suls & T. A. Wills (Eds.), *Social comparison: Contemporary theory and research* (pp. 51–78). Hillsdale, NJ: Erlbaum.

Wilson, A. E., & Ross, M. (2000). The frequency of temporal-self and social comparisons in people's personal appraisals. *Journal of Personality and Social Psychology, 78,* 928–942.

Wilson, T. D., & Brekke, N. (1994). Mental contamination and mental correction: Unwanted influences on judgments and evaluations. *Psychological Bulletin, 116,* 117–142.

Wilson, T. D., Houston, C. E., Etling, K. M., & Brekke, N. (1996). A new look at anchoring effects: Basic anchoring and its antecedents. *Journal of Experimental Psychology, 125,* 387–402.

Windschitl, P. D., Kruger, J., & Simms, E. N. (2003). The influence of egocentrism and focalism on people's optimism in competitions: When what affects us equally affects me more. *Journal of Personality and Social Psychology, 85,* 389–408.

Wittenbrink, B., & Henly, J. R. (1996). Creating social reality: Informational social influence and the content of stereotypic beliefs. *Personality and Social Psychology Bulletin, 22,* 598–610.

Wood, J. V. (1989). Theory and research concerning social comparisons of personal attributes. *Psychological Bulletin, 106,* 231–248.

Wood, J. V. (1996). What is social comparison and how should we study it? *Personality and Social Psychology Bulletin, 22,* 520–537.

Wood, J. V., Michela, J. L., & Giordano, C. (2000). Downward comparison in everyday life: Reconciling self-enhancement models with the mood-cognition priming model. *Journal of Personality and Social Psychology, 79,* 563–579.

Wood, J. V., & van der Zee, K. (1997). Social comparisons among cancer patients: Under what conditions are comparisons upward and downward? In B. P. Buunk & F. X. Gibbons (Eds.), *Health, coping, and well-being: Perspectives from social comparison theory* (pp. 299–328). Mahwah, NJ: Erlbaum.

Wood, J. V., & Wilson, A. E. (2003). How important is social comparison? In M. R. Leary & J. P. Tangney (Eds.), *Handbook of self and identity* (pp. 344–366). New York, NY: Guilford Press.

Wyer, N. A., Sherman, J. W., & Stroessner, S. J. (2000). The roles of motivation and ability in controlling the consequences of stereotype suppression. *Personality and Social Psychology Bulletin, 26,* 13–25.

Wyer, R. S., Jr., & Carlston, D. E. (1979). *Social cognition, inference, and attribution.* Hillsdale, NJ: Lawrence Erlbaum Associates.

Wyer, R. S., & Srull, T. K. (1980). The processing of social stimulus information: A conceptual integration. In R. Hastie, E. B. Ebbesen, T. M. Ostrom, R. S. Wyer, D. L. Hamilton, & D. E. Carlston (Eds.), *Person memory: The cognitive basis of social perception* (pp. 227–300). Hillsdale, NJ: Erlbaum.

Yzerbyt, V. Y., Schadron, G., Leyens, J. P., & Rocher, S. (1994). Social judgeability: The impact of meta-informational cues on the use of stereotypes. *Journal of Personality and Social Psychology, 66,* 48–55.

Zavalloni, M., & Cook, S. W. (1965). Influence of judges' attitudes on ratings of favorableness of statements about a social group. *Journal of Personality and Social Psychology, 1,* 43–54.

Zebrowitz, L. A., Kendall-Tackett, K., & Fafel, J. (1991). The influence of children's facial maturity on parental expectations and punishment. *Journal of Experimental Child Psychology, 52,* 221–238.

Zebrowitz, L., & Lee, S. Y. (1999). Appearance, stereotype-incongruent behavior, and social relationships. *Personality and Social Psychology Bulletin, 25,* 569–584.

Zeigarnik, B. (1935). On finished and unfinished task. In K. Lewin (Ed.), *A dynamic theory of personality* (pp. 300–314). New York: McGraw-Hill.

Zuwerink, J. R., Devine, P. G., Monteith, M. J., & Cook, D. A. (1996). Prejudice toward Blacks: With and without compunction? *Basic and Applied Social Psychology, 18,* 131–150.

Author Index

A

Abele, A. E., 89, 90
Abeles, R. P., 6
Abelson, R. P., 6, 8, 68
Abrams, D., 3, 89, 142
Abramson, L. M., 98
Abramson, P. R., 98
Achee, J. W., 32, 50, 170
Affleck, G., 159, 173
Agostinelli, G., 61, 63
Ahrens, C., 75
Ajzen, I., 6
Albert, S., 173
Alicke, M. D., 58, 59, 74n4, 153, 172, 186
Allen, J. J. B., 124
Allen, V. L., 156
Allison, S. J., 3, 61, 64, 162, 181
Allport, F. H., 60, 67
Ambady, N., 133, 134, 143
Amodio, D. M., 123–24
Andersen, S. M., 68, 70–71, 72, 181
Anderson, N. H., 89
Anderson, R. C., 31
Armor, D. A., 152
Aronson, J., 135, 136, 139, 184
Arrowood, A. J., 151, 153

Ashburn-Nardo, L., 118
Ashmore, R. D., 75
Aspinwall, L. G., 161
Atkins, J. L., 59, 60, 61, 67
Atkinson, J. W., 4, 6
Augoustinos, M., 75

B

Baldwin, M. W., 118, 162
Banaji, M. R., 18, 19, 40, 55, 75, 178
Bandura, A., 6, 120, 121, 124, 126
Bargh, J. A., 9, 10, 11, 13, 19, 20, 57, 72, 98, 134, 135, 136, 137, 143, 145, 184
Barlow, D. H., 60, 62, 74n5, 116
Batson, C. S., 112
Battle, J., 163
Baum, A., 70, 181
Baumeister, R. F., 127
Beattie, A. E., 77, 79, 91
Beauregard, K. S., 58, 59, 181
Bee, H., 130
Beehr, T. A., 104
Beike, D., 55
Bem, S. L., 130
Benassi, V. A., 45

Subject Index

A

Accessibility. *See* Knowledge accessibility
Activation and inhibition model, 84, 182
Assimilation and contrast models. *See*
  Models of assimilation and contrast
Adaptation level (AL), 31
Assimilation and contrast models. *See*
  Models of assimilation and contrast
Assimilation effect
    behavioral, 2, 9, 13, 113, 114, 118, 121,
      122, 127, 135–36, 138, 139, 143
    context and, 9, 16, 18, 22–23, 24, **26**, 37,
      38, 39, 40, 42, 43, 178
    correction and, 25, 26, 38, 179
    definition of, 2
    discrepancies and, 113, 114, 118, 121,
      126, 127
    entitativity and, 16–17
    exemplars and, 68, 69, 71
    expectations and, 4, 8, 44, 45
    false-consensus effect and, 60, 64–66,
      181
    inclusion and, 35–37, 56

internalized standards and, **125**
possible self and, 119, 120
primes and, 8–9, 10, 11, 12, 13, 15, 16,
  17–19, 20, **26–29**, 33, 40, 46, 72,
  135–36, 177–78
self-awareness and, 113–14
self-evaluation and, 2, 48–49
self-other judgements and, 56, 57, 59,
  60, 64–66, 67, 72, 180, 181
self-stereotyping and, 129, 130n, 134,
  135–36, 138, 139–40, 141–42, 143, **144**,
  145, 146n4, 184
standards of comparison and, 2, 20,
  23, 25, **26–29**, 42, 44, 48, 113, 122,
  125, 149, 150, 151, 155, 163, 164–66,
  167–70, 171, 172, 177–78, 183, 184,
  185
stereotyping and, 2, 75, 76, 77, 78, 79,
  81–82, 83, 84, 85–91, 93, 97, 98, **99**,
  100, 101, 103, 104, 105, 106, 107, 182,
  183, 187
targets and, 14–15, 17–18, 20–21,
  33–35, 43, 180
See also Models of assimilation and
  contrast
Associative processing, 46–47